ZAGATSURVEY®

2006

LONDON RESTAURANTS

Edited and Coordinated by
Sholto Douglas-Home and
Susan Kessler

Editor: Troy Segal

Published and distributed by
ZAGAT SURVEY, LLC
4 Columbus Circle
New York, New York 10019
Tel: 212 977 6000
E-mail: london@zagat.com
Web site: www.zagat.com

Acknowledgments

We thank Deborah Bennett, Karen Bonham, British American Business Inc., Jenny Cartwright, Caroline Clegg, Ricki Conway, Alex, Louis and Tallula Douglas-Home, Rosanne Johnston, Larry Kessler, Le Cordon Bleu (London), Pamela and Michael Lester, Leuka 2000, Margaret Levin, Ben and Sheila Miller, Natasha Robinson, Anne Semmes, Steven Shukow, Alexandra Spezzotti, StreetSmart, Peter Vogl, Susan and Jeffrey Weingarten and Annette Wilkinson. We are also grateful to our senior associate editor, Shelley Gallagher, and assistant editor, Victoria Elmacioglu, as well as the following members of our staff: Reni Chin, Larry Cohn, Schuyler Frazier, Jeff Freier, Leah Hochbaum, Natalie Lebert, Mike Liao, Dave Makulec, Robert Poole, Thomas Sheehan, Joshua Siegel, Yoji Yamaguchi and Sharon Yates.

ISBN 1-57006-733-3
Printed in the United States of America

Contents

About This Survey 5
What's New 6
Ratings & Symbols 7
Most Popular 9
TOP RATINGS
Food: Cuisines, Features, Locations 10
Decor: Outdoors, Romance, Rooms, Views .. 15
Service 16
Best Buys 17
RESTAURANT DIRECTORY
Names, Addresses, Phone Numbers, Web Sites, Ratings and Reviews 19
INDEXES
Cuisines 174
Locations 185
Special Features
All-Day Dining 197
Breakfast 198
Brunch 198
Business Dining 199
Celebrity Chefs 201
Cheese Boards 202
Child-Friendly 203
Delivery/Takeaway 205
Dining Alone 207
Entertainment 207
Fireplaces 208
Game in Season 209
Historic Places 210
Hotel Dining 211
Late Dining 212
No-Smoking Sections 213
Noteworthy Newcomers 215
Offbeat 215
Outdoor Dining 216
People-Watching 217
Power Scenes 218
Pre-Theatre Menus 219
Private Rooms 220
Pubs/Microbreweries 222
Pudding Specialists 222
Quiet Conversation 223
Romantic Places 223
Senior Appeal 224
Set-Price Menus 225
Singles Scenes 227
Sleepers 228
Smoking Prohibited 229

Special Occasions 230
Tea Service 231
Trendy 231
Views 233
Visitors on Expense Account 233
Winning Wine Lists. 235
Wine Chart 236

About This Survey

Here are the results of our *2006 London Restaurant Survey,* covering 977 restaurants as tested, and tasted, by 4,844 local restaurant-goers.

This year we celebrate our 10th anniversary in covering London restaurants, a period of extraordinary evolution and creativity for the industry, as well as for the city, the recently appointed, proud host of the 2012 Summer Olympics. It also marks the 26th year that Zagat Survey has reported on the shared experiences of diners like you. What started in 1979 as a hobby involving 200 of our friends rating local NYC restaurants has come a long way. Today we have over 250,000 active surveyors and now cover entertaining, golf, hotels, resorts, spas, movies, music, nightlife, shopping, sites and attractions as well as theatre. All of these guides are based on consumer surveys. Our *Surveys* are also available on PDAs, cell phones and by subscription at zagat.com, where you can vote and shop as well.

By regularly surveying large numbers of avid customers, we hope to have achieved a uniquely current and reliable guide. This year's London participants dined out an average of 2.4 times per week, meaning this *Survey* is based on roughly 615,000 meals. Of these 4,800 plus surveyors, 38% are women, 62% men; the breakdown by age is 14% in their 20s; 31%, 30s; 20%, 40s; 20%, 50s; and 15%, 60s or above. Our editors have synopsised our surveyors' opinions, with their comments shown in quotation marks. We sincerely thank each of these people; this book is really "theirs."

We are especially grateful to our editor/coordinators, who have been with this guide since its first edition: Sholto Douglas-Home, London restaurant critic for over 15 years and an international marketing executive, and Susan Kessler, cookbook author and consultant for numerous lifestyle publications in the U.K. and U.S.

To help guide our readers to London's best meals and best buys, we have prepared a number of lists. See Most Popular (page 9), Top Ratings (pages 10–16) and Best Buys (page 17). In addition, we have provided 40 handy indexes.

To vote in any of our upcoming *Surveys,* just register at zagat.com. Each participant will receive a free copy of the resulting guide (or a comparable reward) when it is published. Your comments and even criticisms of this guide are also solicited. There is always room for improvement with your help. Just contact us at london@zagat.com.

New York, NY
5 September, 2005

Nina and Tim Zagat

What's New

There may be a few souls out there who still see London dining as a staid, slow-moving sort of scene. If so, the city's latest *Survey* results should finally bury that notion: after a three-year reign as the capital's Most Popular, Nobu yields the title to Wagamama, an Asian chain that's the polar opposite of the former *numero uno* – populist, casual and cheap.

Communal Choices: Wagamama's ascendancy is all the more surprising, given that it doesn't take reservations and seats diners at communal tables – hardly the traditional hallmarks of a high-scoring restaurant, yet typical of Londoners' growing desire to dine informally. In fact, fully 50% of surveyors say they're happy to share tables with strangers, which is good news for newcomers featuring the practice, such as the French Bistro Aubaine, the Middle Eastern Ottolenghi and the Chinese Ping Pong.

Poundwise: The popularity of Wagamama also reflects an increased appetite for value – maybe as an antidote to a nearly 5% rise in the cost of an average meal over the last year, from £35.14 to £36.79 (about $64.60). Small wonder that 71% of surveyors say they're spending more when they eat out than they did two years ago. To the rescue come such moderately priced new places as Crazy Homies (a Mexican), Grocer on Warwick (a casual revamp of the Sugar Club) and Wizzy, a Korean from an ex-Hakkasan manager. Each proves that exotic eats can be easy on the wallet.

Mini Morsels: Another sign Londoners are looking for an easy-going experience is the rise of tapas-style menus around town (although only 25% say these places offer better value than traditional restaurants). Diners can Graze in St. John's Wood on New French *petits plats,* or try Tugga's Portuguese *petiscos* in Sloane Square. Debutantes Amaya in Belgravia and Salt Yard in Fitzrovia are also proving popular practitioners of the shared-dish format.

Top Teams: But probably the most prominent premiere among the small-plates purveyors is Maze, which also happens to be the latest colony of Gordon Ramsay's culinary empire. Other notable names are debuting offshoots too. Already up and running with sophisticated New French fare is The Ledbury, from the team behind The Square. Mango Tree's Eddie Lim unveils a smart new Malay eatery in Chelsea later in the year, and Cinnamon Club owner Iqbal Wahhab opens Roast in historic Borough Market.

Horizon-gazing: Meanwhile, Nobu has just unveiled a new, no-reservations branch, Nobu Berkeley. Will this expansion be enough to wrest the Most Popular crown back from Wagamama next time? Stay tuned.

London — Sholto Douglas-Home
5 September, 2005

Ratings & Symbols

Name, Address, Tube Stop, Phone*, Fax & Web Site

Zagat Ratings

Hours & Credit Cards

	F	D	S	C
Tim & Nina's Fish Bar [serves after 11 PM] [closed on Sunday] [no credit cards] ▽	23	5	9	£9

Exeter St., WC2 (Covent Garden), 020-7123 4567; fax 020-7123 4567; www.zagat.com

Open seven days a week, 24 hours a day (some say that's "168 hours too many"), this "chaotic" Covent Garden dive serving "cheap, no-nonsense" fish 'n' chips is "ideal" for a "quick grease fix"; no one's impressed by the "tired, tatty decor" or "patchy service", but judging from its "perpetual queues", the "no-frills" food and prices are "spot-on."

Review, with surveyors' comments in quotes

Top Spots: Places with the highest overall ratings, popularity and importance are listed in BLOCK CAPITAL LETTERS.

Hours: [serves after 11 PM symbol] serves after 11 PM
[closed on Sunday symbol] closed on Sunday

Credit Cards: [no credit cards symbol] no credit cards accepted

Ratings are on a scale of **0** to **30. Cost (C)** reflects our surveyors' estimate of the price of dinner with one drink and service.

F **Food**	D **Decor**	S **Service**	C **Cost**
23	5	9	£9

0–9 poor to fair
10–15 fair to good
16–19 good to very good
20–25 very good to excellent
26–30 extraordinary to perfection
▽ low response/less reliable

For newcomers or survey write-ins listed without ratings, the price range is indicated as follows:

I £20 and below
M £21 to £35
E £36 to £50
VE £51 or more

* When calling from outside the U.K., dial international code + 44, then omit the first zero of the number.

Most Popular

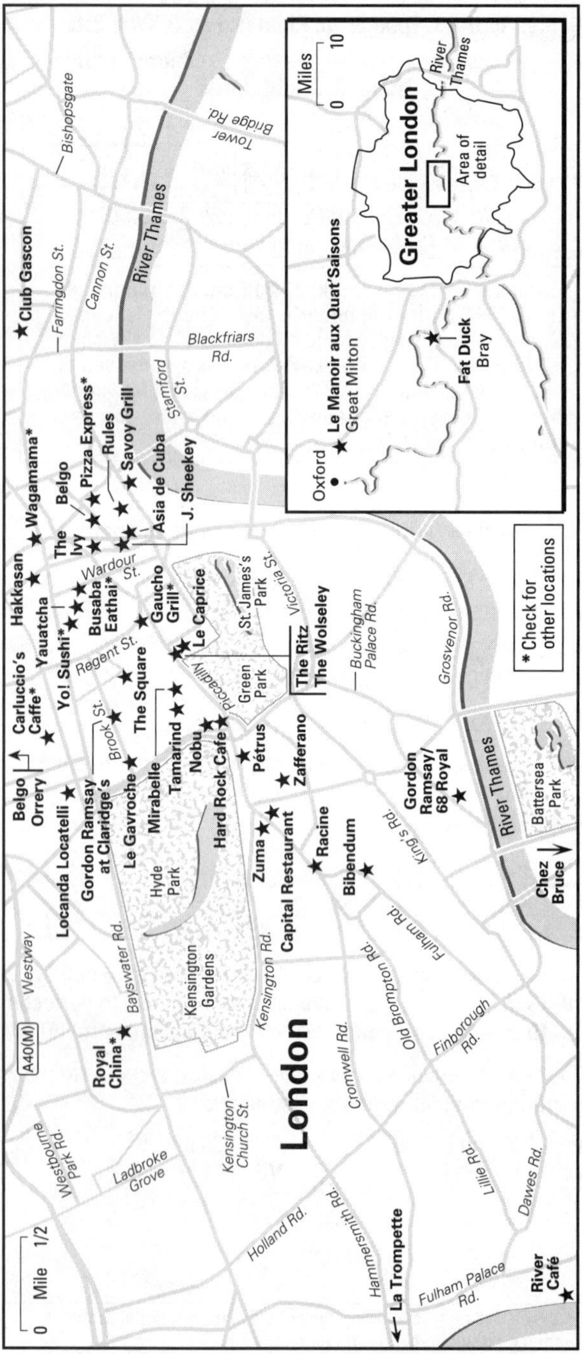

Most Popular

1. Wagamama
2. Nobu
3. Ivy, The
4. Gordon Ramsay/Claridge's
5. J. Sheekey
6. Gordon Ramsay/68 Royal
7. Zuma
8. Hakkasan
9. Square
10. Le Gavroche
11. Zafferano
12. Wolseley
13. Rules
14. Le Caprice
15. Asia de Cuba
16. Capital
17. River Café*
18. Pétrus
19. Royal China
20. Bibendum
21. Pizza Express*
22. Gaucho Grill
23. Yauatcha
24. Savoy Grill
25. Le Manoir/Quat
26. Fat Duck
27. Busaba Eathai
28. Belgo
29. Tamarind*
30. Locanda Locatelli
31. Orrery
32. Ritz
33. Mirabelle
34. Chez Bruce
35. Carluccio's
36. Hard Rock Cafe*
37. Yo! Sushi*
38. La Trompette
39. Club Gascon
40. Racine*

It's obvious that many of the restaurants on the above list are among the most expensive, but if popularity were calibrated to price, we suspect that a number of other restaurants would join the above ranks. Given the fact that both our surveyors and readers love to discover dining bargains, we have added a list of 80 Best Buys on page 17. These are restaurants that give real quality at extremely reasonable prices.

* Indicates a tie with restaurant above

Top Ratings

Excludes places with low voting.

Top 40 Food

29 Gordon Ramsay/68 Royal
28 Chez Bruce
Le Manoir/Quat
Fat Duck
Le Gavroche
Waterside Inn
27 Nobu
Club Gascon
Rasoi Vineet Bhatia
Pétrus
Original Lahore Kebab
Clarke's
Richard Corrigan
Square
Champor
Pied à Terre
La Trompette
Jin Kichi
26 Capital
Defune
Aubergine
Gordon Ramsay/Claridge's
Tom Aikens
L'Oranger
Foliage
St. John
Orrery
River Café
25 Hunan
Ubon
Zuma
Fino
J. Sheekey
Morgan M
Hakkasan
Zafferano
Roussillon
Tentazioni
Greenhouse
Mosimann's (club)

By Cuisine

American
21 Sophie's Steak
19 Bodeans
18 Christopher's
Lucky 7
17 Big Easy

Asian
27 Champor
24 e&o
22 Eight Over Eight
Asia de Cuba
Blakes

British (Modern)
28 Chez Bruce
27 Clarke's
Richard Corrigan
26 St. John
24 Gravetye Manor

British (Traditional)
24 Grill Room
Rhodes 24
23 Wilton's
Mark's Club (club)
Guinea Grill

Chinese
25 Hunan
Hakkasan
Kai Mayfair
24 Mandarin Kitchen
Yauatcha

Chophouses
23 Rib Room
22 Smiths/Top Floor
Rules
21 Notting Grill
Sophie's Steak

Eclectic
25 Mosimann's (club)
24 Lanes
22 Providores/Tapa
Blakes
21 Boxwood Café

Fish 'n' Chips
23 North Sea
Sweetings
21 Two Bros. Fish
Geales Fish
20 Seashell

French (Bistro)
23 La Poule au Pot
Bibendum Oyster
Le Petit Max
L'Escargot
Racine

French (Classic)
28 Le Gavroche
Waterside Inn
25 Oslo Court
24 Ritz
French Horn

French (New)
29 Gordon Ramsay/68 Royal
28 Le Manoir/Quat
27 Club Gascon
Pétrus
Square

Indian/Pakistani
27 Rasoi Vineet Bhatia
Original Lahore Kebab
25 Amaya
Tamarind
24 Vama

Italian
26 River Café
25 Zafferano
Tentazioni
Assaggi
24 Quirinale

Japanese
27 Nobu
Jin Kichi
26 Defune
25 Ubon
Zuma

Lebanese
25 Ishbilia
23 Fakhreldine
Noura
22 Al Sultan
Al Hamra

Mediterranean
26 L'Oranger
25 Moro
24 Ottolenghi
21 Eagle
20 Fifteen

Modern European
28 Fat Duck
26 Foliage
24 Le Caprice
Angela Hartnett's
23 Notting Hill Brass.

Pizza
24 Osteria Basilico
21 Red Pepper
Made in Italy
Oliveto
Spago*

Seafood
25 J. Sheekey
Fish Hoek
23 Bibendum Oyster
One-O-One
Wilton's

Spanish
25 Fino
Moro
23 Cambio de Tercio
21 El Pirata
Eyre Brothers

Thai
25 Patara
24 Pepper Tree
23 Busaba Eathai
22 Blue Elephant
Nahm

Vegetarian
25 Morgan M
Roussillon
24 Rasa
Gate
22 Food for Thought

By Special Feature

Breakfast
24 Cinammon Club
23 St. John Bread/Wine
20 Wolseley
Pat. Valerie
19 Simpson's

Brunch
27 Clarke's
25 Lundum's
24 Le Caprice
Chutney Mary
22 Providores/Tapa

Top Food

Business Lunch Spots
28 Le Gavroche
27 Club Gascon
Square
25 Fino
Greenhouse

Cheese Boards
29 Gordon Ramsay/68 Royal
27 Pétrus
Square
26 Tom Aikens
25 Greenhouse

Child-Friendly
26 River Café
25 Zuma
24 Yauatcha
23 Lucio
21 Berkeley Square

Communal Tables
24 Ottolenghi
23 Baker & Spice
La Fromagerie
Busaba Eathai
21 Chowki Bar

Gastro-Pub
23 Anchor & Hope
22 Churchill Arms
21 Anglesea Arms
Eagle
Cow Din. Rm.

Hotel Dining
28 Le Manoir/Quat
Le Manoir/Quat
Waterside Inn
Waterside Inn
27 Nobu
Metropolitan Hotel
Pétrus
Berkeley Hotel
26 Capital
The Capital Hotel

In-Store Eating
23 Books for Cooks
19 Fifth Floor
18 202
Carluccio's
17 Nicole's

Late Night
25 J. Sheekey
Hakkasan
24 Le Caprice
22 Asia de Cuba
20 Wolseley

Meet for a Drink
25 Zuma
Hakkasan
24 Roka
23 Cellar Gascon
22 Asia de Cuba

Newcomers/Rated
25 Amaya
24 Ottolenghi
Roka
21 Sardo Canale
Cocoon

Newcomers/Unrated
Ledbury
Maze
Pengelley's
Ping Pong
Salt Yard

Offbeat
28 Fat Duck
23 Books for Cooks
St. John Bread/Wine
22 Blue Elephant
21 Crazy Bear

Olde England
24 Ritz (1906)
23 Wilton's (1742)
Sweetings (1889)
22 Rules (1798)
19 Simpson's (1828)

Outdoor
26 River Café
25 Lundum's
23 La Poule au Pot
22 Smiths/Top Floor
20 Spoon

People-Watching
27 Nobu
25 Zuma
Hakkasan
22 Ivy, The
20 Cipriani

Private Clubs – Members Only
25 Mosimann's
23 Mark's Club
Harry's Bar
21 George
Morton's

Private Rooms
27 Pétrus
Square
26 Gordon Ramsay/Claridge's
24 Angela Hartnett's
21 Cocoon

Room with a View
26 Foliage
25 Ubon
24 Rhodes 24
21 Le Pont de la Tour
20 Oxo Tower

Small Plates
27 Club Gascon
25 Fino
Amaya
Moro
21 Le Cercle

Sunday Lunch/Town
28 Chez Bruce
26 Orrery
River Café
25 Morgan M
24 Locanda Locatelli

Sunday Lunch/Country
28 Le Manoir/Quat
Fat Duck
Waterside Inn
24 Gravetye Manor
French Horn

Tasting Menus
29 Gordon Ramsay/68 Royal
28 Fat Duck
27 Club Gascon
Rasoi Vineet Bhatia
26 Tom Aikens

Tea Service
Berkeley Hotel
Capital Restaurant
Connaught Hotel
Lanesborough Hotel
Ritz Hotel

Theatreland
27 Richard Corrigan
25 J. Sheekey
24 Savoy Grill
22 Ivy, The
Asia de Cuba

Winning Wine Lists
27 Pétrus
Square
26 Capital
Tom Aikens
25 Greenhouse

By Location

Belgravia
27 Pétrus
25 Zafferano
Mosimann's (club)
Amaya
Ishbilia

Bloomsbury/Fitzrovia
27 Pied à Terre
25 Fino
Hakkasan
24 Rasa
Passione

Canary Wharf
25 Ubon
23 Royal China
Quadrato
21 Gaucho Grill
19 Moshi Moshi

Chelsea
29 Gordon Ramsay/68 Royal
27 Rasoi Vineet Bhatia
26 Aubergine
Tom Aikens
24 Vama

Chiswick
27 La Trompette
25 Fish Hoek
22 Gourmet Burger
20 FishWorks
17 Giraffe

City
24 Rhodes 24
23 Sweetings
Don
22 Café Spice Namasté
21 Gaucho Grill

Top Food

Clerkenwell
25 Moro
21 Eagle
20 Cicada
Zetter
Clerkenwell

Covent Garden
25 J. Sheekey
24 Savoy Grill
22 Ivy, The
Food for Thought
Rules

Hampstead
27 Jin Kichi
22 Gourmet Burger
21 Bombay Bicycle
Gaucho Grill
ZeNW3

Islington
25 Morgan M
24 Ottolenghi
22 La Trouvaille
20 Masala Zone
Metrogusto*

Kensington
27 Clarke's
24 Locanda Ottoemezzo
Zaika
22 Memories/China
ffiona's

Knightsbridge
26 Capital
Foliage
25 Zuma
Patara
23 One-O-One

Marylebone
26 Defune
Orrery
24 Locanda Locatelli
23 Royal China
La Fromagerie

Mayfair
28 Le Gavroche
27 Nobu
Square
26 Gordon Ramsay/Claridge's
25 Greenhouse

Notting Hill
25 Assaggi
24 Osteria Basilico
e&o
23 Malabar
Books for Cooks

Piccadilly
23 Fakhreldine
Yoshino*
Noura
21 Chowki Bar
Gaucho Grill

Shoreditch/Spitalfields/ Hoxton
23 St. John Bread/Wine
21 Eyre Brothers
Viet Hoa
20 Fifteen
Real Greek

Smithfield
27 Club Gascon
26 St. John
23 Cellar Gascon
22 Smiths/Top Floor
21 Le Café du Marché

Soho
27 Richard Corrigan
25 Patara
24 Yauatcha
23 Mela
L'Escargot

South Kensington
25 Lundum's
Patara
24 L'Etranger
23 Bibendum
Bibendum Oyster

St. James's
26 L'Oranger
24 Quilon
Ritz
Le Caprice
23 Wilton's

In the Country
28 Le Manoir/Quat
Fat Duck
Waterside Inn
24 Gravetye Manor
French Horn

Top 40 Decor

28 Ritz
27 Hakkasan
Home House (club)
26 Le Manoir/Quat
Lanesborough
Criterion Grill
Gravetye Manor
25 Champor
Waterside Inn
Pearl
Wolseley
Les Trois Garçons
Belvedere
Crazy Bear
Gordon Ramsay/Claridge's
Blakes
Pétrus
Mosimann's (club)
24 Foliage
Pasha
Benares
Zuma
Blue Elephant
Momo
Cinnamon Club
Gordon Ramsay/68 Royal
Lanes
Lonsdale
Le Gavroche
Rules
Taman gang
Savoy Grill
Spoon
Oxo Tower Brass.
Sketch/Gallery
Odin's
Mark's Club (club)
Oxo Tower
Grill Room
Angela Hartnett's

Outdoors

Belvedere
Coq d'Argent
La Famiglia
La Poule au Pot
Le Colombier
Ledbury
Le Pont de la Tour
Manicomio
Momo
Oxo Tower
Ritz
River Café
Smiths/Top Floor
Spoon

Romance

Andrew Edmunds
Angela Hartnett's
Blakes
Club Gascon
Lanesborough
La Poule au Pot
Locanda Locatelli
Lundum's
Odin's
Pétrus
Richard Corrigan
Ritz

Rooms

Asia de Cuba
Cocoon
Criterion Grill
Hakkasan
Les Trois Garçons
Momo
Plateau
Ritz
Sketch/Lecture Room
Umu
Wolseley
Zuma

Views

Blue Print Café
Coq d'Argent
Foliage
Inn The Park
Le Pont de la Tour
Oxo Tower
Rhodes 24
Smiths/Top Floor
Ubon
Windows on World

Top 40 Service

28	Gordon Ramsay/68 Royal
27	Lanes
	Le Gavroche
26	Waterside Inn
	Rasoi Vineet Bhatia
	Pétrus
	Le Manoir/Quat
	Capital
	Fat Duck
	Square
	Foliage
	Ritz
	Oslo Court
	Grill Room
	Mark's Club (club)
25	Gordon Ramsay/Claridge's
	Gravetye Manor
	La Trompette
	Mosimann's (club)
24	Harry's Bar (club)
	French Horn
	Savoy Grill
	Lanesborough
	Angela Hartnett's
	Orrery
	Roussillon
	L'Oranger
	George (club)
	Chez Bruce
	Pied à Terre
	Tom Aikens
	Greenhouse
23	ffiona's
	Aubergine
	J. Sheekey
	Clarke's
	Le Soufflé
	Le Caprice
	Richard Corrigan
	Quirinale

Best Buys

Top 40 Bangs for the Buck

1. Food for Thought
2. Books for Cooks
3. Pepper Tree
4. Churchill Arms
5. North Sea
6. Gourmet Burger
7. Little Bay
8. Wagamama
9. Battersea Grill/Chelsea
10. Ed's Easy Diner
11. Busaba Eathai
12. Ye Olde Cheshire
13. Lucky 7
14. Pat. Valerie
15. Original Lahore Kebab
16. La Fromagerie
17. Tokyo Diner
18. La Porchetta
19. Jenny Lo's Tea Hse.
20. Masala Zone
21. Gallipoli
22. Tom's Deli
23. Mela
24. Bodeans
25. Mandalay
26. Pizza Express
27. Nyonya
28. Troubadour
29. Ask Pizza
30. Seashell
31. Ben's Thai
32. Viet Hoa
33. Baker & Spice
34. Chowki Bar
35. Giraffe
36. Two Bros. Fish
37. Meson Don Felipe
38. Khan's/Kensington
39. New Culture Rev.
40. Khan's

Other Good Values

Abbeville
Anglesea Arms
Aperitivo
Belgo
Bloom's
Builders Arms
Buona Sera
Café Japan
Carluccio's
Chiang Mai
Chinese Experience
Chuen Cheng Ku
Crazy Homies
Duke of Cambridge
Eagle
Eat & Two Veg
ECapital
Four Seasons Chinese
Geales Fish
Golden Dragon
Harbour City
Ikkyu
Kulu Kulu Sushi
Made in Italy
Malabar
Maroush
Mr. Kong
Nautilus Fish
Noto
Ottolenghi
Palmerston
Phoenix Palace
Ping Pong
Pizza Metro
Raoul's
Sofra
Strada
Tas
202
Yo! Sushi

Restaurant Directory

Abbaye 16 | 13 | 15 | £22

55 Charterhouse St., EC1 (Farringdon), 020-7253 1612; fax 7251 5259

"When you're in the mood for mussels and beer", this "on-the-dingy-side-of-cosy" venue "across from the Smithfield meat market" "hits the spot" thanks to a "staple", "not-expensive" menu of "comfort food, Belge-style" and a "great range of brews" – just remember to "avoid heavy machinery afterwards"; twice-weekly "jazz nights offer an interesting distraction."

Abbeville, The ∇ 19 | 18 | 17 | £24

67-69 Abbeville Rd., SW4 (Clapham South), 020-8675 2201; fax 8675 2212; www.theabbeville.com

This Clapham gastro-pub makes a "relaxed environment" for "a meal with friends" over a "reasonably priced" Modern European–Traditional British menu ("a bit of a mishmash", but "interesting"); the decor's "much improved after a [recent] refurb", but you may "have to wait patiently for your food, even during slow hours."

Abbey, The – | – | – | M

124 Kentish Town Rd., NW1 (Camden/Kentish Town), 020-7267 9449; www.abbeypub.co.uk

"A great newcomer for the area", this Kentish Town gastro-pub with exposed walls and terra-cotta floors serves simple Modern European–British fare to "the local thirtysomething crowd"; its two snug rooms, garden and rooftop seating area are "very nicely done."

Abbey Road Pub & Dining Room ∇ 15 | 16 | 13 | £27

63 Abbey Rd., NW8 (St. John's Wood), 020-7328 6626; fax 7625 9168

"Classic comfort fare" from a "reliable" Italian menu attracts admirers to this St. John's Wood gastro-pub, which was remodelled last year; but malcontents cite an all-around "mediocrity", noting "I wouldn't find myself here if I didn't live down the street."

Abeno ∇ 21 | 10 | 20 | £27

47 Museum St., WC1 (Holborn), 020-7405 3211; fax 7405 3212

It may be "small and tight", but this "friendly" spot a stone's throw from the British Museum "is a crowd-pleaser" for "funky Japanese dishes", like its "speciality *okonomiyaki*, an omelette-pancake thing, cooked to order at your table"; it's a "unique" experience that's "good for family" meals and groups alike.

Abingdon, The 20 | 16 | 19 | £31

54 Abingdon Rd., W8 (Earl's Ct./High St. Kensington), 020-7937 3339; fax 7795 6388; www.theabingdon.ukgateway.net

"Like your favourite sweater and jeans", this "lively" Kensington haunt "is always comfortable", from the "warm vibe" and "welcoming" staff to "consistently good" Modern European cooking; if pessimists pronounce it "passé" and prone to be "somewhat smoky", all concede it's exactly the kind of "place you want to hang out on a rainy Sunday."

Admiral Codrington, The 18 | 17 | 17 | £30

17 Mossop St., SW3 (South Kensington), 020-7581 0005; fax 7589 2452; www.theadmiralcodrington.co.uk

"Not a gastro-pub, but a pub with a restaurant at the rear", this "civilised", "casual" Chelsea corner is "often packed" with a "youngish, buzzy" crowd enjoying "good-if-not-great" Modern European–British food; if the "service does not shape up" at times, the "cosy fire in winter" and "retracting roof in summer are big plus points"; throw in the "strong fresh fish offerings" and this admiral's admirers say "go for the cod(rington)."

Admiralty, The 19 | 17 | 18 | £43

Somerset House, The Strand, WC2 (Temple), 020-7845 4646; fax 7845 4658

The "swank" entrance through Somerset House's "beautiful courtyard" is "the most spectacular part" of this Strand site featuring "shipshape chandeliers"; supportive sailors say the Modern British fare is "expensive – but when it's good, it's very good", whilst mutinous mateys mutter about a "chilly atmosphere" and maintain the fare "needs a bit of zip."

Alastair Little ◐ ☒ 22 | 14 | 21 | £42

49 Frith St., W1 (Leicester Sq./Tottenham Court Rd.), 020-7734 5183; fax 7734 5206

A "perennial fave" of many, this "low-key", "tiny" Soho stalwart is lauded for "innovative", "carefully orchestrated" Modern British dishes cooked "with flair" and supported by a "competitively priced wine list"; if some claim it is "not the same since Alastair departed" (back in 2003) and suggest the "cramped" digs "need a face-lift", this "unique" spot is "still worth a stop."

Albannach – | – | – | E

66 Trafalgar Sq., WC2 (Charing Cross/Leicester Sq.), 020-7930 0066; fax 7389 9800; www.albannach.co.uk

Adding to the ranks of imposing banks being transformed into sassy-looking restaurants/bars, this large "new find" in Trafalgar Square has a sleek "upstairs dining area" and vaulted booths for private gatherings; the Modern European menu (with Scottish specialities, like "great beef") is served by a tartan-kilted staff, whose "over-friendliness, although unnerving, is charming nonetheless."

Al Bustan 21 | 16 | 19 | £32

68 Old Brompton Rd., SW7 (South Kensington), 020-7584 5805; fax 8563 1036

"Fresh", "decent" Lebanese cooking and "courteous service" are the hallmarks of this bi-level "neighbourhood staple" in South Kensington; although a rise in the Decor score sides with those who feel the "downstairs is odd, yet likeably so", others say it "needs some help" on the furnishings front (it "may have the smallest gents' in town").

Al Duca ☒ 19 | 16 | 18 | £38

4-5 Duke of York St., SW1 (Green Park/Piccadilly Circus), 020-7839 3090; fax 7839 4050; www.alduca-restaurant.co.uk

"Just off Piccadilly", this busy venue serves "dependable Italian specialities" from an "ever-changing menu" to "lots of dark suits" – not to mention a few types on "discreet assignations"; although some "can't get too excited" about the "unremarkable" setting, the "pre-theatre menu can not be beat", along with "efficient" staff to ensure "you make curtain time."

Al Hamra ◐ 22 | 14 | 19 | £35

31-33 Shepherd Mkt., W1 (Green Park), 020-7493 1954; fax 7493 1044; www.alhamrarestaurant.com

"If it's good enough for the gazillionaires who eat here every night [there's a £20 minimum], it's good enough for" me, sums up sentiments about this "friendly", "established Lebanese"; the "fantastic" cuisine's "authenticity can be seen by looking at the customers", and if the "simple", "tight quarters" are "a bit dull" for some, the "outside" tables on Shepherd Market are the "happening place on a nice day."

Allium – | – | – | VE

Dolphin Square Hotel, Chichester St., SW1 (Pimlico), 020-7798 6888; fax 7798 5685; www.allium.co.uk

Assuming command of the Dolphin Square Hotel dining room, co-chef Anton Edelmann (ex Savoy Group) pins his culinary colours to the mast of this smart space with "lush, shiplike decor" (that a few find "cold") and "great", "light" Modern European cooking; for the most part, the "staff try to please."

Alloro ☒ 21 | 19 | 20 | £47

19-20 Dover St., W1 (Green Park), 020-7495 4768; fax 7629 5348

"Someone knows what he's doing in the kitchen" of this "versatile, consistent favourite" that "never fails to satisfy" with its modern Italian menu, supported by a "fab wine list", that's a "pretty decent" value "by Mayfair standards"; a "perfect business venue", it draws a "sophisticated" "art gallery crowd at lunch", but is "more relaxed in the evening" when the "nice bar" fills up with its "following."

Almeida 19 | 18 | 19 | £42

30 Almeida St., N1 (Angel/Highbury & Islington), 020-7354 4777; fax 7354 2777; www.conran-restaurants.co.uk

"Gallic courtesy and Conran Group know-how" combine to make this Islington brasserielike place "perfect [before or] after a play at the Almeida" Theatre next door; most audiences approve of the "accomplished" Classic French cooking – featuring a "heavenly treat of a pâté/charcuterie trolley" – but some snarl that its "patchy" performance amounts to "poor value for the money."

Alounak ◐ | 21 | 9 | 15 | £20

10 Russell Gardens, W14 (Olympia), 020-7603 1130
44 Westbourne Grove, W2 (Bayswater/Queensway), 020-7229 4158; fax 7792 1219

It's "a real hoot when it gets lively" at these "unpretentious" Persians in Olympia and Westbourne Grove, whose "great-value" menu of "excellent, homestyle food" "satisfies a craving for a good mixed grill" amongst other things; "even if the service is on the chaotic side", both offer the added benefit of being BYO – just remember to "book before you go" (Russell Gardens only).

Al Sultan | 22 | 14 | 18 | £36

51-52 Hertford St., W1 (Green Park), 020-7408 1155; fax 7408 1113; www.alsultan.co.uk

Expect "an authentic, no-nonsense experience" of "classic" dishes, including "an excellent array of Middle Eastern tapas", at this Lebanese with a "great location" next to Mayfair's Curzon cinema; whilst many feel "they could work a little more on the decor" ("a bit boring"), the place is "perfect on a drizzly evening" with a "most engaging owner" to jolly things along.

Al Waha ◐ | ▽ 25 | 12 | 20 | £30

75 Westbourne Grove, W2 (Bayswater/Queensway), 020-7229 0806; www.waha-uk.com

"At weekends, prepare to queue" at this "affordable" Bayswater Lebanese for "fabulous", "authentic" cooking ("like grandma used to make") served by "polite" staff who "treat people like royalty"; if the "bland, old-fashioned decor" causes offence, there's "great takeaway too, delivered very attractively."

Amaya | 25 | 23 | 22 | £52

15 Halkin Arcade, Motcomb St., SW1 (Knightsbridge), 020-7823 1166; fax 7259 6464; www.realindianfood.com

"Unlike anything you would expect in an Indian restaurant" – the "decor is spot-on in terms of trendiness", and the open-plan kitchen "specialises in grills rather than traditional" curries – this "hip" Belgravia newcomer from the Chutney Mary team wows with "light", "transcendental food", served in "small, shareable portions" by "helpful waiters"; it may be "hidden" in a shopping arcade, but the "obviously posh clientele" agrees it's "here to last."

Anchor & Hope ⊠ | 23 | 14 | 17 | £28

36 The Cut, SE1 (Waterloo), 020-7928 9898

Representing the "gastro-pub par excellence" (from the team previously at The Eagle), this "super find" close to the Old and New Vics in Waterloo offers "robust", "cutting-edge cooking" from a Modern British menu that's "marvellous for the price"; if the impatient are irked by the "no-reservations policy", stalwarts suggest "settling in for a couple of pints" whilst waiting; P.S. "gets very smoky" at "crowded" times.

Andrew Edmunds 22 | 18 | 21 | £34

46 Lexington St., W1 (Oxford Circus/Piccadilly Circus), 020-7437 5708

It looks a little "ramshackle", but there's "nowhere better" for "effortless romance" than this "intimate experience" in Soho – complete with "the flattering glow of candlelight" – where "hearty, honest" Modern European bistro cooking comes at "bargain prices"; "sitting on your neighbour's lap is not everyone's cup of tea", but the fact it's "increasingly hard to get a table" suggests they're in the minority.

Angela Hartnett's MENU 24 | 24 | 24 | £75

The Connaught Hotel, 16 Carlos Pl., W1 (Bond St./Green Park), 020-7592 1222; fax 7292 1223; www.angelahartnett.com

"Bringing new vibrancy" to the Connaught's "clubby, warm" dining room, "Gordon Ramsay protégée" Angela Hartnett offers "outstanding" Modern European cuisine with some "unusual Italian-inspired dishes", proffered by servers who "know what you want before you do"; naturally, nostalgists are "disappointed", snapping this incarnation is "more self-satisfied than it deserves", but most find the "many amuse-bouches and freebies" make it "worth the steep price."

Anglesea Arms 21 | 16 | 14 | £27

35 Wingate Rd., W6 (Goldhawk Rd./Ravenscourt Park), 020-8749 1291; fax 8749 1254

"One of the most original in London", this Shepherd's Bush "gem of a gastro-pub" is most "notable" for Modern British "comfy food", as well as an "annoying policy of not allowing reservations" – "so get there early for lunch" on weekends; even if "service can be hit-and-miss", it's "a great hangout."

Annabel's ◐ ⊠ 20 | 23 | 22 | £69

Private club; inquiries: 020-7629 1096

"Mingle with the chic, the haughty and the naughty" at this "fabulous private club" in Mayfair that "still has what it takes to be" a "sexy" spot for "dining and dancing till the wee hours"; "attentive service" presents "simple Classic" British–French dishes, and even if the "bill is staggering", patrons profess this "perennial favourite" still has "many years yet to run" – though a vocal minority find "the recent relaxation of the dress code a no-no."

Annie's ▽ 19 | 23 | 22 | £29

162 Thames Rd., W4 (Kew Bridge B.R.), 020-8994 6848
36-38 White Hart Ln., SW13 (Barnes Bridge B.R.), 020-8878 2020; fax 8876 8478

With "idiosyncratic decor" that looks "like someone's front room", this "unpretentious", "bohemian" duo are "perfect neighbourhood restaurants", with "lovely staff" serving "huge portions" of "competent" Modern British fare; being "open all day" (from 10 AM) makes them "worth the trip to Barnes" or Chiswick.

Aperitivo ☒ 20 | 16 | 18 | £25

41 Beak St., W1F (Oxford Circus/Piccadilly Circus), 020-7287 2057; www.aperitivo-restaurants.com

A "delicious" "selection of Italian tapas-style dishes" ("perfect for sharing"), plus "a good choice of vinos", is the main draw of this "spot right in the middle of things" in Soho; it's "ideal for a large group before a night out" or "after the theatre" – although it's advisable to "book ahead at peak times."

Arancia ☒ – | – | – | M

52 Southwark Park Rd., SE16 (Bermondsey), 020-7394 1751; fax 7394 1751

"The kind of neighbourhood restaurant this part of London needs" say Bermondsey boosters of this "fabulous" little place serving "unusual, delicious modern Italian dishes" and wines that make it "a real winner" (despite the "sparse decor") – not the least because it's "excellent value", particularly on the lunch prix fixe.

Archipelago ☒ ▽ 23 | 24 | 20 | £39

110 Whitfield St., W1 (Goodge St./Warren St.), 020-7383 3346; fax 7383 7181

"If you are up for adventure" on a plate, this "strange, but wonderfully intimate" Fitzrovian eatery will "amaze", thanks to an "innovative" Eclectic menu that stars such "weird" delights as "locust salad" and "scorpions in chocolate"; granted, it's "gimmicky", and the "exotic" decor is "like dining in some mad old aunt's living room", but all that "makes a fun date"; P.S. "you can get food without the bugs", too ("but you should try them once just to say you have").

Ark ☒ 17 | 16 | 18 | £34

122 Palace Gardens Terrace, W8 (Notting Hill Gate), 020-7229 4024; fax 7792 8787; www.thearkrestaurant.co.uk

This "low-key" Notting Hill "sleeper" has a loyal following who find it a "good local" option for "inventive" Italian cuisine and a "reasonably priced wine list"; whilst it's "charming" "if the right crowd is there", a fall in the Food and Decor scores supports suggestions the place is "a little worn now."

Arkansas Cafe ▽ 16 | 7 | 8 | £15

Old Spitalfields Mkt., 107B Commercial St., E1 (Liverpool St.), 020-7377 6999; fax 7377 6990

"The charm of American host"/co-chef Bubba Helberg is as much a draw as the "authentic", "amazing" BBQ and burgers for "cheapish" prices at this lunch-only spot at Spitalfields Market; however, "surly" staff and the "ramshackle room" lead several to suggest the place is "past its sell-by date" – "maybe Bubba's lived in Blighty a little too long."

Armadillo ☒ — | — | — | M

41 Broadway Mkt., E8 (Bethnal Green), 020-7249 3633; www.armadillorestaurant.co.uk

Representing "something different in London's sea of Modern European restaurants", this "cosy, unassuming" eatery is "worth a trip" to Hackney for "excellent", "ever-changing" South American fare that's "great value" to boot; "really friendly" service completes the picture for those who "never fail to be impressed."

Artigiano 19 | 16 | 16 | £37

12A Belsize Terrace, NW3 (Belsize Park/Swiss Cottage), 020-7794 4288; fax 7435 2048; www.etruscarestaurants.com

There's "a nice buzz about this comfortable, modern Italian" in "picturesque Belsize Village" (and often full of its "well-known residents"), where "well-cooked, homestyle dishes" and a "good wine selection" make it a "decent" neighbourhood "local"; however, sceptics suggest the "service could be sharper" and find "the cost reflects more the neighbourhood than the food."

ASIA DE CUBA ◐ 22 | 23 | 18 | £49

St. Martin's Lane Hotel, 45 St. Martin's Ln., WC2 (Leicester Sq.), 020-7300 5588; fax 7300 5540; www.chinagrillmanagement.com

"See the beautiful people swan about" at this "chic", "minimalist" dining room "in the über-hip St. Martin's Lane Hotel" where a "fabulous fusion" "celebration of two rich culinary traditions" – Asian and Cuban – comes in large "family-style portions", albeit at "royal family prices"; some snipe the "erratic staff" "think they're destined for the big screen instead of serving quickly", and "things get too noisy for much conversation", but to most, this "achingly trendy" spot "hasn't lost its lustre."

Ask Pizza 16 | 13 | 15 | £17

145 Notting Hill Gate, W11 (Notting Hill Gate), 020-7792 9942
222 Kensington High St., W8 (High St. Kensington), 020-7937 5540; fax 7937 5540
219-221 Chiswick High Rd., W4 (Turnham Green), 020-8742 1323 ◐
121-125 Park St., W1 (Marble Arch), 020-7495 7760; fax 7495 7760
48 Grafton Way, W1 (Warren St.), 020-7388 8108; fax 7388 8112 ◐
Unit 23-24, Gloucester Arcade, SW7 (Gloucester Rd.), 020-7835 0840 ◐
345 Fulham Palace Rd., SW6 (Hammersmith/Putney Bridge), 020-7371 0392
300 King's Rd., SW3 (Sloane Sq.), 020-7349 9123
160-162 Victoria St., SW1 (St. James's Park/Victoria), 020-7630 8228; fax 7630 5218

(continued)
Ask Pizza
216 Haverstock Hill, NW3 (Belsize Park/Chalk Farm), 020-7433 3896; fax 7435 6490 ◐
www.askcentral.co.uk
Additional locations throughout London
Surveyors on "small budgets" say these "middle-of-the-road" Italians are "amazingly good for a chain", with a "varied menu", "quick" service and a "reasonable wine list"; whilst "you're not going to be raving about them", they "always produce the goods", especially "for families of young kids and hungry teenagers."

Assaggi ☒ 25 | 17 | 21 | £48
39 Chepstow Pl., W2 (Notting Hill Gate), 020-7792 5501; fax 08700 512923
"Posing as a rustic Italian above a pub in Notting Hill", this "understated" eatery is actually a "sophisticated", "splendid" site where "everything is perfectly executed", from the "high-end", "unpretentious" cooking "with a Sardinian twist" to the "delightful staff's" "lively service"; a few inevitably think it's "overrated" and many more plead "fix the acoustics" ("can hardly hear"), but the fact it's "always full" speaks loud and clear; P.S. "tip: make your next reservation when you leave."

Atlantic Bar & Grill ◐☒ 16 | 20 | 15 | £38
20 Glasshouse St., W1 (Piccadilly Circus), 020-7734 4888; fax 7734 5400; www.atlanticbarandgrill.com
After the "magnificent bar" and the "grandeur" of the huge, "high ceilinged", art deco room, it's "a pity" that the "frosty" "staff and food are a letdown" at this Modern British–Med "underneath Piccadilly"; still, it's "interesting" for "late-night eating" or "drinks only" amidst the "hopping nightlife" "with a *Footballers Wives* feel" – even if the hip hiss the scene's "outdated" ("I even saw big shoulder pads!").

Aubaine 18 | 17 | 13 | £31
260-262 Brompton Rd., SW3 (South Kensington), 020-7052 0100; fax 7052 0622; www.aubaine.co.uk
"Like sitting on the Left Bank without any of the attitude" sums up the Seine-like scene at this "welcome addition to South Ken" with tightly packed tables (plus a communal one) and a "good all-day menu" (from 7 AM) of "honest" French Bistro fare; even those nonplussed by the "slow, confused service" praise the "patisserie at the front" as "great for carbo-loading on fresh baked goods."

AUBERGINE ☒ 26 | 21 | 23 | £66
11 Park Walk, SW10 (Gloucester Rd./South Kensington), 020-7352 3449; fax 7351 1770; www.atozrestaurants.com
"No hype, just pure consistent quality" is what "those who know" expect from this "class place" off Fulham Road,

which "retains remarkable flair under chef William Drabble"; "excellent, although not for the timid", his New French stylings are served by staff that make you "feel totally pampered"; whilst the "serious" atmosphere strikes some as "stuffy", to most this "gastronomic" getaway is an "ethereal experience"; P.S. it's "rather dear", but the "set lunch is wonderful value."

Aurora ⊠ 19 | 19 | 19 | £54

Great Eastern Hotel, 40 Liverpool St., EC2 (Liverpool St.), 020-7618 7000; fax 7618 7001; www.great-eastern-hotel.co.uk

"One of the decent fancy restaurants in the City", this "large, airy" hotel dining room (part of the Conran Group) with a "flashy" stained-glass Victorian dome is "definitely a banker hangout" with "generous seating", a "keen sommelier" and a Modern British–French menu that's so "surprisingly good", "the bill doesn't feel so difficult to pay" – at least, to those "on expenses"; "but the whole thing is so boring" opponents retort.

Avenue, The 19 | 19 | 17 | £43

7-9 St. James's St., SW1 (Green Park), 020-7321 2111; fax 7321 2500; www.egami.co.uk

"Still slick", still "a kick" puff positives of this "modern, minimalistic" St. James's venue that attracts "City slickers" who "pose at the bar" with its "great sight-lines for people-watching" or consume the "consistent" Modern European fare; main complaint is it's "far too noisy" – perhaps with the calls for "service that's so busy trying to be cool, it couldn't care about the customers."

Axis ⊠ 21 | 21 | 22 | £45

One Aldwych Hotel, 1 Aldwych, WC2 (Charing Cross/ Covent Garden), 020-7300 0300; fax 7300 0301; www.onealdwych.com

"The surroundings make anyone feel special" at this "hip", "neo-modern" address "usefully located underneath" Aldwych, which is "great for business lunches and pre-theatre dinners" (when the service is "super-fast"); although the Modern British–Eclectic fare won't cause the earth to tilt off its axis ("very good but not quite excellent"), most applaud this "steady performer."

Aziz ▽ 19 | 20 | 16 | £29

30-32 Vanston Pl., SW6 (Fulham Broadway), 020-7386 0086; fax 7610 1661

"In a trendy Fulham cobbled lane" this "stylish", modern Middle Eastern eatery is "trying hard and making a good effort" thanks to "much warmer decor since a revamp" and a "real Moroccan feel to the food"; Thursday–Saturdays, there's "live entertainment" (belly dancers) – just "take a pair of earplugs"; P.S. "the adjacent shop is a must" for deli delights.

Babylon ▽ 19 | 21 | 17 | £42

The Roof Gardens, 99 Kensington High St., W8 (High St. Kensington), 020-7368 3993; fax 7938 2774; www.roofgardens.com

"Be sure to walk around the gardens" and see "the excellent views" of South Kensington and beyond from Sir Richard Branson's "elegant" rooftop restaurant; whilst the "quality" Modern European fare seems "quite expensive" ("you'll feel you're subsidising his airline"), most agree this makes a "good place for a special date" – especially on Thursdays and Saturdays when diners can use the private "club downstairs" (£10 fee).

Baker & Spice 23 | 17 | 15 | £22

47 Denyer St., SW3 (Knightsbridge/South Kensington), 020-7589 4734; fax 7589 4734

54-56 Elizabeth St., SW1 (Sloane Sq./Victoria), 020-7730 3033; fax 7730 3188 ⊠

75 Salusbury Rd., NW6 (Queens Park), 020-7604 3636; fax 7604 3646

www.bakerandspice.com

"The smells tempt you from the other end of the street" to this trio around town – "more bakery/cafe than restaurant" – for "seriously addictive", "healthy organic" Med meals and pastries; even "grotesquely" "high prices don't keep the droves away", the reason – along with the "basic", "communal seating" and "shambolic service" – that many "stick to takeaway"; P.S. Elizabeth Street has "no toilets."

Balans ◐ 15 | 14 | 17 | £24

187 Kensington High St., W8 (High St. Kensington), 020-7376 0115; fax 7938 4653

60 Old Compton St., W1 (Leicester Sq./Piccadilly Circus/ Tottenham Court Rd.), 020-7439 2183; fax 7734 2665

239 Old Brompton Rd., SW5 (Earl's Ct.), 020-7244 8838; fax 7244 6226

www.balans.co.uk

"A bohemian thrill for the adventurous", this "crammed", all-day cafe chain attracts a "predominately gay crowd" – although it's "straight-friendly" – with "big portions" of "simple, dependable" Modern British fare (but "the men are tastier than the meals, alas"); "cheerful", "camp staff" add to the appeal – just "don't expect a window seat unless you're one of the pretty people"; N.B. the Old Compton Street site's open all night.

Balham Kitchen & Bar 17 | 21 | 18 | £33

15-19 Bedford Hill, SW12 (Balham B.R.), 020-8675 6900; fax 8673 3965; www.balhamkitchen.com

This "fantastic concept from Nick Jones" (of Soho House fame) is a "stylish, yet casual" "neighbourhood diner" – "just like [its neighbourhood] Balham, in fact" – that serves a "variety of Modern British dishes" "for breakfast through to evening"; aside from the much-praised brunch, "however, the food is nowhere near as special as the place looks" and "the service could do with some re-training."

Baltic 22 | 21 | 19 | £36

74 Blackfriars Rd., SE1 (Southwark), 020-7928 1111; fax 7928 8487; www.balticrestaurant.co.uk

"Worth trekking to Southwark for", this "modern", "elegant" venue in a former coach-builder's workshop ("sister to Wòdka") offers the most "refined", "palatable Eastern European food likely to be found in London"; the "buzzy, busy" "bar scene upfront" is fuelled by "cocktails made to perfection" from a "fabulous vodka selection" – so "make sure you have a designated driver", since you'll "leave feeling well-fed, with no pain."

Bam-Bou ◐ ☒ 18 | 23 | 16 | £36

1 Percy St., W1 (Tottenham Court Rd.), 020-7323 9130; fax 7323 9140; www.bam-bou.co.uk

"Still one of the more stylish in town", this "gorgeous", "colonial"-style "Fitzrovia townhouse" has "several rooms and cosy alcoves" for "a perfect romantic date"; if a minority think "something's lacking" in the "fresh, light" Vietnamese–Southeast Asian cuisine – such as "flavour in your plate" or efficiency from your server – most rate it an "exotic" "experience" that "makes you feel special."

Bank Aldwych 18 | 18 | 17 | £38

1 Kingsway, WC2 (Holborn), 020-7379 9797; fax 7240 7001; www.bankrestaurants.com

A "reliable standby" "for pre- or post-theatre, weekend brunch", "after-work hanging-out" and even breakfast is the bottom line on this "sleek, modern" "stylish venue" serving Modern European cuisine in Aldwych; critical creditors call it costly, "noisy and soulless", but to most, "the deposits at this bank are merited by the quality of the withdrawals."

Bankside 18 | 17 | 17 | £27

32 Southwark Bridge Rd., SE1 (London Bridge), 020-7633 0011; fax 7633 0011

1 Angel Ct., 30 Throgmorton St., EC2 (Bank), 0845-226 0011 ☒

www.banksiderestaurants.co.uk

"Intriguing buzzers at the table side call the attention of a waiter" at this simply decorated Southwark site; if a few feel there's "not much else to recommend it", boosters bank on its "good, honest" Modern British fare; N.B. the new, unrated City sibling is larger, but lacks the table buzzers.

Bank Westminster & Zander Bar ☒ 18 | 19 | 16 | £35

45 Buckingham Gate, SW1 (St. James's Park), 020-7379 9797; fax 7240 7001; www.bankrestaurants.com

It's "nice to have a good bar near Victoria", but beyond this one – at 48 metres, "the longest in the UK" – lies a "beautiful conservatory" "overlooking a courtyard" and decorated with "amazingly alluring balls hanging from the ceiling"; the "solid, respectable" Modern European cuisine comes at "fair prices" though also "with some flaws"; still, it's "lovely on a sunny summer day."

Banquette ◐ ∇ 18 | 21 | 18 | £37

Savoy Hotel, The Strand, WC2 (Covent Garden/Embankment), 020-7420 2392; fax 7592 1601; www.marcuswareing.com

"Perched like a pigeon above the Savoy's motor court" – thus affording "views of the comings and goings of diplomats and tourists" – is this "smart, '50s-style diner"; some applaud the American–Modern European menu's "combo of comfort and luxe" (e.g. "a fabulous Gruyère cheeseburger") whilst others find it a "rip-off par excellence"; all agree, though, "it's handy after nearby theatres."

Barnsbury, The – | – | – | M

209-211 Liverpool Rd., N1 (Angel), 020-7607 5519; fax 7607 3256; www.thebarnsbury.co.uk

"Off the main Islington track", this "stylish, but still homely gastro-pub" – with original oak panelling and "funky glam chandeliers made from wine glasses" – offers a "reliable" Modern British menu that's "excellent value" to boot; it's "not as famous as others in N1", which suits regulars who plead "please keep it a secret!"

Beiteddine ◐ ∇ 20 | 13 | 19 | £39

8 Harriet St., SW1 (Knightsbridge/Sloane Sq.), 020-7235 3969; fax 7245 6335; www.beiteddinerestaurant.com

Its name means 'house of faith', and indeed the faithful come to this unassuming Lebanese just off Sloane Street for "delish" eats served by "helpful" – but "not pushy" – staff; it's particularly "popular with Middle Eastern" visitors, although the "price can rise swiftly if one is not careful."

BELGO 18 | 17 | 15 | £23

50 Earlham St., WC2 (Covent Garden), 020-7813 2233; fax 7209 3212

72 Chalk Farm Rd., NW1 (Chalk Farm), 020-7267 0718; fax 7284 4842

www.belgo-restaurants.com

"Magnificent mussels, awesome ales" and "waiters posing as monks" define this "rather kitsch" Belgian duo in Centraal (Covent Garden) and the Noord (Chalk Farm) with a "raucous warehouse atmosphere" and "communal dining" that's "great for groups"; yes, they're little "more than frites factories" and the service can be "indifferent", but "you can't beat the beat-the-clock special" on weekdays (pay the price of the time you order).

Bellamy's ⊠ ∇ 19 | 19 | 18 | £49

18/18a Bruton Pl., W1 (Green Park/Bond St.), 020-7491 2727; fax 7491 9990

The former supremo of Annabel's et al., Gavin "Rankin knows his stuff" say converts to his "comfortable" "addition to the eating scene" in Mayfair; it proffers "quality" "old French Brasserie favourites" and "tremendous wines at unheard-of, reasonable prices", and whilst some "can't understand the hype" ("sedate" atmosphere, "boring menu"), all applaud the adjacent "fab deli for take-home treats."

Belvedere, The 22 | 25 | 21 | £47

Holland Park, off Abbotsbury Rd., W8 (Holland Park), 020-7602 1238; fax 7610 4382; www.whitestarline.org.uk
Part of "reliable" restaurateur Marco Pierre White's empire, this "beautiful setting in Holland Park" – "like a country manor" surrounded by gardens – houses a "smashing" Modern British–New French menu (with "absolute bargain" prix fixes), served by "gracious" staff in an "elegant" tri-level space with "light streaming through stained glass"; P.S. "make sure to book the terrace in summer" – there are only five sought-after tables.

Benares 23 | 24 | 21 | £46

12 Berkeley Sq., W1 (Green Park), 020-7629 8886; fax 7499 2430; www.benaresrestaurant.com
"Class act" is the consensus on chef-patron Atul Kochhar's "beautifully appointed" Mayfair home (complete with "infinity-edged lotus ponds") where the "inventive" regional Indian cooking ("nouvelle without losing its roots") dished out by "accommodating staff" "won't leave you feeling like you weigh a ton"; it all comes "at a price", so "take a sack of money" – because this "enthralling" spot is "worth it as a treat."

Bengal Clipper ◐ 23 | 19 | 18 | £30

11-12 Cardamom Bldg., 31 Shad Thames, SE1 (London Bridge/ Tower Hill), 020-7357 9001; fax 7357 9002; www.bengalclipper.co.uk
"One street back from the river" Thames at Butlers Wharf, this "upscale" Indian offers "well-executed food"; perhaps the warehouselike room is a tad "awkward", but "if you're lucky, the kitschy pianist will be playing" (Tuesday–Saturday nights) and that "makes the ambience relaxing."

Benihana 17 | 14 | 18 | £39

37 Sackville St., W1 (Green Park/Piccadilly Circus), 020-7494 2525; fax 7494 1456
77 King's Rd., SW3 (Sloane Sq.), 020-7376 7799; fax 7376 7377
100 Avenue Rd., NW3 (Swiss Cottage), 020-7586 9508; fax 7586 6740
www.benihana.com
"Take the kids" to this Tokyo-esque trio where "theatrical" chefs "perform tricks" at the table like "knife-wielding samurais"; but grown-ups gripe "the gimmick's" "getting tired" – especially as the tab's "pretty pricey for pretty average Japanese food"; the need for "better ventilation" means one often emerges "smelling like a french fry."

Ben's Thai 16 | 13 | 18 | £19

93 Warrington Crescent, W9 (Maida Vale/Warwick Ave.), 020-7266 3134; fax 7221 8799

"After a few drinks in the pub downstairs", try the "generous portions" of "reliable" if "typical Thai" fare at "cheapish" prices ("would happily have paid more!") at this "easy-going" Maida Vale venue; the "delightful staff" have earned a rise in the Service score, perhaps because they're "good with young children."

Bentley's ◐ 20 | 18 | 20 | £46

11-15 Swallow St., W1 (Piccadilly Circus), 020-7734 4756; fax 7287 2972

"The fish is fresh and the preparation straightforward" at this "very British" "timeless old-timer" that has occupied the same "tightly packed" Piccadilly premises since 1916; true, "prices have crept up over the years", but everything else – from the "subtle but snappy service" to the signature "Dover sole to die for" – has stayed "astonishingly reliable."

Berkeley Square, The ⊠ 21 | 18 | 18 | £45

7 Davies St., W1 (Bond St.), 020-7629 6993; fax 7491 9719; www.theberkeleysquare.com

"Be daring and try" the "thoughtful", "ambitious" cuisine (and wines suggested by a "helpful sommelier") at this New French near Berkeley Square; it's "perfect for a business lunch" – though some find the decor and service "a bit too business"-like as well ("other than taking our order, there was no dialogue" with staff); still, it's a refreshingly "grown-up" place, and the "summer terrace is a clear advantage."

Bertorelli 17 | 15 | 16 | £30

11-13 Frith St., W1 (Leicester Sq./Tottenham Court Rd.), 020-7494 3491; fax 7439 9431 ◐

19-23 Charlotte St., W1 (Goodge St./Tottenham Court Rd.), 020-7636 4174; fax 7467 8902 ⊠

44A Floral St., WC2 (Covent Garden), 020-7836 3969; fax 7836 1868

1 Plough Pl., Fetter Ln., EC4 (Chancery Ln.), 020-7842 0510; fax 7842 0511 ⊠

www.santeonline.co.uk

When seeking "a dependable, if not daring" meal "at a reasonable price", try this "casual", "cheerful" quartet of "Italian clichés" ("no surprises, and that makes it great"); let the critics carp about the "conveyor-belt" aspects – "great locations" ensure there's always "a good buzz"; P.S. the branch at "Covent Garden is highly recommended for theatrical or operatic evenings."

BIBENDUM ◐ 23 | 23 | 21 | £58

Michelin House, 81 Fulham Rd., SW3 (South Kensington), 020-7581 5817; fax 7823 7925; www.bibendum.co.uk

"A favourite of big wheels", this "renovated Michelin tyre depot" at Brompton Cross is a "sumptuous" setting –

complete with "wonderful stained-glass windows" – for "glorious" New French cuisine served by "efficient, unobtrusive" staff; "with some prices like phone numbers", many motorists question the "value/cost ratio" – but "where better to inflate yourself than the Michelin Man's home?"

BIBENDUM OYSTER BAR 23 18 18 £39

Michelin House, 81 Fulham Rd., SW3 (South Kensington), 020-7589 1480; fax 7823 7925; www.bibendum.co.uk

"All the sensations of the ocean without the sand in your pants" reside at this "wonderfully informal" seafood bistro in the Michelin Building's "former tyre-changing space", which features a "short menu" of "divine seafood platters" and "fabulous oysters"; whilst "teeny-weeny tables" and "neglectful service" have led to Decor and Service score declines, this "true London find" still makes for one "perfect" "pit stop."

Bierodrome 15 15 14 £20

67 Kingsway, WC2 (Charing Cross/Holborn), 020-7242 7469; fax 7242 7493 ⊠

44-48 Clapham High St., SW4 (Clapham North), 020-7720 1118; fax 7720 0288

173-174 Upper St., N1 (Highbury & Islington), 020-7226 5835; fax 7704 0632

www.belgo-restaurants.com

A "fabulous range of obscure speciality ales" to "swill down the mussels" and "Belgian comfort food" is "the main reason to go" to these "fashionable Belgo offshoots" around town; although some say dining here is "more about the fun than the fare", a number of "off-peak deals" (i.e. kids eat free on weekends) means this "lively" chain "won't disappoint" for an "inexpensive" meal.

Big Easy 17 14 16 £26

332-334 King's Rd., SW3 (Sloane Sq.), 020-7352 4071; fax 7352 0844; www.bigeasy.uk.com

"Cajun cuisine meets Chelsea chic" at this "lively" Louisiana shack, "the place to pig out" on "enormous portions" of "good ol'" Yankee vittles accompanied by "U.S. sports on TV" and "live music" every night; it's "appreciated by American expats" and "great for kids" – even if the uneasy argue about the rather unfair prices for only "fair 'cue."

Bingham, The – – – E

Bingham Hotel, 61-63 Petersham Rd. (Richmond), 020-8940 0902; www.binghamhotel.co.uk

Named after former inhabitant Lady Anne Bingham (a 19th-century ancestor of the infamous vanishing Lord Lucan), this handsome Georgian townhouse hotel on the Thames at Richmond has changed hands and undergone a boutique-y revamp; the understated restaurant/bar with huge windows and a covered dining balcony now offers an uncomplicated yet innovative New French–Modern European menu; live jazz fills the rooms at Sunday lunch.

Bistrotheque – | – | – | M

23-27 Wadesdon St., E2 (Bethnal Green), 020-8983 7900; fax 8880 6433; www.bistrotheque.com

Although it's "situated in an unexpected location" (an old Bethnal Green factory), it's "worth the search" to find this large yearling, already "attracting the fashionable" with its "simple French Bistro" fare, a bar serving the usual "hip" cocktails and live entertainment several nights a week.

Bistrot 190 ◐ ∇ 17 | 18 | 16 | £36

Gore Hotel, 190 Queen's Gate, SW7 (Gloucester Rd./South Kensington), 020-7581 5666; fax 7589 8127; www.gorehotel.com

"After a concert at the Royal Albert Hall" around the corner, this "low-key" hotel venue makes a "pleasant" option for "consistent" French–Modern British "offerings" and "a good glass of wine"; reports on the room, however, range from "cosy" to "cramped", which is why some prefer the "interesting" "bar scene" across the corridor.

Black & Blue 17 | 16 | 17 | £27

215-217 Kensington Church St., W8 (Notting Hill Gate), 020-7727 0004; fax 7229 9359
90-92 Wigmore St., W1 (Bond St.), 020-7486 1912; fax 7486 1913
105 Gloucester Rd., SW7 (Gloucester Rd.), 020-7244 7666; fax 7244 9993
205-207 Haverstock Hill, NW3 (Belsize Park), 020-7443 7744; fax 7443 7744
www.blackandblue.biz

"When you need a fix" of beef, this chain is "a good place to meat" profess punsters who, with their "carnivorous children", admire the American menu of steaks, burgers and "great spinach-artichoke dip"; despite "reasonable" prices, sceptics snap your mood and "your wallet will be black-and-blue" after a trip here – perhaps the "soulless" ambience and "inexperienced staff" seem "poor value for money."

Blah! Blah! Blah! ⊠ ∇ 24 | 11 | 19 | £19

78 Goldhawk Rd., W12 (Goldhawk Rd.), 020-8746 1337; fax 7328 3138

"One of London's best-kept secrets", this "little" Shepherd's Bush venue "puts vegetarian food firmly on the map" thanks to an "inexpensive" menu of "wonderful tastes and textures" (the "desserts are worth the visit alone"); a "warm welcome" overpowers the "positively medieval decor."

Blakes ◐ 22 | 25 | 20 | £70

Blakes Hotel, 33 Roland Gardens, SW7 (Gloucester Rd./South Kensington), 020-7370 6701; fax 7373 0442; www.blakeshotels.com

"Clad in black and lacquer", this "effortlessly chic" hotel dining room "away from the madding crowd" in Kensington is "one of London's sexiest" spots for a "dark", "romantic" assignation; after a sabbatical, "chef Neville Campbell is back" to oversee a new "delicious, exotic" Eclectic-Asian menu served by "efficient, if clinical service"; it's "sooo expensive", "but worth it."

Blandford Street ∇ 18 | 17 | 21 | £40

5-7 Blandford St., W1 (Bond St.), 020-7486 9696; fax 7486 5067; www.blandford-street.co.uk

"Excellent for a quiet night out", this Marylebone Modern European offers a "frequently innovative" menu and "pleasant" service; despite doubters who declare it should be dubbed "Bland"-ford Street, it makes "a nice standby when you don't know what you're in the mood for"; N.B. a post-*Survey* refurb may outdate the Decor score.

Bleeding Heart ☒ 22 | 20 | 19 | £38

19 Greville St., EC1 (Farringdon), 020-7404 0333; fax 7831 1402

4 Bleeding Heart Yard, off Greville St., EC1 (Farringdon), 020-7242 8238; fax 7831 1402

www.bleedingheart.co.uk

"Hidden away" in a cobbled courtyard off Hatton Garden, this "atmospheric" New French has an "intimate dining room" downstairs ("a great romantic hideaway") and a "crowded, noisy" ground-floor bistro that works "for business or pleasure"; the "hearty cooking" is "always good", and the "staff know their stuff" – though they can also appear "on the cusp of snooty"; P.S. the Tavern sibling off Greville Street serves "top-quality pub food."

Bloom's 20 | 9 | 15 | £22

130 Golders Green Rd., NW11 (Golders Green), 020-8455 1338; fax 8455 3033; www.bloomsrestaurant.co.uk

"One of the few places to head when you need a chopped liver fix", this traditional Golders Green deli (over 40 years at this location) is "the only place for salt beef" and other kosher "heavy Jewish" dishes "the way your grandma made"; the sentimental sigh the "place has seen better days", but positives proclaim it a "London legacy."

Bluebird Club and Dining Rooms 17 | 19 | 16 | £44

350 King's Rd., SW3 (Sloane Sq.), 020-7559 1129; fax 7559 1202

This Chelsea "Conran Group location" actually houses two eateries: the original Bluebird, an "airy", "brightly lit industrial floor" and "trusty fallback" for "enjoyable" Modern European fare with a "nifty bar" attached; and the Dining Rooms next door, "a great newcomer" run by Tom Conran with a "modern take on Traditional British" cooking in a "smart", "clublike room" (in fact, this is a "refurb" of the old private club – "no need to join now!"); both can be quite "a bit of fun – [particularly] if someone else is paying."

Blue Elephant ◐ 22 | 24 | 21 | £42

3-6 Fulham Broadway, SW6 (Fulham Broadway), 020-7385 6595; fax 7386 7665; www.blueelephant.com

"The kitsch decor is a hoot" at this "Disney-esque jungle" in Fulham, with "wild tropical" plants and "wood bridges" over "koi-filled streams" serving as backdrop for "charming service" and "authentic" Thai cooking that "never fails to impress"; of course this "Southeastern Asia extravaganza" comes "at a price", and a few find it all rather "OTT", but most concede this "movie set" is "a real experience"; P.S. there are "football specials on [Chelsea] match days."

Blue Print Café 18 | 20 | 17 | £40

Design Museum, Butlers Wharf, 28 Shad Thames, SE1 (London Bridge/Tower Hill), 020-7378 7031; fax 7357 8810; www.conran.com

"Go at night" and "get a window table" to make the most of the "fabulous view of Tower Bridge" at this "busy" Conran Group entry in the Design Museum with its "bright, clean-lined" decor and Modern European menu that's long on "fresh seafood"; however, "so-so service" and "inflated prices" cause some surveyors to sing the blues.

BODEANS 19 | 14 | 17 | £19

10 Poland St., W1 (Oxford Circus), 020-7287 7575; fax 7287 4342
169 Clapham High St., SW4 (Clapham Common), 020-7622 4248; fax 7622 3087
www.bodeansbbq.com

"When you just want a messy pig-out" on "finger-licking" "ribs and burnt ends", these BBQ places in Soho and now Clapham make an "awesome" choice for "American comfort food at its best" – and at "damn cheap" prices too; perhaps the "basic decor" is reminiscent of "a Holiday Inn" but most "lonely expats" just concentrate on the tube in the "TV room dedicated" to U.S. sports.

Boisdale ⊠ 18 | 19 | 18 | £42

15 Eccleston St., SW1 (Victoria), 020-7730 6922; fax 7730 0548
Swedeland Ct., 202 Bishopsgate, EC2 (Liverpool St.), 020-7283 1763; fax 7283 1664
www.boisdale.co.uk

"If you can't get to Scotland for dinner, at least go to" these tartan-clad twins in Victoria and Bishopsgate for "a little bit of Caledonian bliss" – "even down to the haggis and 200 single-malt whiskies" – in a "gentleman's club–type" atmosphere; a wee drop in the Food score supports those who say the British grub "has gone downhill in recent years", but carnivores counsel "stick to the beef and you'll do fine."

Bombay Bicycle Club 21 | 18 | 19 | £31

128 Holland Park Ave., W11 (Holland Park), 020-7727 7335

(continued)

(continued)
Bombay Bicycle Club
95 Nightingale Ln., SW12 (Clapham South), 020-8673 6217; fax 8673 9100
3A Downshire Hill, NW3 (Hampstead), 020-7435 3544; fax 7794 3367
www.thebombaybicycleclub.co.uk
Although it's "now part of a chain", this "cosy" Clapham colonial-style Indian has suffered "no noticeable drop in quality after the owners sold out" (and in fact, a "fresh look" has elevated the Decor score); it's still a stop for "curry a cut above the rest" and "adventurous" alternatives, with staff who "make suggestions for those of a sensitive palate."

Bombay Brasserie ◐ 23 | 23 | 21 | £39
Courtfield Rd., SW7 (Gloucester Rd.), 020-7370 4040; fax 7835 1669; www.bombaybrasserielondon.com
A "grand selection" of "exceptional" dishes ("the vegetarian selection is noteworthy"), "opulent" "colonial-style decor" and "high-class service" add up to a "great Raj experience" at this "spacious" South Kensington Indian; hipsters say it "seems a little dated now" ("doesn't quite attract the A-list celebs it used to"), but to most, this "upmarket" address remains "dependably stellar" after 24 years.

Books for Cooks ⊠ 23 | 17 | 20 | £16
4 Blenheim Crescent, W11 (Ladbroke Grove/Notting Hill Gate), 020-7221 1992; fax 7221 1517; www.booksforcooks.com
"If you love cookbooks", this "cute, cramped" bookshop/ cafe near Portobello Market is a "must-do", with its "tiny laboratory kitchen" creating "invariably imaginative" Eclectic lunches – "different each day", depending on the Portobello Market nearby – using recipes from the tomes; the "staff help you a lot" and it's "so cheap" – just "be careful you don't end up spending more on books than on food"; P.S. "get there early to get one of the few tables."

Boxwood Café 21 | 20 | 20 | £53
Berkeley Hotel, Wilton Pl., SW1 (Knightsbridge), 020-7235 1010; fax 7235 1011; www.gordonramsay.com
Devotees declare executive chef-owner "Gordon Ramsay hits the mark" at his "less formal" but still "smart" split-level Belgravia venue featuring an Eclectic–Modern British menu of "upscale" "comfort food cooked incredibly well"; the "disappointed" deem it all "dull" (which may reflect seating, as "some tables are definitely better than others"), but most just "enjoy" all the Ramsay "quality at a much less price."

Brackenbury, The ▽ 19 | 17 | 21 | £31
129-131 Brackenbury Rd., W6 (Goldhawk Rd./Hammersmith), 020-8748 0107; fax 8748 6159
"In a quaint, off-the-beaten path location", this cosy Hammersmith "hideout" comes "highly recommended" for

its "reliable" Modern European fare ("the lunch menus are a steal"), "served by warm, attentive staff"; sentimentalists scold it's "a shadow of its former self", but still "nice in summer to sit out" on the patio; N.B. there's valet parking.

Bradley's ▽ 19 | 17 | 18 | £40

25 Winchester Rd., NW3 (Swiss Cottage), 020-7722 3457; fax 7435 1392

"A bit of sophistication in an unexpected location" "behind Swiss Cottage tube", this "neighbourhood find" has a "surprisingly good" French–Modern British menu, and if some feel it costs "a little more than it should", the "great lunch and pre-dinner deals" hit the mark.

Brasserie Roux ◐ 20 | 21 | 19 | £38

Sofitel St. James London, 8 Pall Mall, SW1 (Piccadilly Circus), 020-7968 2900; fax 7389 7647; www.sofitelstjames.com

The "elegant", high-ceilinged dining room (a former bank) of this "gorgeous" St. James's hotel offers an Albert Roux–designed "classic", "fine" French Brasserie menu with "bargain" prix fixe options and "interesting wine pairings"; however, some have their "high expectations disappointed" by what they find to be rather "typical fare."

Brasserie St. Quentin 18 | 17 | 19 | £36

243 Brompton Rd., SW3 (Knightsbridge/South Kensington), 020-7589 8005; fax 7584 6064; www.brasseriestquentin.co.uk

As "unpretentious as it should be", this "time-tested, authentic French brasserie" well-positioned "between Harrods and the V&A" "hits just the right notes" thanks to "reliable" cooking, "gracious service" and a "you-might-be-in-Paris" atmosphere; but it's "not as good as it was" cry critics citing a "cliché menu" – strictly for those who "don't want to be challenged culinarily" – and "little ambience."

Brian Turner Mayfair ☒ 22 | 18 | 22 | £56

Millennium Mayfair Hotel, 44 Grosvenor Sq., W1 (Bond St.), 020-7596 3444; fax 7596 3443; www.millenniumhotels.com

Celebrity chef Brian "Turner still knows how to show English food at its best" cheer converts to the Traditional cuisine, enhanced by "efficient", "professional service", showcased at this "relaxed, sophisticated" venue; given the Millennium Mayfair location, the menu and the 150-label-strong wine list are, no surprise, "limited at the value end", but otherwise this makes a "good choice, [especially] if residing at the hotel."

Brinkley's ▽ 16 | 15 | 13 | £32

47 Hollywood Rd., SW10 (Earl's Court), 020-7351 1683; fax 7376 5083; www.brinkleys.com

"Catering to a still-rockin' middle-aged crowd" after 27 years, this "buzzing" "local bistro" in Chelsea "remains a staple" for Eclectic–Modern British grub that's "a notch up from decent home cooking", especially when washed down with "ultracheap wine" from their shop next door.

Browns 16 | 17 | 17 | £30

47 Maddox St., W1 (Bond St./Oxford Circus), 020-7491 4565; fax 7497 4564
82-84 St. Martin's Ln., WC2 (Leicester Sq.), 020-7497 5050; fax 7497 5005
Shad Thames, SE1 (London Bridge), 020-7378 1700; fax 7378 7468
9 Islington Green, N1 (Angel), 020-7226 2555; fax 7359 7306
Hertsmere Rd., E14 (Canary Wharf/West India Quay), 020-7987 9777; fax 7537 1341
8 Old Jewry, EC2 (Bank), 020-7606 6677; fax 7600 5359 ☒
www.browns-restaurants.com

"For a spur-of-the-moment meal out" that's "competently done and reasonably priced" (albeit with no "surprises, good or bad"), look no further than this "no-nonsense" Traditional British bistro chain; "despite their harried existence, staff are eager to please", but "don't take any hard-of-hearing grannies" to happy hour when some "big, bustling" and "bland"-looking branches get "very noisy."

Brunello ∇ 21 | 23 | 16 | £74

Baglioni, 60 Hyde Park Gate, SW7 (Gloucester Rd./High St. Kensington), 020-7368 5900; fax 7368 5701

Opposite Kensington Palace, this luxury hotel houses a "happening restaurant" in a "beautiful", "spacious" chandelier-hung dining room; the kitchen prepares "a fine selection" of Italian-skewed Eclectic cuisine, supported by an "excellent, if expensive wine list" that runs to over 400 bins; P.S. "the bar is a lovely place to start the evening."

Builders Arms, The 17 | 16 | 15 | £24

13 Britten St., SW3 (Sloane Sq./South Kensington), 020-7349 9040; fax 7351 3181; www.geronimo-inns.co.uk

This "gem of a gastro-pub" "hits the spot" for Traditional British fare ("tasty", if "secondary to the good-looking Chelsea crowd"), served at "big tables and sofas to slouch on"; for those up in arms about a scene "so noisy and smoky, you can't see or hear, much less dine", there's always the "pleasant outdoor seating"; P.S. "no reservations, but queuing is part of the atmosphere."

Buona Sera ◐ 16 | 17 | 16 | £23

22-26 Northcote Rd., SW11 (Clapham Junction B.R.), 020-7924 1666; fax 7228 1114
289A King's Rd., SW3 (Sloane Sq.), 020-7352 8827; fax 7352 8827

There's "always" a "happy atmosphere" at this "welcoming" Italian duo in Battersea and Chelsea (with quirky double-decker tables "reached via a ladder so, girls, no miniskirts") that remains "as good as ever" for "solid", "wholesome food" at "cheap" prices; "basic, but fun", especially "with a large group."

BUSABA EATHAI 23 | 20 | 16 | £20

106-110 Wardour St., W1 (Piccadilly Circus/Tottenham Court Rd.), 020-7255 8686

22 Store St., WC1 (Goodge St.), 020-7299 7900; fax 7299 7909

8-13 Bird St., W1 (Bond St.), 020-7518 8080

"Busaba makes me to want to eathai everyday" confide converts to this "clean-cut" trio with an "unbeatable combo" of "imaginative, subtle" Siamese fare, "affordable prices" and a "cool", "youthful vibe"; the "canteen-style" "communal tables" – "perfect for ogling dishes next door" – "take table-sharing to a high art"; "they don't accept reservations", but at least the "quick turnover" means you can "ignore the queue outside – it goes quickly."

Busabong, The ◐ – | – | – | M

1A Langton St., SW10 (Fulham Broadway/Sloane Sq.), 020-7352 7414; fax 7352 7534

Around the corner from World's End, this "low-key Thai" in a Chelsea townhouse with "many levels" is appreciated for "generous dishes" served by "lovely people" – even if "prices have sparked up a bit."

Bush Bar & Grill ◐ ▽ 20 | 22 | 19 | £31

45A Goldhawk Rd., W12 (Goldhawk Rd./Shepherd's Bush), 020-8746 2111; fax 8746 7114; www.bushbar.co.uk

A "lively, fun crowd" ensures there's quite "a buzz down the Bush" at this "industrial-looking" "old warehouse" beside Goldhawk Road tube station with a "great bar scene" and "accomplished", "reliable" Modern European cooking for when "you don't want to venture into town."

Butlers Wharf Chop House 20 | 17 | 17 | £38

Butlers Wharf Bldg., 36E Shad Thames, SE1 (London Bridge/ Tower Hill), 020-7403 3403; fax 7940 1855; www.conran.com

"Tough to beat on a summer's evening", this Conran Group venue has a "great view" "over the Thames at Tower Bridge"; most agree "you can't go wrong" with the "truly Traditional English" fare of "meat, meat and more meat", but the "boring interior" "is a bit public-school" ("wedged in regimented tables, I was closer to my neighbours than I've ever been to my own family") and the "friendly staff" sometimes "can't handle the crowds."

Cafe at Sotheby's ⊠ 16 | 15 | 18 | £30

Sotheby's Auction House, 34 New Bond St., W1 (Bond St./ Oxford Circus), 020-7293 5077; fax 7293 6993; www.sothebys.com

You "never know which mystery bidder you'll see" at Sotheby's small, "sedate" weekday cafe, which offers a "light" Modern British menu and "unhurried service"; whilst it's "not a destination restaurant" – "after all's said and done, it's cafeteria food" and, "like many an auctioned item, overpriced" – it's "convenient" "when there's a viewing or sale", and "pleasant for lunch or tea" (but closed for dinner).

Café Boheme ◐ 17 | 17 | 16 | £26

13-17 Old Compton St., W1 (Leicester Sq./Tottenham Court Rd.), 020-7734 0623; fax 7434 3775; www.cafeboheme.co.uk

"Understated Gallic charm oozes like a warm Brie" at this "bustling", "bohemian" Soho all-day cafe that starts with "a quiet breakfast" and ends serving steak and chips "in the wee small hours"; the "easy French Bistro food" comes at "decent prices", and even if "service is erratic", there's plenty of "people-watching" to pass the time.

Café des Amis ◐ ⊠ 18 | 17 | 18 | £32

11-14 Hanover Pl., WC2 (Covent Garden), 020-7379 3444; fax 7379 9124; www.cafedesamis.co.uk

"Useful" for "pre-theatre"/"pre-opera" "pit stops", this "casual" Covent Gardener ("a little tricky to find" in a side street) serves "decent" New French and Brasserie fare, augmented by "smiling staff" and a "downstairs wine bar for lovely apéritifs"; "nothing inspired", but still "mellow."

Cafe Fish 18 | 14 | 17 | £30

36-40 Rupert St., W1 (Leicester Sq./Piccadilly Circus), 020-7287 8989; fax 7287 8400; www.santeonline.co.uk

This Soho seafooder has "a menu so broad, don't be surprised if you find Nemo on it" gush fans who find it "fintastic" for "fresh fish" served in a "central location" that's ideal "on your way to a show"; contrarians concede it's "convenient for the theatre, but no more than that", especially given the "basic decor."

Café Japan 21 | 7 | 15 | £25

626 Finchley Rd., NW11 (Golders Green), 020-8455 6854; fax 8455 6854

"Fantastic sushi at a snip" is the appeal of this diminutive, "basic" Golders Green Japanese, which "stands the test of time" for "mouth-watering" meals ("they've brought hot food back" onto the menu, too); pity about the "patchy service" (as confirmed by a four-point fall in the Service score) and the "poor, smoke-filled atmosphere."

Cafe Lazeez 18 | 14 | 16 | £26

21 Dean St., W1 (Leicester Sq.), 020-7434 9393; fax 7434 0022 ◐ ⊠

93-95 Old Brompton Rd., SW7 (Gloucester Rd./South Kensington), 020-7581 9993; fax 7581 8200 ◐

88 St. John St., EC1 (Farringdon), 020-7253 2224; fax 7253 2112 ⊠

www.cafelazeez.com

There's a "good mix of traditional and funky new Indian food" to be found at these "modern", "upmarket curry venues" whose staff are "amicable" if "slow" ("I almost starved waiting for my food)"; "trying hard to be cool", Soho and South Ken are "open late" with "after-hours drinking", prompting opponents to observe it "can't make up its mind if it's a cafe or bar."

Cafe Med 16 | 15 | 14 | £27

21 Loudoun Rd., NW8 (St. John's Wood), 020-7625 1222 ◐
370 St. John St., EC1 (Angel), 020-7278 1199
"They let you stay as long as you like" at these "funky" "Med-inspired" Eclectic cafes near Angel and in St. John's Wood (with a "lovely open fire") serving "generous portions" of comfort food with "specials worth paying attention to"; "abrupt staff let down an otherwise reliable" experience.

Cafe Pacifico ◐ 19 | 15 | 15 | £24

5 Langley St., WC2 (Covent Garden), 020-7379 7728; fax 7379 5933; www.cafepacifico-laperla.com
"In a city void of good Mexican food", this Covent Garden cantina is "as close as it gets to the real deal" according to amigos of the "decent", "reasonably priced" fare – whose Food score has jumped – which "tastes even better after" an "excellent margarita" made by "jovial, flirtatious bar staff"; it all "makes being away from home bearable" attest the Americans who "pack" the "lively, loud" digs.

Café Rouge 13 | 14 | 13 | £22

31 Kensington Park Rd., W11 (Ladbroke Grove/Notting Hill Gate), 020-7221 4449; fax 7792 3064
98-100 Shepherd's Bush Rd., W6 (Shepherd's Bush), 020-7602 7732; fax 7603 7710
227 Chiswick High Rd., W4 (Chiswick Park), 020-8742 7447; fax 8742 7557
15 Frith St., W1 (Tottenham Court Rd.), 020-7437 4307; fax 7437 4442
34 Wellington St., WC2 (Covent Garden), 020-7836 0998; fax 7497 0738
39 Park Gate Rd., SW11 (Clapham Junction/Sloane Sq.), 020-7924 3565; fax 7924 3773
40 Abbeville Rd., SW4 (Clapham South), 020-8673 3399; fax 8673 2299
27-31 Basil St., SW3 (Knightsbridge), 020-7584 2345; fax 7584 4253
120 St. John's Wood High St., NW8 (St. John's Wood), 020-7722 8366; fax 7483 1015
10 Cabot Sq., 29-35 Mackenzie Walk, E14 (Canary Wharf), 020-7537 9696; fax 7987 1232
www.caferouge.co.uk
Additional locations throughout London
"Drop in anytime" to this "informal" chain that "manages to retain an intimate French feel while popping up all over the place", sticking to a "classic formula" of "good value" Bistro "staples"; whilst some see *rouge* over the food ("mediocrity reigns") and staff ("service is trying at times"), most sum it up as "dependable, never excellent, convenient in every way."

Café Spice Namasté ☒ 22 | 17 | 19 | £32

16 Prescot St., E1 (Aldgate/Tower Hill), 020-7488 9242; fax 7488 9339; www.cafespice.co.uk
"Taste every spice" in chef-owner Cyrus Todiwala's "innovative" Indian menu with "specialities you don't get

anywhere else"; the "colourful", slightly "wacky" Tower Bridge location is "a bit far off the beaten track" for some preferences, but "definitely worth venturing east" for.

Caldesi ☒ — | — | — | E

15-17 Marylebone Ln., W1 (Bond St.), 020-7935 9226; fax 7935 9228; www.caldesi.com

The "funny waiters" "aim to please", "making you feel at home" at this "small, warm" Marylebone trattoria with frescoed walls and wooden flooring and a "solid" Italian menu of "mostly Tuscan specialties", served in "ample portions"; it's "not noisy, so it's a good place for a discreet dinner", and they also own a "great cafe" around the corner.

Cambio de Tercio ● 23 | 16 | 21 | £40

163 Old Brompton Rd., SW5 (Gloucester Rd./South Kensington), 020-7244 8970; www.cambiodetercio.co.uk

"Proving that Spanish food is more than tapas", this "lively", "crowded bistro" in South Ken "never fails to delight", with a "genuine", "creative" menu and "killer wine list", along with "attentive" staff who "treat you like family"; "some days they display a large pig leg in the window that amuses passers-by"; N.B. across the road is a "BYO tapas bar" under the same ownership.

Camden Brasserie 18 | 14 | 19 | £28

9-11 Jamestown Rd., NW1 (Camden Town), 020-7482 2114; fax 7482 2777

"Exactly as a brasserie should be" say loyalists of this 23-year-old Camden haunt where the "formula's old, but not stale", offering "honest", "cheapish" Mediterranean fare, a "buzzy" atmosphere – although some warn the "noise can be deafening" – and "fun, friendly" staff.

Camerino ☒ — | — | — | E

(fka Paolo)

16 Percy St., W1 (Tottenham Court Rd.), 020-7637 9900; www.camerinorestaurant.com

Renamed after owner Paolo Boschi's birthplace, this low-key, red-and-white attired Fitzrovian yearling is a "favourite" haunt of "media types", yet "intimate enough for an evening date"; the "excellent" Italian regional "menu changes regularly" ("go for truffles") and is "great value for the quality."

Cantaloupe ● 16 | 16 | 16 | £28

35-42 Charlotte Rd., EC2 (Old St.), 020-7729 5566; fax 7613 4111; www.cantaloupe.co.uk

"Packed with City suits" and a "lively" crowd, this "industrial chic" Shoreditch venue has a "great buzz" about it, with a "trendy bar" at the front leading to a "warm interior"; the "interesting", "decent" Mediterranean dishes arrive in "ample servings" to "keep hunger at bay"; P.S. "you should probably enjoy loud music to enjoy this place."

Cantina del Ponte 15 | 14 | 12 | £36

Butlers Wharf Bldg., 36C Shad Thames, SE1 (London Bridge/Tower Hill), 020-7403 5403; fax 7403 4432; www.conran.com
An "enjoyable terrace (that is, if you can find a table)" and "reasonable prices" allow you to "watch Tower Bridge open for cheaper than the next-door" establishments when you visit this Butlers Wharf Italian; but whilst the cuisine is "competent", "sloppy service" might drive you – view or no view – to "get the pizza to go."

Cantina Vinopolis 16 | 18 | 16 | £34

Vinopolis Museum, 1 Bank End, SE1 (London Bridge), 020-7940 8333; fax 7940 8334; www.cantinavinopolis.com
The trump card of this "little-bit-different" eatery in "light, airy" quarters under the "wonderful" "brick railway arches" of the Vinopolis Museum of Wine is an "outstanding world-wide wine list" "with many you'd not get elsewhere"; there's a "very competent" Eclectic-Med menu but, in truth, it comes "second to the great selection" of bottles; "ok service" could "be more attentive."

Canyon 17 | 23 | 14 | £39

Tow Path, Riverside, near Richmond Bridge (Richmond), 020-8948 2944; fax 8948 2945
"Check if it's going to be sunny, and book an outside table" at this "gorgeous" setting on "the water's edge" near Richmond Bridge; the "interesting" Eclectic-Med menu is "decent", if "quite pricey", but a drop in the Service rating supports those who find the "stunning location is marred by slap-dash servers."

CAPITAL RESTAURANT, THE 26 | 23 | 26 | £66

The Capital Hotel, 22-24 Basil St., SW3 (Knightsbridge), 020-7589 5171; fax 7225 0011; www.capitalhotel.co.uk
"Dark suits, ties and jewels" are on display at this capital place that, after 35 years, is still "impeccably elegant" – but "now more comfortable" after a "great face-lift"; chef Eric Chavot's "fantastic", "faultless" New French cuisine is supported by "astonishing wines" and "exemplary" staff who "make you feel like a regular even if you only visit once a year"; it's "not a place to let your hair down" – this is Knightsbridge, after all – and you may need to "mortgage your flat before you come" – but it's "worth every penny."

Caraffini ◐ ⊠ 22 | 17 | 21 | £37

61-63 Lower Sloane St., SW1 (Sloane Sq.), 020-7259 0235; fax 7259 0236; www.caraffini.co.uk
Just "off Sloane Square", this "perfect neighbourhood hangout" is "always packed", thanks to "high-quality" Italian cooking ("the daily specials are sure to please") that "does not break the bank", and staff who "make you feel like a long-lost son" or daughter; the "cosy" interior gets a bit "noisy", but happily it's "great to sit outside" too.

Caravaggio ⊠ | 18 | 17 | 15 | £44

107-112 Leadenhall St., EC3 (Bank/Monument), 020-7626 6206; fax 7626 8108; www.etruscagroup.co.uk

"You can still see bankers polishing off their lunches at 4 o'clock in the afternoon" at this "favourite City hangout" (celebrating its 10th birthday) offering "decent", "traditional Italian" eats and "plenty of choice on the wine list"; however, critics charge "it tends to be expensive and not always worth the expense" – especially as "service slips when they get busy."

CARLUCCIO'S CAFFE | 18 | 14 | 14 | £23

5-6 The Green, W5 (Ealing Broadway), 020-8566 4458; fax 8840 8566
St. Christopher's Pl., W1 (Bond St.), 020-7935 5927
Fenwick, New Bond St., W1 (Bond St.), 020-7629 0699; fax 7493 0069
8 Market Pl., W1 (Oxford Circus), 020-7636 2228; fax 7636 9650
3-5 Barrett St., W1 (Bond St.), 020-7935 5927; fax 7487 5436
Putney Wharf, SW15 (Putney Bridge), 020-8789 0591; fax 8789 8360
236 Fulham Rd., SW10 (Fulham Rd.), 020-7376 5960; fax 7376 3698
305-307 Upper St., N1 (Angel/Highbury & Islington), 020-7359 8167; fax 7354 9196
2 Nash Ct., E14 (Canary Wharf), 020-7719 1749; fax 7513 1197
12 West Smithfield, EC1 (Farringdon), 020-7329 5904; fax 7248 5981
www.carluccios.com
Additional locations throughout London

"Everyone's having a good time" at chef Antonio Carluccio's "bustling", burgeoning chain (which "doesn't feel like a chain") of "casual" all-day cafes, thanks to a "short menu" of "inventive, rustic Italian" fare "at sensible prices" and staff that are "admirably patient in a harried environment" (some "unbelievably slow" exceptions aside); a few feel its "rapid expansion is affecting quality" (e.g. "increasingly basic fare"); still, the deli "takeaway food is outstanding."

Carpaccio ◐⊠ | 19 | 16 | 16 | £43

4 Sydney St., SW3 (South Kensington), 020-7352 3433

"Gorgeous punters" (it "could be nicknamed Silicone Valley") are "tightly packed" into this "humming" Chelsea haunt where the "exuberant" ambience has a "Continental buzz about it" and the "high-standard" Italian menu features the eponymous "carpaccio – but it's nothing special" (as this year's lower Food score suggests); "smoke and noise can be an issue" for some, but at least this "chaotic-chic" site puts "you in the mood to party."

Casale Franco ◐ | ▽ 21 | 19 | 20 | £34

134-137 Upper St., N1 (Angel/Highbury & Islington), 020-7226 8994; fax 7359 1114

An "Italian's Italian" in Islington, this "authentic" "rustic" is run by "interesting host" Franco Pensa who "stalks around tables of arty media [types] proffering advice on everything, from the choice of wine to what to wear"; it's "quirky", no doubt, but *amici* agree it "always pleases."

Cecconi's 22 | 20 | 21 | £58

5A Burlington Gardens, W1 (Green Park/Piccadilly Circus), 020-7434 1500; fax 7494 2440; www.cecconis.co.uk

"Feels like Milano" (though it's actually Mayfair) attest *amici* of this "slick", "stylish" "well-laid-out dining room" where "carefully prepared", "creative approaches to traditional Italian" dishes are "a pleasure"; but some sigh it seems "less special" since Soho House acquired it, with "service dependent on staff mood"; indeed, you might be "happier in the bar enjoying the James Bond–type characters swaning around"; P.S. it was poised to reopen in the fall after a redo by the "new ownership."

Cellar Gascon ◐ Ⓢ 23 | 17 | 16 | £33

59 West Smithfield, EC1 (Barbican/Farringdon), 020-7796 0600; fax 7796 0601

"Sharing the same kitchen" as its legendary *frère,* Club Gascon, next door, this "decent watering hole" in Smithfield combines an "impressive wine list" with "sinful tastes" of "sophisticated" New French cuisine in trademark "tapas-portion" sizes (notably "superb foie gras"), which are "more affordable than the main restaurant's"; even if it's "not a very comfortable space", most agree it's a "great place to meet after work."

Chalcot – | – | – | E

40 Chalcot Rd., NW1 (Chalk Farm), 020-7483 0077

The Primrose Hill street corner that once housed Pukka Bar is now the site of this easy-going neighbourhood place serving homestyle Med-orientated Modern European fare, matched by an undemanding wine list; the bi-level space, decorated with atmospheric photos of Italian landscapes, has a handful of wooden tables on a ground-floor mezzanine and a more intimate room with an antique stone floor below.

Chamberlain's Ⓢ ▽ 21 | 15 | 16 | £41

23-25 Leadenhall Mkt., EC3 (Bank/Monument), 020-7648 8690; fax 7648 8691; www.chamberlains.org

Behind a characterful Victorian facade within Leadenhall Market, this tri-level seafooder (with vaulted basement bar) offers "wonderfully fresh fish, originally presented" from an "excellent, but expensive" menu; sit "outside in summer for a great business lunch."

CHAMPOR-CHAMPOR Ⓢ 27 | 25 | 23 | £36

62-64 Weston St., SE1 (London Bridge), 020-7403 4600; www.champor-champor.com

"For something different and off the beaten track", this "treasure hidden" near London Bridge is "worth writing home about", with an "esoteric", "campy" "art-house-film" interior – with the "attentive staff as the cast" – and "adventurous" Malay-Asian dishes (think "ostrich, octopus and frogs' legs") at "reasonable prices", along with a "quirky drinks list" ("Indian bubbly", anyone?); P.S. "for special occasions *à deux,* book the romantic table on the balcony."

Chancery, The ☒ ▽ 22 | 19 | 22 | £42

9 Cursitor St., EC4 (Chancery Lane), 020-7831 4000; www.thechancery.co.uk

The Clerkenwell Dining Room team offers Holborn this "tastefully decorated" site with floor-to-ceiling windows; reviewers pass favourable judgment on the "adventurous business lunches" and dinners of "innovative" Modern European fare, served by "informative, but not in the least intrusive" staff; "why are they only open during the week?"

Chelsea Bun 15 | 10 | 15 | £13

Limerstone St., SW10 (Sloane Sq.), 020-7352 3635; fax 7731 4821; www.chelseabun.co.uk

Battersea Grill

70 Battersea Bridge Rd., SW11 (Sloane Sq.), 020-7738 9009

"Kick-start your weekends" with a "good English fry-up – it "hits the spot" "when you're hung over" – at Chelsea's "cheap and cheerful" "American-style coffee shop" with a "ridiculously large menu" of "sturdy food, and salads" too, served amid "good divey ambience"; just "get there early" because the "crowds spill out the door"; P.S. though substantially the same, the "cheap, cheerful" Battersea branch is now separately owned.

Cheyne Walk Brasserie 24 | 23 | 21 | £45

50 Cheyne Walk, SW3 (Sloane Sq./South Kensington), 020-7376 8787; fax 7376 5878; www.cheynewalkbrasserie.com

"A great open fire" for grilling "huge amounts of meats and fish" and a "contemporary, yet classical" brasserie setting create a "casual", "warm atmosphere" at this "former pub" on the Chelsea Embankment; most appreciate the "rural French cooking" and "friendly, efficient staff" even if "prices are steep"; P.S. a "trendy crowd" can be found in the "divine bar upstairs" with "views of the river."

CHEZ BRUCE 28 | 21 | 24 | £55

2 Bellevue Rd., SW17 (Balham/Wandsworth Common B.R.), 020-8672 0114; fax 8767 6648; www.chezbruce.co.uk

"Every mouthful is special" on the Modern British menu of "kitchen-master" Bruce Poole, whose "unpretentious" venue (ok, it's a bit "cramped") is "one of London's best", with its "inventive", "beautifully executed" dishes, "fantastic wine list", "and, oh, did we mention the cheese board?"; all's "well run" by "staff that manages to be both formal and friendly", and whilst it's in "out-of-the-way" Wandsworth, it's definitely "worth venturing to" – so "bring a foodie date, and splurge."

Chez Gérard 17 | 16 | 15 | £33

8 Charlotte St., W1 (Goodge St./Tottenham Court Rd.), 020-7636 4975; fax 7637 4564 ◐
31 Dover St., W1 (Green Park), 020-7499 8171; fax 7491 3818 ◐
Opera Terrace, The Market, 1st fl., 45 E. Terrace, WC2 (Covent Garden), 020-7379 0666; fax 7497 9060 ◐
119 Chancery Ln., WC2 (Chancery Ln.), 020-7405 0290; fax 7242 2649 ⊠
Thistle Hotel, 101 Buckingham Palace Rd., SW1 (Victoria), 020-7868 6249
9 Belvedere Rd., SE1 (Waterloo), 020-7202 8470; fax 7202 8474
1 Watling St., EC4 (Mansion House/St. Paul's), 020-7213 0540 ⊠
14 Trinity Sq., EC3 (Tower Hill), 020-7480 5500; fax 7480 5588 ⊠
64 Bishopsgate, EC2 (Bank/Liverpool St.), 020-7588 1200; fax 7588 1122 ⊠
www.santeonline.co.uk

"It may be a chain, but it takes a lot to beat" the "satisfying", "old-style" French fare ("tender steaks, tasty frites", etc.) argue *amis* of these "relaxed", "mock brasseries" around town (special kudos to the Covent Garden Opera Terrace with its "excellent views of the bustle below"); but snipers snap the chain "needs to smarten itself up" – especially the "comically rude" staff.

Chez Kristof ◐ – | – | – | E

111 Hammersmith Grove, W6 (Hammersmith), 020-8741 1177; www.chezkristof.co.uk

"One of Hammersmith's best-kept secrets", this "worthwhile newcomer" from Jan Woroniecki of Wòdka and Baltic fame has a "great atmosphere" and "excellent" Classic French menu of "fancy Bistro cooking"; some say "service is pretty patchy, but considerably better if you're with a celebrity."

Chiang Mai 20 | 13 | 16 | £27

48 Frith St., W1 (Leicester Sq./Tottenham Court Rd.), 020-7437 7444; fax 7287 2255

"For a good Thai fix, it does the trick well" say champions of this quarter-century "old fave"; true, the modest Soho "location does not inspire confidence", but the "spicy, tasty and hot" cuisine at "solid value" and "friendly, fast service" "make up for the surroundings", which at least are ideally situated "for a pre- or post-theatre dinner."

Chinese Experience ∇ 19 | 15 | 16 | £23

118 Shaftesbury Ave., W1 (Leicester Sq.), 020-7437 0377; www.chineseexperience.com

This "welcome addition" to "tourist-trappy Chinatown" is a "contemporary", glass-fronted venue that's "decent pre/post-theatre", offering a "different take on Shanghai and Szechuan food, with some unusual dishes" "done very well."

Chino Latino — | — | — | E

Riverbank Park Plaza Hotel, 18 Albert Embankment, SE1 (Waterloo), 020-7769 2500; www.riverbankparkplaza.com

Filling a culinary void on the Albert Embankment near Lambeth Bridge, this new granite-floored brasserie boasts a globe-spanning Eclectic menu with not one, but two chefs: David Massey (ex Fifth Floor Cafe) prepares Med meals, whilst a former Nobu toque, Jimmy Nakamura, looks after the Asian cuisine, including dim sum, tempura and sashimi.

Chor Bizarre ◐ 20 | 22 | 19 | £37

16 Albemarle St., W1 (Green Park), 020-7629 9802; fax 7493 7756; www.chorbizarre.com

The "quirky", artefact-crammed decor (which "is always changing as everything is for sale") "elevates this Indian above the run-of-the mill" cheer chaat converts about this "cheerful" site with "nice and spicy" dishes buoyed by "interesting wine selections"; still, some find it "cheesy" ("makes you think you're at your Indian grandmother's, if you had one") and "expensive for what it is" – though "cheap for the area" (Mayfair).

Chowki Bar & Restaurant ◐ 21 | 15 | 16 | £21

2-3 Denman St., W1 (Piccadilly Circus), 020-7439 1330; fax 7287 5919; www.chowki.com

"Giving lots of opportunity to try regional favourites" on a "regularly changing" Indian menu that "average curryheads might not experience", this Piccadilly Punjab "stands out from the crowd"; not everyone warms to the environs – with "communal tables", "backless benches" and service that "feels rushed at times" – but "who's complaining" at these "stupidly cheap prices", including a three-course lunch for less than £11.

Christopher's Covent Garden 18 | 16 | 16 | £39

18 Wellington St., WC2 (Covent Garden), 020-7240 4222; fax 7240 3357; www.christophersgrill.com

"A staple in an area" "full of tourist traps", the eponymous Christopher Gilmour's "civilised" Victorian venue near Covent Garden remains "popular" "pre- and post-theatre" and for "business meals" of "consistently good" American surf 'n' turf classics; still, doubters say it "feels tired now", citing "excruciatingly average" eats and "erratic service."

Chuen Cheng Ku ◐ 19 | 9 | 14 | £22

17 Wardour St., W1 (Leicester Sq./Piccadilly Circus), 020-7437 1398; fax 7434 0533

"Forget you're in London" at this 26-year-old Chinatown citizen more valued for its "first-rate dim sum" offered on traditional trolleys, "Hong Kong–style" ("don't get run over by the eager cart girls!"), than for its "nondescript" decor and "curt" staff – although some say that "the servers have learned to smile" of late.

Churchill Arms 22 | 16 | 14 | £15

119 Kensington Church St., W8 (High St. Kensington/ Notting Hill Gate), 020-7727 4242; www.fullers.co.uk

It "has a cult following", "so expect to wait for a table" at this "rowdy", flowers-filled venue "at the back of a great pub" in Notting Hill; fans find it worth it, as the "enormous portions" of "brilliant Thai" fare are "ridiculously cheap" ("where else do you get change from a tenner?"); others, however, are up in arms over "the militant time limit" ("you'll be in and out in 30 minutes tops") and "overwhelming smoke" (though that's a "problem endemic to UK pubs").

Chutney Mary ◐ 24 | 22 | 21 | £43

535 King's Rd., SW10 (Fulham Broadway), 020-7351 3113; fax 7351 7694; www.realindianfood.com

"No longer the trendiest, but still one of the best" claim fans of this "sophisticated, sensual" Chelsea "institution" where "mouth-watering", "light" Indian dishes "nuanced with creative flavours" make a "divine experience for the tongue" (particularly those of "Westernised palates"); the servers seem "eager to help you enjoy your food" too; P.S. for a "*Bombay Dream* date", romantics recommend you "try for a conservatory" table.

Chutney's ◐ ▽ 23 | 12 | 15 | £14

124 Drummond St., NW1 (Euston Sq.), 020-7388 0604; fax 7209 0627

"Large portions" of "cheap, reliable food" from "friendly staff" sum up this unassuming Indian-vegetarian in Euston; in particular, the "amazing" £5.95 daily lunch buffet alone has "sufficient variety to justify repeat visits"; it's "full of children on Sundays" when the price is fixed all day, hence "not a place for a quiet meal" then.

Cicada ⊠ 20 | 16 | 16 | £31

132-136 St. John St., EC1 (Farringdon), 020-7608 1550; fax 7608 1551; www.cicada.nu

This "Eastern-inspired" Clerkenwell cousin of e&o boasts a "funky" opium-den-like decor and a "tasty fashion-food" Asian menu (including "delicious small plates") and "cocktails like the lycheetini"; on the "downside, it can get noisy and smoky", which means it's "fantastic for a party night" rather than "an intimate dinner for two."

Cigala ▽ 22 | 13 | 16 | £36

54 Lamb's Conduit St., WC1 (Holborn/Russell Sq.), 020-7405 1717; fax 7242 9949; www.cigala.co.uk

"In an area short of class restaurants", this "crowded", almost "canteen"-like Bloomsbury address is "a real find for lovers of Spanish cuisine", with "nuevo" dishes and a "fascinating wine list"; snipers say the food can be "hit-and-miss", but "when on form", it's "a treat from tapas to dessert."

Cinnamon Club ☒ 24 | 24 | 21 | £50

The Old Westminster Library, 30 Great Smith St., SW1 (St. James's Park/Westminster), 020-7222 2555; fax 7222 1333; www.cinnamonclub.com

Set in the "dignified surroundings" – "Bollywood meets the British bankers' club" – of a cleverly "refurbished library", this "winning" Westminster venue offers "outstanding modern reinterpretations of Indian" cuisine, albeit at "eye-popping prices"; expect to find "expense-accounters" and MPs mingling with a "young stylish crowd", who also avail themselves of the "sexy" members' "bar downstairs"; service is "gracious", "even if you're not a politico."

Cipriani 20 | 21 | 19 | £65

25 Davies St., W1 (Bond St.), 020-7399 0500; fax 7399 0501; www.cipriani.com

"If you're nostalgic about the Venetian" original, this "absolutely buzzing new addition" "is the place to go" for a taste of "la dolce vita" Mayfair-style and to see "beautiful, pampered" types "showing off their diamonds (and that's just the men)"; the "plentiful", "understated" Italian fare is "pricey" – many say "crazily" so – and service can range from "friendly" to "snooty" (reflecting perhaps one's "celebrity status"), but "since you'll feel great to have [gotten] a table, you're guaranteed a good evening."

Circus ◐☒ 18 | 19 | 18 | £40

1 Upper James St., W1 (Piccadilly Circus), 020-7534 4000; fax 7534 4010; www.egami.co.uk

Fans say this "swanky" Soho spot (approaching its 10th anniversary) is "still a delight", with "lighting that makes everyone look good" and an "interesting" Modern European menu; critics carp the "food is nothing remarkable for the price" and "staff can be a little stand-offish", but all approve of the "hip bar downstairs", with the added benefit of "no alcopop crowds."

Citrus 21 | 20 | 21 | £38

Park Lane Hotel, 112 Piccadilly, W1 (Green Park), 020-7290 7364; www.sheraton.com/parklane

With its across-the-street "views of Green Park" offering "a peaceful respite in busy Piccadilly", this "bright, cheery" Park Lane restaurant "deserves more recognition" for its "upscale", "creative" Med menu converts claim; the tart-tongued say the "standard fare" and service "never get beyond that hotel-dining-room feel"; still, it's a "more-than-acceptable" "backup", and "children are welcome" too.

City Miyama ☒ ▽ 20 | 9 | 19 | £36

17 Godliman St., EC4 (St. Paul's), 020-7489 1937; fax 7236 0325

"Japanese tourist buses" make a beeline for this cramped, bi-level eatery (which "could do with a lick of paint") "tucked away" near St. Paul's Cathedral, where "wonderful" "fresh sushi" and "good tempura" compensate for the fact there's "no atmosphere" – unless you count the chefs cooking in front of you; P.S. the "£35 all-you-can-eat deal is good value."

CLARKE'S ☒ 27 | 19 | 23 | £53

124 Kensington Church St., W8 (Notting Hill Gate), 020-7221 9225; fax 7229 4564; www.sallyclarke.com

"A foodies' paradise without the pretence", Sally "Clarke's tiny refuge from the madding crowd" in Kensington offers an "understated" but "highly imaginative", "ingredient-driven" Modern British menu that's "set each night" – so "if you like what they're serving, you're in for a treat", "otherwise you have a problem" (though "they're hugely obliging if there's anything" you can't eat); P.S. there are choices at lunch and brunch, or "pick up all sorts of goodies at the deli next door."

Clerkenwell Dining Room & Bar ☒ 20 | 19 | 20 | £41

69-73 St. John St., EC1 (Farringdon), 020-7253 9000; fax 7253 3322; www.theclerkenwell.com

"With a simplistic elegance" and "warm atmosphere", this "upscale", contemporary Clerkenwell eatery is "good for business lunches and dinners", with a "quality" Modern European menu that "is pleasingly difficult to choose from"; and most think there's "potential" for it to "get better and better", with such features as the £19 three-course prix fixe already "offering value for money."

CLUB GASCON ☒ 27 | 20 | 22 | £56

57 West Smithfield, EC1 (Barbican/Farringdon), 020-7796 0600; fax 7796 0601

Situated beside Smithfield Market, this "veritable shrine to foie gras" has fans "ready to indulge" and "drool over" a "heavenly", "inventive" New French small-plates menu featuring "something different" (or actually, a lot of different little somethings), and a "well-chosen list of Southwestern" wines; on the flip side, it's "pretty pricey", and the service "somewhat perfunctory" "if you're not a regular", but most urge goose-liver "lovers not to miss this hot spot."

Coach & Horses ▽ 20 | 12 | 16 | £27

26-28 Ray St., EC1 (Farringdon), 020-7278 8990; fax 7278 1478; www.thecoachandhorses.com

"Essentially an old-fashioned pub" with a "gastro-pub vibe", this "cosy" Clerkenwell venue is "in the vanguard" for British-Med "food that's excellent, if a little short on choice"; citing "slow service", some wags suggest it "should be renamed [Coach and] Snail", but the "relaxed" ambience just makes it "perfect for lazy weekends."

Cocoon ◐ 21 | 23 | 19 | £48

65 Regent St., W1 (Piccadilly Circus), 020-7494 7600; www.cocoon-restaurants.com

"Seriously comfy" cocoon-shaped chairs and tables inlaid with "gorgeous rose petals" are all part of the "sexy",

"*Austin Powers*" look of this "great addition" to Piccadilly that's attracting a "happening crowd" with "innovative" Pan-Asian "shareable dishes" ("the blowtorched sushi is a cute gimmick"); only the "painfully chic, untrained" servers have yet to morph; P.S. there's also a "hip" bar "full of wannabe *Footballers' Wives*."

Collection, The ◐ 11 | 19 | 14 | £39

264 Brompton Rd., SW3 (South Kensington), 020-7225 1212; fax 7225 1050; www.the-collection.co.uk

"Make a late dinner reservation and wear your dancing shoes" to this Brompton Cross venue; a "useful dining area" with "big tables" and an Eclectic menu "overlooks a cool bar" where a "young, very loud crowd" gyrates to "throbbing music"; the scene's "still trendy" to supporters, but "yesterday's news" to naysayers, whilst a drop in the Food score supports those who "collect here for a drink, nothing more."

Como Lario ⊠ 17 | 15 | 20 | £42

18-22 Holbein Pl., SW1 (Sloane Sq.), 020-7730 2954; fax 7730 9046; www.comolario.uk.com

"Very much a place for locals, not tourists", this trattoria "well hidden" behind Sloane Square is "always lively, always fun" and rising in the ratings; whilst the "traditional" Italian cuisine "won't blow your socks off", its "quality is stable" and its "specials are fresh"; "but the secret to this place is its staff", an "entertaining" lot with "lots of banter"; the "new decor is quite nice", though the digs remain "cramped."

Coq d'Argent 18 | 22 | 16 | £49

1 Poultry, EC2 (Bank), 020-7395 5000; fax 7395 5050; www.conran.com

"Crowded" with "City slickers" looking to "impress clients" (or just "to catch the sunset with a glass of champagne"), the Conran Group's "upscale" Poultry rooftop "retreat" boasts "beautiful roof gardens" and "fantastic" *centre-ville* views; few folks "quibble with the victuals" on the "reliably" "good" New French menu; the only cuckoo in this "expense-account" nest is the service, which takes "haughty to new heights."

Costas Grill ⊠≠ ▽ 19 | 11 | 21 | £23

12-14 Hillgate St., W8 (Notting Hill Gate), 020-7229 3794

"Thumbs up" for this "convivial", "homey place" in Notting Hill, run for over 50 years by the same family that dishes out "hefty" portions of "fresh", "excellent-value" Greek-Cypriot dishes to a "fair share of regulars who are all a bit eccentric"; a few think it's an "unsophisticated" "dinosaur", but everyone appreciates the "beautiful back patio" with "a grape-bearing vine – what more could you ask in the centre of London?"

Cow Dining Room, The 21 | 16 | 16 | £31

89 Westbourne Park Rd., W2 (Westbourne Park), 020-7221 0021; fax 7727 8687

Tom Conran's "unique" gastro-pub, "a favourite haunt of bohemian-chic Notting Hill-billies", has a "traditional", "relaxed upstairs" dining room where a "tiny kitchen produces tremendous Modern British delights" for dinner and weekend lunch; the "cosy" downstairs bar offers "simple", "fresh" seafood and Belgian brews all day.

Crazy Bear, The ⊠ 21 | 25 | 19 | £40

26-28 Whitfield St., W1 (Goodge St.), 020-7631 0088; fax 7631 1188; www.crazybeargroup.co.uk

"A surprising find" say supporters of this "atmospheric" Fitzrovian (the cub of a popular Oxford haunt) whose "sumptuous surroundings" in an art deco–styled dining room offer a "good selection" of "delicious Thai" dishes; the "beautiful bar downstairs" is "a must for drinks beforehand"; just "watch the wallet, as it's about to take a hit"; P.S. don't leave without "checking out" the "funniest loos in London."

Crazy Homies ⊄ – | – | – | M

125 Westbourne Park Rd., W2 (Royal Oak/Westbourne Park), 020-7727 6771; fax 7727 6798

As miniature as its next-door sibling, Lucky 7 (and sharing the same phone number), Tom Conran's "lively" Notting Hill newcomer has a "tiny" menu of some of "the best Mexican food around"; but as they take "no reservations", expect to "wait a long" while for one of the handful of tables – though the "excellent margaritas" should help pass the time.

Criterion Grill ⊠ 18 | 26 | 16 | £43

224 Piccadilly, W1 (Piccadilly Circus), 020-7930 0488; fax 7930 8380; www.whitestarline.org.uk

"The ravishing decor" – complete with "delightful murals" and a "gorgeously preserved" neo-Byzantine ceiling – adds a "real sense of occasion" to this "oasis in the middle of frenetic Piccadilly" (part of the Marco Pierre White empire); though "nice enough", the Modern European menu of "well-executed New French dishes incorporating the best British ingredients" "doesn't live up to the fabulously decadent setting, sadly", and the service "needs a lot of tightening up" ("we practically had to do handstands to get the bill").

Cru 19 | 19 | 15 | £32

2-4 Rufus St., N1 (Old St.), 020-7729 5252; fax 7729 1070; www.cru.uk.com

With "that unique gift of being cosy in winter and light and airy in summer", this "slick warehouse conversion" in Hoxton has "a brilliant wine list", accompanied by an "above-average" Med menu that includes "amazing, tapas-style" bar snacks; but it's "disappointing" to a few who prefer to "go for the vino and think about food later."

Daphne ◐ ⊠ ▽ 19 | 14 | 21 | £23

83 Bayham St., NW1 (Camden Town), 020-7267 7322; fax 7482 3964

Now comfortably into its third decade, this popular haunt in "old Camden Town" is "always reliable" for "good-value" Greek-Cypriot fare that "often strays interestingly off the beaten track"; the service is "warm and friendly" and the "roof terrace is a delight" in the summer.

Daphne's ◐ 20 | 19 | 18 | £49

112 Draycott Ave., SW3 (South Kensington), 020-7589 4257; fax 7581 2232; www.daphnes-restaurant.co.uk

"Daphinitely delicious" declare devotees about the Italian cuisine at this "elegant" Brompton Cross "haunt" of the "rich, the famous" (hence "a lot of rubber-necking") and "romantics"; though foes who find the fare "unimaginative" and the service "brusque" are "confused why it's so popular", for most it's "always a treat."

Daquise 18 | 11 | 15 | £20

20 Thurloe St., SW7 (South Kensington), 020-7589 6117

An "absolute classic" that looks "like something from East Berlin in the '50s", this "cheap and cheerful" Polish specialist above the South Ken tube station "feels like home" to anyone seeking "huge portions" of "honest" "comfort food" that tastes like it's "right out of grandma's kitchen"; the "slightly grumpy waitresses are part of the charm."

De Cecco ▽ 15 | 15 | 18 | £34

189 New King's Rd., SW6 (Parsons Green), 020-7736 1145; fax 7371 0278; www.simpsonsofmayfair.com

"Where smart city types living in SW6 go when they're off duty", this Parsons Green trattoria offers "classic" Italian "staples", such as "excellent lobster pasta", that are "unlikely to disappoint"; a few frown at the "tired" menu and feel the "bustling atmosphere", "bright lights" and "closely packed tables make it a terrible choice for romance."

deep – | – | – | E

Imperial Wharf, The Boulevard, SW6 (Fulham Broadway), 020-7736 3337; fax 7736 7578; www.deeplondon.co.uk

Next to Chelsea Harbour, this minimalist white-walled eatery is buoyed by floor-to-ceiling windows with riverside views; the upscale seafood menu spreads its net far and wide, including small dishes of less familiar species (zander filet, anyone?) to encourage experimentation; N.B. there are two terraces for alfresco dining.

DEFUNE 26 | 16 | 22 | £57

34 George St., W1 (Baker St./Bond St.), 020-7935 8311; fax 7487 3762

"For sheer indulgence in top-notch" sushi and "excellent cooked food", this "discreet" Marylebone Japanese "definitely gets things right"; "occasional celeb sightings" liven up a scene with "no vibe" to speak of otherwise and it's "ridiculously expensive", but cognoscenti swear it stands up to "the best in Tokyo's Ginza"; P.S. it's "no longer a secret – so be advised to book at night."

Del Buongustaio ⊠ ∇ 22 | 15 | 19 | £34

283-285 Putney Bridge Rd., SW15 (East Putney/Putney Bridge), 020-8780 9361; fax 8780 9361; www.delbuongustaio.com

It's "like stepping straight into rustic Italy" at this Putney trattoria that's "worth a venture" for a monthly changing menu of "original" Italian cooking and "friendly" service; other plus points include an "excellent prix fixe dinner with a good range of options" (£21 for three courses) and a next-door patisserie.

Deya ⊠ ∇ 28 | 21 | 21 | £35

34 Portman Sq., W1 (Marble Arch), 020-7224 0028; www.deya-restaurant.co.uk

A "fabulous treat" "for the tired shopper or business luncher" in Marylebone, this "interesting newcomer" in a "beautiful room" just off Oxford Street offers "inventive", modern Indian dishes with "spectacularly refined flavours" at a "reasonable price for the location"; "well-meaning" staff operate "without being intrusive", but can be "a little slow"; N.B. its backers include Sir Michael Caine.

dim t 16 | 15 | 15 | £20

1A Hampstead Ln., N6 (Highgate), 020-8340 8800; fax 8648 1671

Groupies gush this "modern-hip" Highgate Chinese "always comes up trumps" with a "wholesome", "versatile" menu and "fantastic dim sum", served in a "busy, happy" setting; even those who see "nothing special" about it concede that "you can't ask for much with these prices."

Dish Dash ∇ 17 | 20 | 13 | £28

11-13 Bedford Hill, SW12 (Balham B.R.), 020-8673 5555; www.dish-dash.com

"Ask the waiter to surprise" you with "something different" from the "great selection of dishes" on the midpriced Persian-Lebanese menu at this "busy" restaurant/bar in Balham; the "service could be better", though, and if you "move your chair back half an inch, you're sitting at the next table"; P.S. the cocktails are "divine."

Diverso ◐ 18 | 18 | 19 | £38

85 Piccadilly, W1 (Green Park), 020-7491 2222; fax 7495 1977

"Well situated" just opposite Green Park, this veteran Piccadilly Italian offers "consistent" "classic Italian" cuisine and "unfailingly good service" in an interior that resembles a "modern" "Tuscan villa", with enough "space between the tables to carry on a conversation"; though a divergent contingent call it "uninspired", for others it's an altogether "comfortable experience."

Don, The ⊠ 23 | 20 | 22 | £45

The Courtyard, 20 St. Swithins Ln., EC4 (Bank/Cannon St.), 020-7626 2606; fax 7626 2616; www.thedonrestaurant.co.uk

"Well-produced, quality" Modern European cuisine "never disappoints" at Bleeding Heart's "hard-to-find" sibling on Cannon Street, "discreetly" housed in a sherry importer's "warehouse from another time" (1798, to be precise); the sommelier "knows his wines", and the "friendly" staff provide "superb service"; P.S. there's an "unusual" bistro in the "fantastic cellar."

Draper's Arms, The 18 | 17 | 15 | £29

44 Barnsbury St., N1 (Highbury & Islington), 020-7619 0348; fax 7619 0413; www.thedrapersarms.co.uk

Housed in a handsome Georgian building "in the quiet side of Islington", this "very chilled" gastro-pub is a "great place to lounge around" "for the young and elderly alike", with a beer garden that "can't be beat"; when it comes to "innovative" Modern European cooking at "a good price" and "helpful" service, it "delivers results", though the cognoscenti caution "it can have off days."

Drones 19 | 20 | 20 | £46

1 Pont St., SW1 (Sloane Sq.), 020-7235 9555; fax 7235 9566; www.whitestarline.org.uk

Private club; inquiries: 020-7491 0576

"Popular with illustrious types and celebrities", this highly "civilised" Marco Pierre White production in Belgravia is "not super-lively", but it is "an excellent choice" for "dependable" Modern European cuisine, a "well-balanced wine list" and "efficient service"; dissenters deem it "just average", however, and see "no reason to return"; P.S. the Mayfair establishment, owned with entrepreneur Piers Adam, is a "great private club full of interesting people."

Duke of Cambridge 18 | 15 | 15 | £27

30 St. Peter's St., N1 (Angel), 020-7359 3066; fax 7359 1877; www.singhboulton.co.uk

"If organic is your thing, you can't do much better" than this "chilled" gastro-pub in Islington where "crunchy, tasty upscale dishes" made from organic produce comprise a "constantly changing" Modern British menu; some flinch at paying "such a premium" to dine "with a clear conscience" and the service gets mixed responses ("lovely" vs. "off-putting"), but dog owners give it "extra points" for the "pooch-friendly" bar area.

Duke of Clarence, The ▽ 16 | 18 | 18 | £18

148 Old Brompton Rd., SW5 (Gloucester Rd./South Kensington), 020-7373 1285

"Decent" Modern British cooking and "well-maintained" quarters attract a "warm crowd" of regulars to this South

Kensington gastro-pub (same owners as the Builders Arms) whose "comfortable couches" make it a "great place to spread the papers out on a Sunday"; however, sceptics who find the fare "nothing special" claim it's "better for a pint."

Eagle, The 21 | 13 | 15 | £22

159 Farringdon Rd., EC1 (Farringdon), 020-7837 1353; fax 7689 5882

Widely regarded as London's "Ur-gastro-pub", this "rough and ready boozer" in Clerkenwell is "always buzzing" with an "eclectic mix of patrons" who come for "hearty", "reasonably priced" Med "comfort" fare, served "without pretensions" in a "basic" room that "could use a revamp"; there are no reservations, so "getting a table can be a long wait – nothing another pint won't deal with."

E&O 24 | 21 | 19 | £41

14 Blenheim Crescent, W11 (Ladbroke Grove), 020-7229 5454; fax 7229 5522; www.eando.nu

"Bookings are hard to come by" at Will Ricker's "star-spotters" paradise in Notting Hill offering an "awesome" Pan-Asian menu replete with an "array of tastes and textures" that will "delight even the most difficult" of palates, a "great cocktail list" and "funky" "minimalist" decor; the "prices may cause some panic", however, and whilst fans praise the "superlative" staff, detractors deride them as "model wannabes" with "too much attitude."

Eat & Two Veg 15 | 15 | 15 | £22

50 Marylebone High St., W1 (Baker St.), 020-7258 8595; www.eatandtwoveg.com

The marriage of "U.S. diner with a vegetarian menu" at this "bright", "noisy" Marylebone all-day venue is an "interesting format" that strikes a chord with many who praise the fare as "inventive", but rings hollow for others who find it "bland" and "lifeless"; the "efficient" staff win praise for their "child-friendly" approach, especially at weekends, but critics note there are "lots of smokers – a bit odd for a healthy restaurant."

Ebury Dining Room & Brasserie ▽ 17 | 18 | 18 | £32

11 Pimlico Rd., SW1 (Sloane Sq./Victoria), 020-7730 6784; fax 7730 6149; www.theebury.co.uk

"A young crowd" frequents this "fun, handy" gastro-pub near Pimlico Green; the ground-floor brasserie/bar offers seafood "temptingly put on display" and a "great wine selection by the glass", whilst upstairs houses a lesser-known, airy Modern European dining room – leading some to say "this place needs to decide if it's a restaurant or bar."

Ebury Wine Bar & Restaurant 18 | 18 | 17 | £31

139 Ebury St., SW1 (Sloane Sq./Victoria), 020-7730 5447; fax 7823 6053; www.eburywinebars.co.uk

This "cute", rather "retro" vino bar near Victoria Station, "a warm, welcoming place for neighbours and tourists alike", boasts 33 years of providing "surprisingly tasty", "inventive" Eclectic cuisine, along with "good Australian choices" on the "excellent wine list"; it's "always crowded", hence service can be "really slow."

ECapital ◐ 20 | 13 | 21 | £23

8 Gerrard St., W1 (Leicester Sq./Piccadilly Circus), 020-7434 3838; fax 7434 9991

It's got "decor that's worse than a hospital ward", "but do not underestimate the food quality" at this "quirky" Chinatown venue with an "adventurous menu (try the pigs' ears)" that includes "excellent vegetarian choices" and "some Shanghai-style dishes not found elsewhere"; don't fret if you're "uninitiated": "helpful service will guide you through the menu."

Eco ▽ 19 | 14 | 18 | £17

4 Market Row, SW9 (Brixton), 020-7738 3021; fax 7720 0738 ☒
162 Clapham High St., SW4 (Clapham Common), 020-7978 1108; fax 7720 0738
www.ecorestaurants.com

"The real deal" say lovers of these "popular", "packed" pizza "institutions" in Brixton Market (BYO) and Clapham, with a "cheap" selection of "unusual, tasty" toppings (like "divine truffle") and "cheerful" service; "loud, dancey music" adds to the "buzzing" experience.

Edera ▽ 21 | 17 | 18 | £42

148 Holland Park Ave., W11 (Holland Park), 020-7221 6090

"Manager Roberto" Pisano has taken over this "wonderful little Italian in a stretch of Holland Park" not well-endowed with culinary delights, and introduced an "impeccable", "authentic" new menu that's "just what the doctor ordered"; the "modern" space is "a bit cramped" and "soulless" for some tastes, but many appreciate the "great thought that has gone into the wine list."

Ed's Easy Diner 15 | 16 | 15 | £15

12 Moor St., W1 (Leicester Sq./Tottenham Court Rd.), 020-7439 1955; fax 7494 0173
London Trocadero Ctr., 19 Rupert St., W1 (Piccadilly Circus), 020-7287 1951; fax 7287 6998
362 King's Rd., SW3 (Sloane Sq.), 020-7352 1956; fax 7352 4660
O_2 Ctr., 255 Finchley Rd., NW3 (Finchley Rd.), 020-7431 1958; fax 7431 9837
www.edseasydiner.co.uk

"Jukeboxes, Formica tables and faux red leather seats" create a "kitschfest" at this "retro" American-themed chain with a "classic diner" menu of "greasy-spoon comfort food" (e.g. "classic" chili dogs, "posh burgers and lovely sides"); those uneasy about recent experiences emphasise that it "used to be good"; but even they concede it's still a "great choice for kids" or "after a particularly hard night out."

Efes Kebab House ◐ 19 | 13 | 19 | £23

175-177 Great Portland St., W1 (Great Portland St.), 020-7436 0600; fax 7636 6293
80 Great Titchfield St., W1 (Oxford Circus), 020-7636 1953; fax 7323 5082 ⊠

For a "change of pace", this "warm, friendly" Turkish duo just north of Oxford Street offers a "jolly good night out" – especially at Great Portland Street, where there's live music every night and "great belly dancers"; even if "the decor is '70s hell, the food is new-millennium heaven", and all comes "at a fair price"; P.S. "they'll cook anything" to your liking.

1880 ⊠ ▽ 26 | 23 | 23 | £65

The Bentley Hotel, 27-33 Harrington Gardens, SW7 (Gloucester Rd.), 020-7244 5361; fax 7259 2121; www.thebentley-hotel.com

Buried in the basement of this "smart" South Kensington hotel is "a hidden gem" where chef Andrew Turner and "helpful" staff oversee an "excellent" New French–Modern European bill of fare, including an "unbelievable 10-course tasting menu" and "possibly the best bread basket in London"; not everyone is "into the kitsch Louis XIV decor", but most rank this a "superb all-round experience"; N.B. for casual dining, there's Peridot, an all-day brasserie, upstairs.

1802 ▽ 15 | 18 | 14 | £29

Museum of Docklands, 1 West India Quay, Hertsmere Rd., E14 (Canary Wharf/West India Quay), 0870-444 3886; fax 7350 1748; www.searcys.co.uk

With a "wonderful warehouse setting", this old Canary Wharf tea-sorting house adjacent to the Museum of Docklands has a "split personality": during the day, it's "the kind of place to sit and read", nibbling Modern British "fancy cafe food" from caterers Searcy's, whilst at night it becomes a "cool venue", complete with "resident DJ, who makes it too noisy to talk" (Wednesdays–Fridays).

Eight Over Eight 22 | 19 | 18 | £45

392 King's Rd., SW3 (Sloane Sq.), 020-7349 9934; www.eightovereight.nu

This "stylish, sophisticated" Chelsea site is "a photocopy" of its "sister e&o in all respects" – from the "great people-watching" to the "buzzing" bar and "creative", "expensive" Asian menu of "beautifully presented, fragrant" dishes that are "ideal for sharing" ("designer food for designer people"); on the downside, "service can be sketchy", and expect "long waits for tables" even if you book.

El Blason ⊠ ▽ 19 | 14 | 19 | £38

8-9 Blacklands Terrace, SW3 (Sloane Sq.), 020-7823 7383; fax 7589 6313

"Everybody knows your name" at this low-key joint just off King's Road, where "crazy owner Carlos" Ulloa is "worth the admission cost" alone, as are his "dependably Spanish" dishes, including "paella to die for"; that said, a few fret "it's a tired place."

Electric Brasserie, The 18 | 19 | 14 | £31

191 Portobello Rd., W11 (Ladbroke Grove/Notting Hill Gate), 020-7908 9696; fax 7908 9595; www.the-electric.co.uk

With "guaranteed celebrity sightings" and an electric "vibe", this "bustling brasserie" on Portobello Road "gets packed" – not least as it's an "easy rendezvous spot"; whilst the "consistently good" Eclectic menu features "everything you could possibly want to eat", a few feel the Soho House–owned site is "masquerading as something more special than it is" – especially given the "impersonal service" (it's "perhaps too crowded for its own good").

Elena's l'Etoile ⊠ – | – | – | E

30 Charlotte St., W1 (Goodge St.), 020-7636 1496; fax 7637 0122; www.elenasletoile.co.uk

"Elena Salvoni herself hovers around, greeting old friends" with "a warm welcome" at this "classic bistro" in Fitzrovia "with nicotine-coloured walls and photos of celebrities of yesteryear", plus "exquisitely prepared" French and Italian dishes from a "traditional" menu.

El Gaucho 18 | 13 | 14 | £31

30 Old Brompton Rd., SW7 (South Kensington), 020-7584 8999
Chelsea Farmers Mkt., 125 Sydney St., SW3 (Sloane Sq./ South Kensington), 020-7376 8514 ⊄

"A good destination for those carnivorous days", this "casual" South Kensington duo "feels like a cattle station on the pampas", turning out "authentically Argentinean" steaks "with no fuss" and "at good prices"; however, disgruntled gauchos growl the "inconsistent food" and "sometimes spotty service" are "not worth it"; N.B. no reservations at Chelsea Farmers Market.

Elistano 16 | 13 | 16 | £34

25-27 Elystan St., SW3 (South Kensington), 020-7584 5248; fax 7584 8965

Near Chelsea Green, this "popular party" place gets so "packed" that the "charming comments of staff are difficult to decipher over the roar of the diners"; it elicits criticism from those who feel it "has lost its lustre" (especially now that it's "no longer cheap"), but even if the "unpretentious Italian" cooking can be "hit-and-miss", at least it comes in "huge portions."

El Pirata ◐⊠ 21 | 16 | 19 | £27

5-6 Down St., W1 (Green Park), 020-7491 3810; www.elpirata.co.uk

It may be "hard to find" in "one of Mayfair's tiny side streets" ("and doesn't look like much from the outside"), but this "casual", "crowded" "Spanish gem" is "a winner" thanks to "terrific tapas" that "won't break the bank", "great sangria" and "smiling waiters" who "work as a seamless team"; and if "it would be unremarkable in Andalusia", it "hits the spot" as far as Londoners are concerned.

Embassy ◐ ☒ 20 | 20 | 15 | £48

29 Old Burlington St., W1 (Green Park/Piccadilly Circus), 020-7851 0956; fax 7734 3224; www.embassylondon.com

"Beautiful people meet haute cuisine" at this "trendy, but not intimidating" Mayfair venue where chef/co-patron Garry Hollihead presides over an "attractive", glass-fronted dining room with a "surprisingly good" Modern European menu, whilst downstairs is a "fun nightclub" full of "Page 3 'stunnas' and rejects from *Footballers' Wives*"; P.S. the club is members-only but "dinner gets you in" for the evening.

Emporio Armani Caffe ☒ 17 | 20 | 17 | £33

Emporio Armani, 191 Brompton Rd., SW3 (Knightsbridge), 020-7581 0854; fax 7823 8854

The "all-in-black set" like to "drop in, do some shopping, then have a light lunch" at this "relaxing" "pit stop" on the first floor of the "very cool" Knightsbridge designer store; on offer is a "classic Italian" menu of "decent" fare, although "maybe helpings are small because the patrons need to fit into Armani's clothes"; N.B. closes at 5:30 PM.

Engineer, The 18 | 17 | 16 | £28

65 Gloucester Ave., NW1 (Chalk Farm), 020-7722 0950; fax 7483 0592; www.the-engineer.com

"Upstairs in winter, garden in summer" is the way to go at this "crackin' gastro-pub" in Primrose Hill with a "lively", "clubby atmosphere"; a "great value" Modern British menu hits the mark for most ("imaginative, unusual"), but leaves a handful hissing it's "losing its edge"; the staff also divide diners: "good-natured" vs. "pleased with themselves."

Enoteca Turi ☒ 24 | 19 | 23 | £41

28 Putney High St., SW15 (Putney Bridge), 020-8785 4449; fax 8780 5409

"Conjuring the spirit of Florence", this Putney "perfect neighbourhood restaurant" offers "accomplished", yet "unpretentious" Italian cooking that makes "use of seasonal produce", along with a "mind-boggling wine list"; "enthusiastic service" is "welcoming to regulars", adding to the "homey" appeal of this "family-run" spot.

Enterprise, The 20 | 19 | 18 | £33

35 Walton St., SW3 (Knightsbridge/South Kensington), 020-7584 3148; fax 7584 2516; www.christophersgrill.com

"Really more of a restaurant in a pub than a gastro-pub", this "convivial" Chelsea haunt is "always packed" with a "surprisingly elegant crowd" enjoying "quality" Eclectic fare that's "not too fancy", and "reasonably priced"; the "service, though casual", is "efficient"; pity the "lively, noisy bar scene can detract from the dining experience."

Esarn Kheaw – | – | – | M

314 Uxbridge Rd., W12 (Shepherd's Bush), 020-8743 8930; fax 7243 1250

"Ignore the fact that you are crammed elbow-to-elbow" and "savour the true flavours of the Far East" at this "hole-in-the-wall" Shepherd's Bush Thai; a menu of "authentic regional specialties" that "vary from your standard" and "reasonable service" trumps the "rather dismal" decor.

Essenza ◐ ▽ 22 | 16 | 19 | £33

210 Kensington Park Rd., W11 (Ladbroke Grove), 020-7792 1066; fax 7229 7980; www.essenza.co.uk

"Gorgeous waiters and a beautiful clientele" add to the lustre of this Notting Hill "neighbourhood trattoria" (part of the Mediterraneo stable) where the combo of "huge portions" of "tasty Italian fare" and a "warm, friendly atmosphere" make it a "great little place" for "dinner with a few friends or a romantic candlelit" encounter – plus "you can often get a booking on the day"; now, if only "they would go nonsmoking."

Eyre Brothers 21 | 18 | 18 | £42

70 Leonard St., EC2 (Old St.), 020-7613 5346; fax 7739 8199; www.eyrebrothers.co.uk

"Out of the way, but worth the trek" is the consensus on this "interesting place" in Shoreditch from "hospitable owners" David and Robert Eyre (the founders of the Eagle), which serves "upmarket Spanish" "food with a wonderful homemade feeling" and "unusual" global wines; other features are "wood decor" with the retro-look of "'70s speaker cabinets" and a "great music" system that sets a "hip" mood, depending on the night.

Fairuz 21 | 16 | 20 | £29

27 Westbourne Grove, W2 (Bayswater/Queensway), 020-7243 8444; fax 7243 8777 ◐

3 Blandford St., W1 (Baker St./Bond St.), 020-7486 8108; fax 7935 8581

"Whilst the menu is not inventive", everything is "enjoyable" at this "down-to-earth" Lebanese pair in Bayswater and Marylebone; although they "can get hectic when full", the "super-friendly", "simpatico staff" ensure a "fun" time, and if a few feel the fare's "starting to look pricey for its type", the "huge portions" mean they "can make a meal" out of the "marvellous mezze."

FAKHRELDINE ◐ 23 | 19 | 20 | £40

1st fl., 85 Piccadilly, W1 (Green Park), 020-7493 3424; fax 7495 1977; www.fakhreldine.co.uk

Now "a fabulous place to hang out" after a "funky" "face-lift" a while back, this "evergreen" 27-year-old Lebanese "overlooking Green Park" is "the place to discover Arabic cuisine beyond mezze", thanks to "tantalising", "authentic" dishes; although some now find the place "a tad too expensive", "attentive service" compensates; P.S. "don't skip the coffee – you'll be ready to go all night!"

Farm, The 19 | 20 | 18 | £37

18 Farm Ln., SW6 (Fulham Broadway), 020-7381 3331; www.thefarmfulham.co.uk

"Achingly cool (for Fulham at least)", this newcomer makes a "welcome" "change from the standard gastro-pub", with its "atmospheric" dark-wood decor and a quite "decent" British menu from a former Greenhouse chef that features "traditional dishes with a modern twist"; "service is sporadic", however – and "what's with the cash-only bar?"

FAT DUCK, THE 28 | 21 | 26 | £79

High St., Bray, Berkshire, 01628 580333; fax 01628 776188; www.fatduck.co.uk

Chef Heston Blumenthal – who has "the soul of an artist" or "a mad scientist" – lives up to his reputation for "dramatic, breathtaking" Modern European dishes at this "cute" Berkshire cottage; even if the cuisine is "a challenge to even the most sophisticated diner" (chocolate-and-cauliflower risotto, anyone?), all agree the "stunning attention to detail", both in the kitchen and on the floor, makes it "a must" "at least once"; N.B. Blumenthal now has a nearby pub, the Hind's Head, under his wing.

ffiona's 22 | 17 | 23 | £32

51 Kensington Church St., W8 (High St. Kensington/ Notting Hill Gate), 020-7937 4152; www.ffionas.com

"Once a favourite, always a favourite" ffind ffriends of Ffiona Reid-Owen's "small", "homey" if "a bit dark" Kensington eatery; the owner is "quite a character" – she "tells you what to order" from the "hearty" Modern British menu – and directs the "personable", if "erratic" service; a "quirky" place, but most are "ultimately charmed" by having "home cooking without the hassle of cleaning up."

Fifteen 20 | 18 | 19 | £54

15 Westland Pl., N1 (Old St.), 0871-330 1515; fax 7251 2749; www.fifteenrestaurant.com

"Beyond all Jamie Oliver's hype", his "hip, happening" Hoxton venue is a "worthy cause" that acts "as a training camp for chefs-to-be" on a nonprofit basis ("don't expect any charity from the prices", though); the apprentices produce a tasting menu of "interesting" if "erratic" Med dishes in the "funky" downstairs venue, whilst the "casual upstairs" all-day trattoria serves "refreshing" Italian fare; "service is still not up to scratch", but overall, most say "well-done, Mr. Oliver."

Fifth Floor 19 | 18 | 18 | £39

Harvey Nichols, 109-125 Knightsbridge, SW1 (Knightsbridge), 020-7235 5250; fax 7235 7856; www.harveynichols.co.uk

The "smashing" look of an "oval spaceship" adds "uplift" to this "busy, bristling" department-store dining room where a "chic" crowd "can always count on a good Modern British meal" during or "after a hard day's shopping" in "the Harvey Nics inferno"; "service varies between pretentious and lovely" and it's certainly "pricey for what it is" – though "the entertainment, in the form of your fellow diners, is free."

Fifth Floor Cafe 18 | 14 | 15 | £27

Harvey Nichols, 109-125 Knightsbridge, SW1 (Knightsbridge), 020-7823 1839; fax 7823 2207

"Perfect for escaping the Knightsbridge hustle and bustle", this "light, airy" cafe offers "something for everyone" on a "consistent" all-day Modern British–Med menu; just recall that it's in "a busy store, and adjust your expectations accordingly"; P.S. "tables are on top of each other", but the "tiny veranda" makes amends as a "nice summer" treat.

Fifty ◐ – | – | – | VE

Private club; inquiries: 0870-415 5050

Lavishly transformed by restaurateur Robert Earl, this centuries-old St. James's gambling haunt is once again the site of the action, with a kitchen overseen by celebrated chef Jean-Georges Vongerichten; on the ground floor is Rama, a classily hip Asian eatery, whilst upstairs is V, a fine-dining space serving the chef's trademark Eclectic mix of Franco-Asian fare; a chic club, stylish bar and grand casino cap it all.

Fina Estampa ⊠ ▽ 22 | 16 | 20 | £30

150 Tooley St., SE1 (London Bridge/Tower Bridge), 020-7403 1342; fax 7403 1342

"Every neighbourhood should have a Peruvian restaurant" say those who discover this "well-kept secret" near Tower Bridge that's "quite a find" for "authentic, tasty" cooking at "reasonable prices"; and what it "lacks in decor, it makes up in service" from "eager-to-please staff", as well as in the "perfect drinks" from the downstairs bar.

FINO ⊠ 25 | 19 | 21 | £42

33 Charlotte St., W1 (Goodge St./Tottenham Court Rd.), 020-7813 8010; fax 7813 8011; www.finorestaurant.com

"Too-good-to-be-true tapas" and other Iberian dishes with "fresh-as-a-daisy ingredients" make this "legendary place" in a "contemporary" Fitzrovia basement "better than bars in Spain" (and with a bonus of "patient, friendly menu explanations"); virtually every surveyor warns the cost "of those little plates does add up" – "you could fly to Seville for the price!" – especially when you succumb to the "irresistible wine and sherry list"; P.S. the "tricky-to-find" entrance is on Rathbone Street.

Fiore ☒ — | — | — | E

33 St. James's, SW1 (Green Park), 020-7930 7100; fax 7930 4070; www.fiore-restaurant.co.uk

Housed in the narrow, modern space that "used to be Pétrus", experienced restaurateur Claudio Pulze (of Zaika) has joined with chef Umberto Vezzoli to unveil this addition to St. James's; the "welcome's warm", and a "reliable, if not outstanding" Italian menu "delivers the goods."

First Floor 16 | 20 | 14 | £31

186 Portobello Rd., W11 (Ladbroke Grove/Notting Hill Gate), 020-7243 0072; fax 7221 9440; www.firstfloorportobello.co.uk

This "cool", "interesting Gothic space" with a "shabby-chic" look above a Portobello Road pub makes a "funky hangout" – one that's "excellent for parties"; but most agree the place is "let down by excruciatingly slow and uninterested service" and a Modern British menu that, though "honest", seems increasingly "hit-or-miss."

fish! 19 | 17 | 17 | £30

Cathedral St., Borough Mkt., SE1 (London Bridge), 020-7407 3803; fax 7357 8636; www.fishdiner.co.uk

In a glass-and-steel pavilion "looking out on Borough Market and Southwark Cathedral", this "casual" Traditional British seafooder is "a safe bet" for "simple, delicious dishes" (even fans wish they were "a bit more creative") and "solicitous, but not annoyingly so" staff; though technically, it's "not too shabby on the wallet", the fin-icky fuss it still seems "too expensive for what it is – a glorified fish diner."

FISH HOEK 25 | 15 | 22 | £36

6-8 Elliott Rd., W4 (Turnham Green), 020-8742 0766; fax 8742 3374

"South African flair" (down to the "proper tomato sauce") applied to "superb" "exotic" seafood is the hoek that makes this spot "worth the trek" to Chiswick; the "knowledgeable staff know their fish" – "is there anywhere else you have this amount of choice?" – and "though it's not inexpensive", "their early-bird specials" offer "more moderate pricing."

Fishmarket ☒ ▽ 17 | 14 | 16 | £35

Great Eastern Hotel, 40 Liverpool St., EC2 (Liverpool St.), 020-7618 7200; fax 7618 7201; www.great-eastern-hotel.co.uk

"Stuck between two bars" in the Great Eastern Hotel, this low-key, pastel-coloured seafooder has a "decent" Modern British seafood menu – much of which is displayed on a handsome bar; it works best as a business venue, even though the service can be "slapdash" on occasion.

Fish Shop on St. John St. 19 | 15 | 18 | £36

360-362 St. John St., EC1 (Angel), 020-7837 1199; fax 7837 3399; www.thefishshop.net

"If you're still mourning the Upper Street Fish Shop", this Clerkenwell offshoot run by the same team is "your salvation", offering an "interesting", "unusual" selection of British seafood that's "a tad on the pricey side", but "always very fresh"; however, a sceptical minority (sick of being "packed like sardines in the cramped rooms") suggest it's "not living up to its potential – or pedigree."

FishWorks 20 | 14 | 16 | £37

6 Turnham Green Terrace, W4 (Turnham Green), 020-8994 0086; fax 8994 0778
89 Marylebone High St., W1 (Baker St.), 020-7935 9796; fax 7935 8796
www.fishworks.co.uk

"Can't go wrong" for "simple, but well-cooked" fin fare direct from Cornwall, profess fans of these two "lively" Chiswick and Marylebone outposts of a bourgeoning chain that feature "their own fishmonger at the front" (in fact, nearby tables can "get a bit too fishy"-smelling); but critics decry the "cold decor" and "prices that have crept up" whilst the menu remains "predictable."

Floridita ◐ ☒ 18 | 23 | 20 | £43

100 Wardour St., W1 (Tottenham Court Rd.), 020-7314 4000; fax 7314 4040; www.floriditalondon.com

Seeking to re-create the famous Havana haunt, El Floridita, this "stunning" Soho newcomer offers a "dinner/dancing combination" of "good" Cuban cookery, "live music" every night, 40 types of rum for your mojitos and "cigars to finish up with"; dissenters are "disappointed" with the "bland" fare, but it's the "Latin party feel" in "grey London" that gets "the glam crowd flocking" here.

FOLIAGE 26 | 24 | 26 | £65

Mandarin Oriental Hyde Park, 66 Knightsbridge, SW1 (Knightsbridge), 020-7201 3723; fax 7235 4552; www.mandarinoriental.com

"Knockout cooking, knockout views" are the trump cards at the Mandarin Oriental's "tranquil", "beautiful dining room" "overlooking Hyde Park"; "culinary wizard" Chris Staines' "creative", "caringly produced" French–Modern European cuisine comes courtesy of "knowledgeable", "perfectly paced" service and preferably "with an intriguing selection from the fabulous, all-glass wine cellar" on display; those concerned by "astronomical prices" seek refuge in the "divine lunch" prix fixe.

Food for Thought ⊄ 22 | 10 | 14 | £11

31 Neal St., WC2 (Covent Garden), 020-7836 9072

Ignore the "drab surroundings and do-it-yourself service" – this "compact" Covent Garden "cubby hole", again voted the *Survey*'s No.1 Bang for the Buck, is "an absolute must" for "amazing, hearty" vegetarian fare that "will please even the fiercest carnivore"; it's "not a place to linger" – the "communal tables" mean "you're crammed amongst strangers in awkward positions" – but there's always "good takeaway" if you can't face the "queues down the road."

Food Room, The ☒ – | – | – | E

123 Queenstown Rd., SW8 (Clapham Common), 020-7622 0555; fax 7622 9543

Making "a worthy replacement for the Stepping Stone" (which closed on these Battersea premises in 2004), this "stark" site run by a "friendly" husband-and-wife team offers "flavoursome, well-executed" Mediterranean meals and a "short wine list with some excellent stuff on it"; as with many novices, however, "little things are irksome" – mainly the "unimpressive service."

Fortnum's Fountain ☒ 18 | 17 | 19 | £27

Fortnum & Mason, 181 Piccadilly, W1 (Green Park/ Piccadilly Circus), 020-7973 4140; fax 7437 3278; www.fortnumandmason.com

"British nostalgia at its best" lives at this "sentimental favourite", a "convenient", "unchanging" (since 1950) all-day "ground-floor cafe in the famous emporium" that offers the "upper crust of comfort food" ("particularly good Welsh rarebit"); true, "service can vary" and the decor's "looking a bit tired" – but most relish the fact "it's just like it was when my parents took me here"; P.S. on the fourth floor is St. James's Restaurant, a larger, more formal option serving luncheon and the "quintessential English tea."

43 South Molton ◐ – | – | – | E

43 S. Molton St., W1K (Bond St.), 020-7647 4343; www.43southmolton.com

Now occupying Khew's old corner, this multilevel venue in Mayfair comprises a variety of spaces; decorated like a general store, the all-day cafe on the ground floor serves pricey Modern European bistro-style fare, from breakfast and dinnertime tapas, whilst upstairs, a private members club goes for a funky country-house look; the basement houses a versatile room for private parties.

Four Seasons Chinese ◐ 24 | 8 | 9 | £21

84 Queensway, W2 (Bayswater), 020-7229 4320; fax 7229 4320

"The queues outside are testament" to the popularity of this "bustling" Bayswater venue that's "legendary to Chinese foodies around the world" thanks to the "fabulous Peking duck" and other "exceptional" Mandarin specialities; even if the "decor hasn't changed since the beginning of the Cold War", and it "can feel like you're in Hong Kong with such brusque service", it still has many "adoring fans."

1492 ◐ ▽ 19 | 15 | 18 | £30

404 North End Rd., SW6 (Fulham Broadway), 020-7381 3810; fax 7381 1402; www.1492restaurant.com

"Mixing Mexican, Peruvian, Colombian and all sorts of cuisines" from South America, this adventuresome Fulham haunt has its supporters; but sceptics scoff there's "nothing extraordinary" about the "pseudo-Latin" experience – except, perhaps, the "incredibly noisy" atmosphere.

Frankie's Italian Bar & Grill 17 | 19 | 17 | £36

3 Yeoman's Row, downstairs, SW3 (Knightsbridge), 020-7590 9999; fax 7590 9900

This "barn"-sized underground room in Knightsbridge (formerly Chez Max) has been transformed by Marco Pierre White and top jockey Frankie Dettori into a "fun, frivolous and family-friendly" venue with "flashy disco decor" (down to the "giant", "sparkly" balls on the ceiling); the Italian mains and hamburgers are "seriously good" – "but for the price you're paying, you should get better" foes fume – and at times the "noise is horrific."

Frederick's ☒ 20 | 19 | 18 | £41

106 Camden Passage, N1 (Angel), 020-7359 2888; fax 7359 5173; www.fredericks.co.uk

After 37 years, "everyone knows" this "Camden Passage stalwart", appreciating its "delightful" qualities for a "romantic" "first date" and "great outdoor seating in summer"; the "enjoyable", if "pricey" Modern British–European menu is "consistent" "year after year", but some warn "the service can be painfully slow."

French Horn 24 | 23 | 24 | £57

French Horn Hotel, Sonning-on-Thames, Sonning, Berkshire, 01189 692204; fax 01189 442210; www.thefrenchhorn.co.uk

Surveyors sound the trumpets for this "special-occasion" site, a "fabulous" family-run hotel where "conservative British elegance, with the right French notes in the food", makes guests feel "transported to another time and place"; amidst the "gorgeous" Thames-side setting in Berkshire, "always-attentive staff" serve the "perfectly cooked" classic fare – such as "duck roasting on an open fire in the bar"; oh, and they've got "great rooms if you can't get home" that night (or don't want to).

French House, The ☒ 15 | 16 | 17 | £35

49 Dean St., W1 (Piccadilly Circus/Tottenham Court Rd.), 020-7437 2477; fax 7287 9109

"An absolute charmer up above a pub" in Soho, this "small, atmospheric" dining room gets "packed" on account of its "richly satisfying" French Bistro dishes "at a reasonable price"; even if some feel "service could be a bit warmer", this popular "hangout for the French and Francophiles" remains "perfect for a lunch rendezvous."

Friends ▽ 18 | 13 | 16 | £28

6 Hollywood Rd., SW10 (Fulham Broadway/South Kensington), 020-7376 3890; fax 7352 6368

"Dependable brick-oven pizzas" with "good ingredients and flavour combinations" and a "friendly", "relaxed" attitude are what makes this "easy" Chelsea eatery "always a pleasant experience", even if the "tables are a bit close together" for comfort.

Frontline ▽ 17 | 20 | 16 | £31

13 Norfolk Pl., W2 (Paddington), 020-7479 8960; fax 7479 8961; www.frontlinerestaurant.com

It's "a real find in the otherwise dreary Paddington area" say intrepid reviewers who've sniffed out this Modern British–Med co-owned by TV cameraman Vaughan Smith – hence the "beautiful building's" decor of "oversized ceiling lampshades" illuminating the "war photography" on the walls; the ground-floor restaurant serves "not great, but good food"; afterwards, you can "trot upstairs for first-rate political discussions" held by the private journalists' club.

Fung Shing ● 21 | 11 | 17 | £31

15 Lisle St., WC2 (Leicester Sq.), 020-7437 1539; fax 7743 0284

"A Chinatown standout" smile fans of this thirtysomething stalwart where "upscale, creative" Cantonese cooking is "prepared with care and finesse"; the "staff are helpful with suggestions" over the menu, ensuring an experience "great for groups" as well as "when you dine alone"; "just close your eyes whilst you're eating (decor needs a major redo")."

Galicia ● ▽ 18 | 12 | 15 | £26

323 Portobello Rd., W10 (Ladbroke Grove), 020-8969 3539

This "raunchy, smoky den seems to have been plucked from Spain and set down" in Portobello Road, offering a "hectic" scene in which to sample "simple" Iberian fare, including a "good selection of tapas" and "paella that satisfies the soul"; the main problem: you "never know if you're gonna get smiling or sulky service."

Gallipoli 18 | 15 | 19 | £19

102 Upper St., N1 (Angel), 020-7359 0630; fax 7704 0496
107 Upper St., N1 (Angel), 020-7226 5333; fax 7704 0496 ●
120 Upper St., N1 (Angel), 020-7359 1578; fax 7704 0496
www.gallipolibazaar.com

"So popular it's spread across" Upper Street, this "cheery" Turkish trio "tends to be a noisy affair, ending with people dancing on the bar" after indulging in "generous portions" of "decent" Middle Eastern fare that "just keeps on coming", along with "a bottle or two of their reasonable wines"; true, "the decor is slightly down-at-heel – but what do you expect for the price?"

Garbo's ▽ 19 | 16 | 20 | £26

42 Crawford St., W1 (Baker St./Marylebone), 020-7262 6582; fax 7262 6582

"A must for those who like to try" different cuisines, this low-key Scandinavian in Marylebone has "some real pleasures waiting" on an "unmistakably Swedish" menu that includes an "impressive" smorgasbord and other "traditional dishes

Swedes can't live without", overseen by a chef-owner who's "a real character ("don't miss the elk on the wall"); "it won't break the bank" either.

Gate, The ☒ 24 | 20 | 21 | £28

51 Queen Caroline St., W6 (Hammersmith), 020-8748 6932; www.thegate.tv

"Whether or not you're a vegetarian", the Modern European fare at this "magical" eatery is "delicious, inventive" – and "good enough to convert die-hard carnivores" to the cause; situated in an "old artists' studio", it's "worth the effort to find" (hidden behind Hammersmith's Apollo Theatre), especially as there's "a lovely outdoor courtyard" too.

GAUCHO GRILL 21 | 17 | 17 | £36

19 Swallow St., W1 (Piccadilly Circus), 020-7734 4040; fax 7734 1076 ◐

125-126 Chancery Ln., WC2 (Chancery Ln.), 020-7242 7727; fax 7242 7723 ☒

89 Sloane Ave., SW3 (South Kensington), 020-7584 9901; fax 7584 0045

64 Heath St., NW3 (Hampstead), 020-7431 8222; fax 7431 3714 ◐

29 Westferry Circus, E14 (Canary Wharf), 020-7987 9494; fax 7987 9292

1 Bell Inn Yard, EC3 (Bank/Monument), 020-7626 5180; fax 7626 5181 ☒

www.thegauchogrill.co.uk

"Dedicated to all that is bovine-tastic", right down to the "cowboy decor" and "cowhide seats", this burgeoning chain grills up "hearty, unpretentious" chophouse fare, including "Argentinean steak so tender you can cut it with a spoon"; grouchy gauchos grimace at "sometimes sloppy service" and "expensive prices", but most "meat junkies" rate this a "pleaser from start to finish"; N.B. a big Broadgate branch was set to open in late summer, and Canary Wharf has just instituted delivery – via rickshaw.

Gay Hussar ☒ 20 | 19 | 20 | £35

2 Greek St., W1 (Tottenham Court Rd.), 020-7437 0973; fax 7437 4631

"A true landmark with all the paprika-laced trimmings", this Hungarian haunt "after 50 years is still grinding out" "the favourites"; with its "heavy" cuisine, "charming service" and "long, narrow hall", eating here is "like stepping back in time", but that makes a "welcome change from trendy spots in Soho" – especially since the "rich pictorial history of liberal politicos" on the walls is often augmented by real-life sightings of "interesting celebs" too.

Geales Fish Restaurant 21 | 12 | 17 | £22

2 Farmer St., W8 (Notting Hill Gate), 020-7727 7528; fax 7229 8632

"When you get that urge for fish 'n' chips", this "homely" Notting Hill Gate "institution" is "still a favourite" to old salts who "stuff" themselves on "crusty, moist" seafood; but lachrymose landlubbers snap "if you like boring food", "service with a frown" and decor that "could use smartening up", "this is your place."

George ☒ 21 | 21 | 24 | £57

Private club; inquiries: 020-7491 4433

Attracting a "definitely chic, but not ostentatious" crowd, this "more casual" (but still "civilised") Mayfair "member of the well-run [private] Mark Birley clubs" has a "winning formula" of "truly welcoming staff" who "cater to your needs" with "genuinely well-prepared and -presented" Modern European cuisine; some sigh "shame it's members only", but to others, it's "best to be a guest", given the "expensive" prices; N.B. the recently expanded downstairs bar now has its own membership option.

Getti ☒ 16 | 16 | 18 | £31

42 Marylebone High St., W1 (Baker St./Bond St.), 020-7486 3753; fax 7486 7084

16-17 Jermyn St., SW1 (Piccadilly Circus), 020-7734 7334; fax 7734 7924

www.getti.com

A "no-nonsense eatery" for "no-fuss Italian" fare sums up the situation at this "decent" duo in Marylebone and St. James's; all praise the "pleasing service", but what positives applaud as "reliable" cooking, pessimists proclaim is "rather too predictable", whilst opinions on the decor range from "pleasant" to "poor."

Ginger ▽ 21 | 15 | 17 | £30

115 Westbourne Grove, W2 (Notting Hill Gate), 020-7908 1990; fax 7908 1991; www.gingerrestaurant.co.uk

For a "different take on Indian food", this Bangladeshi "on the border of Notting Hill and Bayswater" offers an "appealing", "good-value-for-money" menu; and even if it is "atmospherically challenged", it's "unique, and so, more fun than the usual" subcontinental standards.

Giovanni's ☒ – | – | – | M

10 Goodwin's Court, WC2 (Covent Garden), 020-7240 2877

It's "hard to find" in a mews off St. Martin's Lane, but this "small, intimate" family-run Italian, in the same unassuming quarters since 1950, is "popular with the after-theatre crowd" or anyone looking for "delicious food at a modest price"; "top-notch service" and "attention from proprietor Pino Ragona on the wine selection" also get the thumbs up.

Giraffe 17 | 14 | 17 | £20

7 Kensington High St., W8 (High St. Kensington), 020-7938 1221; fax 7938 3330

270 Chiswick High Rd., W4 (Turnham Green), 020-8995 2100; fax 8995 4204

(continued)

(continued)
Giraffe
6-8 Blandford St., W1 (Baker St./Bond St.), 020-7935 2333; fax 7935 2334
27 Battersea Rise, SW11 (Clapham Junction/Clapham Common), 020-7223 0933; fax 7223 1037
46 Rosslyn Hill, NW3 (Hampstead), 020-7435 0343; fax 7431 1317
348 Muswell Hill Broadway, N10 (Highgate), 020-8883 4463; fax 8883 1224
29-31 Essex Rd., N1 (Angel), 020-7359 5999; fax 7359 6158 ◐
30 Hill St., Twickenham (Richmond), 020-8332 2646; fax 8332 9171
www.giraffe.net
There's "something for everyone" on the "uncomplicated", "eco-savvy" and economical Eclectic menu of these "cheeky" all-day cafes, many with "canteen-style benches" and world music, that are "family friendly earlier in the day and more of a date place at night"; it's "a great concept, if a little rough around the edges" – and "a bit of a zoo due to the kid factor", though the "smiley staff" are "accommodating" (even to "screaming babies").

Glas ☒ – | – | – | E
3 Park St., SE1 (London Bridge), 020-7357 6060; fax 7357 6061; www.glasrestaurant.com
In small, cosy digs under the railway arches near London Bridge, this quirky Scandinavian newcomer (the name is Swedish for 'glass') has sprung up; run by a mother-daughter team, it's a relaxed spot with a few grand touches, like a crystal chandelier and old paintings and mirrors; but the menu is quite modern, with such ambitious dishes as venison with liquorice jus and gin-and-lingonberry mousse.

Glasshouse, The 24 | 19 | 21 | £46
14 Station Parade, Kew (Kew Gardens), 020-8940 6777; fax 8940 3833; www.glasshouserestaurant.co.uk
"A good reason to move to Kew" – "you can tell the locals, they are the ones not dressed up" – agree admirers of this "sophisticated, calm" corner (under the same ownership as Chez Bruce) where the "subtle, imaginative" Modern British menu offers a "wonderful mélange of tastes"; whilst it's "never a cheap or fast option", and can feel "slightly cramped", few stones get thrown at this glass house.

Globe ▽ 17 | 14 | 17 | £28
100 Avenue Rd., NW3 (Swiss Cottage), 020-7722 7200; fax 7722 2772; www.globerestaurant.co.uk
"Some fun touches" – like drag-act "cabaret nights", led by owner and self-styled 'queen bee' Neil Armishaw most Thursdays – make this "pleasant, light" eatery "that little bit different"; the "fairly priced" Modern British menu is "good, if not terribly original", whilst "always welcoming" staff are appreciated; P.S. situated next door to Hampstead Theatre, it's handy "for pre-show dining."

Golden Dragon ◐ 20 | 11 | 15 | £22

28-29 Gerrard St., W1 (Leicester Sq./Piccadilly Circus), 020-7734 2763; fax 7734 1073

Unless you "go after the theatre", "waiting for a table is not unusual" at this "crowded", "basic"-looking Chinatown venue; whilst the "well-priced" multiregional menu (with "especially fresh dim sum" during the day) will "not blow your mind", it "delivers the standards well" and is "served in good time", albeit by "indifferent" staff.

Good Earth, The 21 | 15 | 19 | £31

233 Brompton Rd., SW3 (Knightsbridge/South Kensington), 020-7584 3658; fax 7823 8769 ◐

143-145 The Broadway, NW7 (Mill Hill B.R.), 020-8959 7011; fax 8959 1464

"As the name suggests, it's good" at this "down-to-earth" Chinese duo, a 23-year-old "staple in Knightsbridge" and Mill Hill for "traditional dishes done that much better"; although a few think it's "rather pricey for what you get", the "friendly service" gets a pat on the back; N.B. there are also delivery-only outposts in Wimbledon, Richmond and Hampstead.

Gopal's of Soho ◐☒ ▽ 19 | 9 | 16 | £25

12 Bateman St., W1 (Leicester Sq./Tottenham Court Rd.), 020-7434 1621; fax 7434 0840

This "standby" is seen as a "safe bet" for a "dependable" Indian meal, and even if the "dimly lit room could use refreshing", most agree this "consistent" spot is a "no-brainer" when in Soho, especially "before/after the theatre."

GORDON RAMSAY AT CLARIDGE'S 26 | 25 | 25 | £80

Claridge's Hotel, 45 Brook St., W1 (Bond St.), 020-7499 0099; fax 7499 3099; www.gordonramsay.com

In a "dining room worthy of Claridge's" ("art deco deluxe!"), Gordon Ramsay's "sumptuous" venture offers a "well-choreographed show" starring "rich" New French dishes with "extraordinary flair in their presentation", supported by "a most amazing cheese selection" and "fantastic wine list"; it's "not at the level of its Chelsea sibling", perhaps, but to most it's "worth every pound" (and it costs "a lot of them"); P.S. try "the chef's table in the kitchen – a once-in-a-lifetime experience."

GORDON RAMSAY AT 68 ROYAL HOSPITAL RD. ☒ 29 | 24 | 28 | £95

68 Royal Hospital Rd., SW3 (Sloane Sq.), 020-7352 4441; fax 7352 3334; www.gordonramsay.com

His "empire grows, but this remains the mecca of the Gordon Ramsay world", a "divine dining experience" that's "still the best" – and still the *Survey*'s No.1 for Food and Service; within "discreet" modern Chelsea digs, the "gastronomically orgasmic" New French cuisine "boggles the mind" with its "classic perfection", whilst service is "impressive, yet without fuss"; true, "reservations are nearly impossible" ("call exactly one month ahead") and it's "not cheap – but would you expect it to be?"

Goring Dining Room 21 | 21 | 23 | £45

The Goring Hotel, 15 Beeston Pl., SW1 (Victoria), 020-7396 9000; fax 7834 4393; www.goringhotel.co.uk

"For traditional, if slightly eccentric dining", take a "step back in time" to this "civilised" Victoria hotel dining room where "lovely" Traditional British fare (there's an "extra-special breakfast", "but don't ignore their afternoon teas") is presided over by "smooth" service; it's an equally suitable "place to take your mother-in-law" or "to quietly meet with government officials."

Gourmet Burger Kitchen 22 | 11 | 14 | £15

15-17 Hill Rise, TW10 (Richmond), 020-8940 5440
131 Chiswick High Rd., W4 (Turnham Green), 020-8995 4548
50 Westbourne Grove, W2 (Bayswater/Royal), 020-7243 4344
333 Putney Bridge Rd., SW15 (Putney Bridge), 020-8789 1199
44 Northcote Rd., SW11 (Clapham Junction B.R.), 020-7228 3309
49 Fulham Broadway, SW6 (Fulham Broadway), 020-7381 4242
331 West End Ln., NW6 (West Hampstead), 020-7794 5455
www.gbkinfo.co.uk

Doing "exactly what it says on the tin", this chain of "tightly packed" eateries is credited with "redefining the burger experience", producing "real, proper" Aberdeen-Angus beef patties (and "good alternatives") with "grown-up" trimmings, "nice fat fries" and "awesome milkshakes"; there's a "confusing ordering system", so have "patience."

Gravetye Manor 24 | 26 | 25 | £67

Gravetye Manor Hotel, Vowels Ln., East Grinstead, West Sussex, 01342 810567; fax 01342 810080; www.gravetyemanor.co.uk

"Worth the drive" for its "out-of-this-world" Sussex setting alone, this "beautiful manor" house hotel is "dark" and "formal", but "exudes warmth" thanks to "superb" Modern British cuisine and "friendly, attentive staff" (two of whom – the chef and general manager – now own the joint); "it's at its most wonderful on a summer's evening, when dinner can be preceded by a drink in the lovely gardens."

Graze – | – | – | E

215 Sutherland Ave., W9 (Maida Vale/Warwick Avenue), 020-7266 3131; www.graze.co.uk

The old Otto Dining Lounge has gotten a funky makeover by owner Soren Jessen (noble rot., 1 Lombard Street), resulting in this relaxed resident of St. John's Wood; its Eclectic–New French menu is dominated by grazing-style dishes (hence the name), whilst blood-red walls and impressive antique chandeliers create a quirky, bohemian feel; N.B. there's a 1 AM bar license Tuesdays–Saturdays.

Great Eastern Dining Room ◐ ☒ ▽ 20 | 16 | 19 | £35

54 Great Eastern St., EC2 (Liverpool St./Old St.), 020-7613 4545; fax 7613 4137; www.greateasterndining.co.uk

With a "cool interior" shaped from an 1800s warehouse and two bars – one open until 1 AM – this trendoid owned by Will Ricker (Cicada, e&o) "could so easily be superficial, but it surprises with rather good" Asian fare and "all-around" "atmosphere" for both Shoreditch diners and "the after-work crowds."

GREENHOUSE, THE ☒ 25 | 23 | 24 | £68

27A Hay's Mews, W1 (Green Park), 020-7499 3331; fax 7499 5368

Now "firing on all cylinders" after the ministrations of new owner Marlon Abela (Morton's, Umu), this "class act" – "well-hidden" in a Mayfair mews – showcases the talents of "impressive chef" Bjorn van der Horst, whose "stunning", "highly inventive" New French dishes are supported by an "incredibly extensive wine list" and "astonishing service"; catering to a "nice mix of locals and sophisticated tourists" ("not for the celebrity-spotting, midriff-baring crowd"), it's "exactly what an expensive meal should be."

Green Olive, The ▽ 24 | 21 | 21 | £39

5 Warwick Pl., W9 (Warwick Ave.), 020-7289 2469; fax 7289 2463

"Don't be deceived by the exterior": this Maida Vale "relative of Red Pepper" is a "lovely little neighbourhood" address, serving "upscale", "inspiring" Tuscan treats in an "intimate setting" ("like eating in someone's uncluttered living room"); the staff's slightly "weird" but "warmly welcoming" anyway.

Green's 21 | 18 | 21 | £46

36 Duke St., SW1 (Green Park/Piccadilly Circus), 020-7930 4566; fax 7930 2958; www.greens.org.uk

"Quintessentially British, in a hounds-and-foxes kind of way", this "comfortable" "non-changing" St. James's stalwart (approaching its 25th anniversary) is a "favourite" for "dependable seafood" "and classic dishes" ("the best club food served outside a club") served by "attentive" staff in the "traditional" style; however, a Decor score drop confirms the setting – and indeed, "the whole place – needs a face-lift."

Grenadier, The 16 | 21 | 17 | £30

18 Wilton Row, SW1 (Hyde Park Corner), 020-7235 3074; fax 7235 3400

"Once you find its hidden location" in a "cobblestone mews", join the "Belgravia locals" and "American tourists" at this "historic" tavern – once "the site of the Duke of Wellington's mess hall", now home to an "old ghost" – whose "fireplaces and atmosphere make up for" the "remarkably average" British "pubby food"; it's more "a place to imbibe", really, but those dining "best make a reservation" as they've "just a few tables."

Greyhound, The — | – | – | M

136 Battersea High St., SW11 (Clapham Junction), 020-7978 7021; fax 7978 5911; www.thegreyhoundatbattersea.co.uk

"Run by two Aussies", this "Battersea newcomer" is "excellent for gastro-pub lovers", with a spick-and-span space comprising a bright bar with leather sofas, a skylit room and a small courtyard for alfresco dining; the short Modern European menu is enlivened by quirky touches (e.g. a goats' curd salad) and a varied wine list reflecting the owner's experience as a sommelier at The Greenhouse.

GRILL ROOM, THE 24 | 24 | 26 | £61

The Dorchester, 53 Park Ln., W1 (Hyde Park Corner/Marble Arch), 020-7629 8888; fax 7317 6464; www.dorchesterhotel.com

The Dorchester's dining room sets "a living example of old-school luxury", from the "faultless, friendly service" to a "tempting" Traditional British menu of "freshly baked breads" and "ravishing roast beef" "from the trolley" ("a nice touch"); the young and trendy may deem it "out-of-date", but "you can't go wrong with a class restaurant in a class hotel"; N.B. scores don't reflect the post-*Survey* arrival of Olivier Couillaud (ex La Trompette) or the new Scottish-themed decor, set to be unveiled in the fall.

Grocer on Warwick, The ⊠ – | – | – | M

(fka Sugar Club)

21 Warwick St., W1 (Piccadilly Circus), 020-7437 7776; www.thegroceron.com

Just off Regent Street, owners Ashley Sumner and Vivienne Hayman have converted their respected Sugar Club into a bustling venture that houses a shop-front deli, a rear restaurant and a coffee bar sandwiched in between; in the simply appointed, skylit dining room, Soho-ites can sample an array of Asian and Pacific Rim edibles from the wok, grill and tandoor.

Groucho Club, The ⊠ 18 | 18 | 20 | £39

Private club; inquiries: 020-7439 4685

"If you can get in, you might get a sighting of an artist", author or actor at Joel Cadbury's "cool", "amusing" private members' club in Soho where the "wine and conversation" are as much a part of the Modern British menu as the "rather good" fare; both it and the service are "on something of a comeback."

Grumbles ∇ 18 | 13 | 18 | £28

35 Churton St., SW1 (Pimlico/Victoria), 020-7834 0149; fax 7834 0298; www.grumblesrestaurant.co.uk

"Popular" in Pimlico, this "'60s survivor with unchanged bistro decor" remains a "cramped" but "cosy", "convivial" corner for "comfort food" of both the British and French varieties; the "really reasonable" prices ensure that "even finicky mothers like it" here.

Guinea Grill ☒ 23 | 18 | 21 | £49

30 Bruton Pl., W1 (Bond St.), 020-7499 1210; fax 7491 1442; www.theguinea.co.uk

Whether "charcoal-grilled" or in a "genuine kidney pie", "steaks are the thing" at this "charming", "old-school" dining room in "a quaint mews off Berkeley Square"; the Traditional British menu "does what it does well", and the "spot-on service" is "as convivial as the setting", though a few feel it "needs to tone down the prices."

Gun, The ▽ 21 | 21 | 17 | £32

27 Coldharbour, E14 (Canary Wharf), 020-7515 5222; www.thegundocklands.com

"Doubling as a local pub and posh restaurant", this "much-needed addition to the Canary Wharf scene" – a "revamped old" 1750 tavern that hosted Lord Nelson – boasts "stunning river views" from its "alfresco" terrace and "interesting" Modern British "gastro-pub grub"; "service can be slow" when it's under the gun at busy times.

Gung-Ho ◐ ▽ 18 | 12 | 15 | £30

330 West End Ln., NW6 (West Hampstead), 020-7794 1444; fax 7794 5522

"Great for all occasions", this "friendly" "neighbourhood Chinese" serves up "consistent quality" Szechuan cooking for "reasonable prices" in brightly coloured if "a bit cramped" digs; though "mostly frequented by locals", it's "worth the cab ride" to Hampstead.

HAKKASAN ◐ 25 | 27 | 18 | £51

8 Hanway Pl., W1 (Tottenham Court Rd.), 020-7927 7000; fax 7907 1889

"Your date will be impressed" by Alan Yau's "fabulously decorated, opium den"–"dark" Bloomsbury basement down "a dead-end alley", where a "too-too hip" crowd and "celebrities galore" enjoy "delicate" "fresh dim sum" or "creative", Chinese mains and "sexy cocktails"; some sharpen their chopsticks over "slow" staff who then "quickly kick you out" for the next table, but the fact "reservations trade on the futures market" proves this venue is so "sublime", "you don't even notice the drain on your wallet."

Halepi 22 | 14 | 21 | £29

18 Leinster Terrace, W2 (Lancaster Gate/Queensway), 020-7262 1070; fax 7262 2630 ◐

48-50 Belsize Ln., NW3 (Belsize Park/Swiss Cottage), 020-7431 5855; fax 7431 5844

"Robustly satisfying Greek" fare, "welcoming" waiters "who are not reticent in assisting with your order" and "a lively atmosphere" are the hallmarks of this "oh-so-very-nice family"-run pair in Bayswater (a 40-year-old stalwart) and Belsize Park; "the ambience is nothing great", but "it's a treat" nonetheless.

Harbour City ◐ | 18 | 12 | 13 | £22

46 Gerrard St., W1 (Leicester Sq./Piccadilly Circus), 020-7439 7859; fax 7734 7745

A "solid, traditional Chinatown classic" claim converts who appreciate the Cantonese fare and "good dim sum" at lunch; but those harbouring doubts decry the "slightly run-down" digs and warn it's "a crapshoot in terms of service" ("staff are experts at avoiding eye contact and frantic waves"); P.S. "don't get shuffled upstairs" – it's social "Siberia."

HARD ROCK CAFE ◐ | 13 | 19 | 15 | £24

150 Old Park Ln., W1 (Green Park/Hyde Park Corner), 020-7629 0382; fax 7629 8702; www.hardrock.com

"You either love it or hate it" (or perhaps love to hate it) – "the original cafe off Piccadilly" that's fostered a "famous" chain with "throbbing" music, "amazing [rock 'n' roll] memorabilia" and "predictable" American eats; many are pretty hard on it ("why eat here when London has so much to offer?"), "but sometimes predictable is all you need", and it remains "a must" "if you have restless kids/teens in tow."

Harlem ◐ | 14 | 18 | 14 | £23

78 Westbourne Grove, W2 (Bayswater/Queensway), 020-7985 0900; fax 7985 0901

469 Brixton Rd., SW9 (Brixton), 020-7326 4455; fax 7326 4488

www.harlemsoulfood.com

The brainchild of American music producer Arthur Baker, this "relaxed", "easy-going" eatery in Westbourne Grove has seen its Southern "soul food" – served "all day" – rise in the ratings; but sceptics say it still seems "ordinary", and given the "spacey" service, many prefer just "to head downstairs" to the "groovy bar in the evenings"; N.B. the new Brixton Road branch is unrated.

Harry's Bar ◐ ⊠ | 23 | 22 | 24 | £68

Private club; inquiries: 020-7408 0844

For "members only" (and "how lucky they are"), this "clubby" Mayfair "standby for the rich and famous" – like "*Vanity Fair* come to life" – remains "as discreet as ever", with "superb servers" proffering the "artistically presented" "essence of Italian" cucina; "outrageous prices" and "tiny tables and low chairs" cause a frisson of frustration, but all's eased by a signature "peach Bellini from barman Mario."

Havelock Tavern ⌿ | ▽ 25 | 18 | 15 | £25

57 Masbro Rd., W14 (Olympia/Shepherd's Bush), 020-7603 5374; fax 7602 1163; www.thehavelocktavern.co.uk

"They take the classics and cook them very well" on a "constantly changing" Modern British menu at this Brook Green gastro-pub; despite "the usual drawbacks – noisy (very) and smoky (even worse)" – this no-reservations venue is "ever reliable", whether it be for "a Sunday lunch chilling with the papers" or "simple dinner with friends."

Hi Sushi | 13 | 9 | 10 | £23

40 Frith St., W1 (Leicester Sq.), 020-7734 9688; fax 7734 9882
16 Hampstead High St., NW3 (Hampstead), 020-7794 2828; fax 7794 7328

Those who "prefer this small mom-and-pop place to the chain sushi haunts" hail this Hampstead and Soho duo; but sliding scores support sceptics who slam the "rather unremarkable" food, "nothing-special" service and "budget space-age decor", "wishing it would become Bye Sushi."

Homage | – | – | – | M

The Waldorf-Hilton, 22 The Aldwych, WC2 (Holborn), 020-7759 4080; www.homagegrandsalon.co.uk

As part of a £30 million revamp, the Waldorf-Hilton (built in 1908) has unveiled a handsome new restaurant whose pillar-dominated decor pays homage to the grand Continental cafes of yore; alongside a patisserie and bar, the main dining room serves midpriced Modern British–European fare from breakfast through to post-theatre supper.

Home House ◐ | 20 | 27 | 22 | £44

Private club; inquiries: 020-7670 2100

"Impeccably located" in Portman Square, this "beautiful townhouse mansion" caters to "lots of pretty people"; in its "calm", high-ceilinged dining room, there's a "solid offering of Modern British–European cuisine" for that "good old 'at home' dinner-party feel" – though some stick to snacks in the Bison Bar or "nice afternoon tea" in the Drawing Room.

Hoxton Apprentice | – | – | – | M

16 Hoxton Sq., N1 (Old St.), 020-7749 2828; fax 7749 2829; www.hoxtonapprentice.com

"A similar idea to Jamie Oliver's Fifteen", this Hoxton venture in a "beautifully restored Victorian building" aims to "train people from difficult backgrounds to become qualified" in the restaurant business; all applaud "the good cause", but whilst positives praise the "simple" Eclectic "food done well" and "adept service", antagonists argue it's "average."

HUNAN ☒ | 25 | 13 | 21 | £43

51 Pimlico Rd., SW1 (Sloane Sq.), 020-7730 5712; fax 7730 8265

"Enjoy a whirlwind tour of Chinese delights" – "mainly, small dishes of Hunan and Szechuan origin" – at this "quirky", "sparse" Pimlico venue with "not much elbow room"; "you trust" chef-owner Michael Peng to "choose what to bring you, and the food keeps coming until you say stop"; just "be careful", the "tailor-made" approach is "not cheap."

Hush ☒ | 17 | 19 | 17 | £43

8 Lancashire Ct., W1 (Bond St.), 020-7659 1500; fax 7659 1501; www.hush.co.uk

There's "nothing hushed" about this "crowded" venue "discreetly placed" in a "cobblestone courtyard off Bond

Street" that's "beautiful for summer" dining; on the ground floor is a "relaxed", "reliable" Modern British brasserie ("vegetarians will struggle") and "trendy bar" that grabs the "rich set" (but "no celebs in sight these days"); upstairs, the recently refurbished Le Club dining room offers rustic, "expensive" French fare; "scatty service" is the main gripe.

Ifield, The – | – | – | M

59 Ifield Rd., SW10 (Earl's Ct./Fulham Broadway), 020-7351 4900; fax 7351 1100

In Earl's Court, this "classic gastro-pub" is an "inviting spot" with a "cosy" rear dining area with chandeliers and candelabras serving "decent" Modern British fare; whilst it may "not be first choice for a meal", all agree a "good crowd makes for a fun bar."

Ikeda ☒ 22 | 9 | 18 | £47

30 Brook St., W1 (Bond St.), 020-7629 2730; fax 7490 5992

"Don't be put off by the room, the food makes up for it" at this "little secret" in Mayfair, whose "serious" sushi and sashimi attracts "Japanese residents in town" – and even "from Tokyo"; a £16 prix fixe lunch placates those who go "ouch on the prices."

Ikkyu 21 | 7 | 15 | £22

67A Tottenham Court Rd., W1 (Goodge St.), 020-7636 9280

"Venture down hidden stairs" on Tottenham Court Road and "be instantly transported to Tokyo" at this "grotty", "offbeat" eatery where the traditional "menu is written in Japanese on the walls"; whether cooked or raw, the "amazing" fare is all at a "reasonable price", so "it's advisable to book to be sure to get in."

Il Bordello 21 | 14 | 19 | £30

81 Wapping High St., E1 (Wapping), 020-7481 9950

"It's a bit cramped for space, especially when they bring out the [huge] pizzas" and "massive portions" of "wholesome Italian fare" at this "noisy", "value-for-money" venue in a "Wapping warehouse"; but it's "often overcrowded" with a "mix of Eastenders, Canary Wharf suits and local residents", "and service suffers"; N.B. the opening of sibling La Figa, 45 Narrow Street, may ease the squeeze.

Il Convivio ☒ 23 | 20 | 23 | £49

143 Ebury St., SW1 (Sloane Sq./Victoria), 020-7730 4099; fax 7730 4103; www.etruscarestaurants.com

Bavarian-born chef Lucas Pfaff "experiments" – black spaghetti with lobster, *signore*? – "but also keeps classic dishes" on the "interesting, nonstandard Italian" menu – accompanied by "a serious wine list at serious prices" – at this "charming" Belgravia townhouse that boasts a "bright conservatory" whose "roof opens on nice days"; a score rise confirms that "service has improved", and is "as friendly as the name may suggest."

Il Falconiere ◐ ⊠ ▽ 16 | 15 | 16 | £33

84 Old Brompton Rd., SW7 (Gloucester Rd./South Kensington), 020-7589 2401; fax 7589 9158; www.ilfalconiere.co.uk

"A good solid choice, with no weaknesses" sums up loyalists' view of this "fair-value", *famiglia*-owned South Ken Italian, in peach-coloured digs with "tables close together"; the set lunch is "not bad for treating parents."

Il Portico ⊠ – | – | – | M

277 Kensington High Street, W8 (High St. Kensington), 020-7602 6262

"An absolute find" in Kensington, this "cosy Italian gets votes" for its "unobtrusive atmosphere" and "authentic", "good-value" cucina that's "delicious without being fussy", along "with affordable wine"; expect "jovial interaction between customers" and the "friendly, professional staff."

Imperial China ◐ 21 | 20 | 17 | £25

25A Lisle St., WC2 (Leicester Sq./Piccadilly Circus), 020-7734 3388; fax 7734 3833; www.imperial-china.co.uk

"Set back in a [Chinatown] courtyard, this huge restaurant" is "hugely improved after the renovation" in 2004; also on the upswing is the "above-average" Cantonese cuisine (starring "fresh, tasty dim sum" at lunch) at prices that are "a steal"; "not the smiliest service" is the main moan.

Imperial City ⊠ 17 | 17 | 17 | £37

Royal Exchange, Cornhill, EC3 (Bank), 020-7626 3437; fax 7338 0125; www.orientalrestaurantgroup.co.uk

In an "interesting space" – the Royal Exchange's vaulted basement ("nice arches") – this "decent Chinese" is "great for feeling you're not in the City"; whilst the "Westernised" Mandarin fare comes at "haute prices", most agree this "consistent performer" makes an "excellent location for entertaining clients" or dining in "large groups."

Incognico ⊠ 19 | 17 | 19 | £44

117 Shaftesbury Ave., WC2 (Leicester Sq./Tottenham Court Rd.), 020-7836 8866; fax 7240 9525; www.incognico.com

"There's an air of contentedness about" this "discreet", "laid-back" Theatreland venue with its "upscale crowd", "thoughtful service" and "interesting" New French menu that includes "simple" Brasserie fare as well as more "sophisticated" "combinations"; if a few find the food and "dark" digs "underwhelming for the price", all concede it has "one of the best pre/post-theatre menus around."

Indigo ◐ 22 | 21 | 22 | £42

One Aldwych Hotel, 1 Aldwych, WC2 (Charing Cross/ Covent Garden), 020-7300 0400; fax 7300 1001; www.onealdwych.com

A "secret find" "overlooking the buzzy lobby bar of One Aldwych Hotel", this "less-expensive sister" of Axis is a "relaxed", "low-ceiling space", with "chairs that are the ultimate tush cush"; it's open all day, offering "surprisingly good" Modern European cuisine and a "very acceptable wine list"; the "solid service" has "quirky" moments, but "they get you out in time for the theatre."

Iniga ⊠ – | – | – | E

2A Pond Pl., SW3 (South Kensington), 020-7589 6589

Noura Salloum, a 24-year-old restaurant debutante, is the latest to run this basement on a narrow South Ken street that's seen several ventures come and go; the theatrically colourful setting includes a comfy bar bearing a bruschetta menu from £4.75 and a sunken dining area with red leather banquettes and sensibly priced modern Italian eats; live music plays Thursdays–Saturdays.

Inn The Park 17 | 19 | 14 | £35

St. James's Park, SW1 (St. James's Park), 020-7451 9999; fax 7451 9998; www.innthepark.com

"Cafeteria by day, restaurant at night", this "basic"-looking wood-and-glass "pavilion" "in the midst of St James's Park" makes a "superb setting on a sunny day"; whilst they're "glad it's here", surveyors sigh it "could be so much better" – from the "safe, but not exciting" Traditional British menu (overseen by Oliver Peyton) to the "lackadaisical service" and "uncomfortable seating."

ISHBILIA 25 | 12 | 17 | £34

Harrods, 87-135 Brompton Rd., 2nd fl., SW1 (Knightsbridge), 020-7893 8598 ⊠

9 William St., SW1 (Knightsbridge), 020-7235 7788; fax 7235 7771; www.ishbilia.com ●

For an "ample selection" of "outstanding", "authentic" Lebanese fare, plus weekend belly dancing, "short of Beirut, there's no better" than this Knightsbridge address; and if the "bare setting" and "difficult servers" (whose score has dropped) are "not worth it", remember "takeout is always an alternative"; N.B. a Harrods branch opened post-*Survey.*

Island Restaurant & Bar – | – | – | M

Royal Lancaster Hotel, Lancaster Terrace, W2 (Lancaster Gate), 020-7551 6070; fax 7551 6071; www.islandrestaurant.co.uk

Natural light floods in from huge windows at this "very modern", split-level spot next to Lancaster Gate tube station, and whilst there aren't "any inspired moments" on the "good" Modern British menu, most feel this newcomer is "wellnamed, given its emergence in an area lacking in dining options."

I-Thai ▽ 23 | 24 | 23 | £42

Hempel Hotel, 31-35 Craven Hill Gardens, W2 (Lancaster Gate), 020-7298 9000; fax 7402 4666; www.the-hempel.co.uk

In a "beautifully minimalistic", "Zen-like" dining room within this "ultracool" Bayswater hotel, expect to encounter an "expensive" but "fantastic", "flavoursome" "Asian mixture of food", "served with flair"; and if those tired of playing I-Spy snap the "lighting could be improved, you can hardly see what's on the plate" – others enjoy the "romantic little secret" ambience.

itsu 18 | 15 | 14 | £26

Vogue House, 1 Hanover Sq., W1 (Bond St./Oxford Circus), 020-7491 9799; fax 7491 7193
103 Wardour St., W1 (Leicester Sq./Piccadilly Circus), 020-7479 4794; fax 7479 4795
118 Draycott Ave., SW3 (South Kensington), 020-7590 2400; fax 7590 2403
Jubilee Place Mall, 28A Jubilee Pl., E14 (Canary Wharf), 020-7512 9650
Cabot Pl. E., level 2, E14 (Canary Wharf), 020-7512 5790; fax 7512 5791
www.itsu.co.uk

At "the high end of conveyor-belt-delivered morsels" maintain mavens of this "minimalist", "funky" Japanese chain; but whilst loyalists love the "Euro-sushi's" combo of "quality and originality", critics carp it's "not as innovative as it used to be"; the real problem, though, is "how you just keep eating and eating – and the bill grows exponentially."

IVY, THE ◐ 22 | 21 | 22 | £53

1 West St., WC2 (Leicester Sq.), 020-7836 4751; fax 7240 9333; www.caprice-holdings.co.uk

With "more stars than in heaven (and just about as hard to get into, as well)", this "true icon" of "glamorous" London dining "is still the place" for a "convivial", "cheek-by-jowl bustle", Modern British–European dishes "done extremely well" and "pleasant staff" "who never let you feel anything less than special"; foes huff this long-running Theatrelander needs to "get its act together", citing "outdated" eats and "tired" decor; nevertheless, like its namesake vine, this "popular" perennial happily hangs in there.

Iznik ◐ ▽ 21 | 19 | 19 | £25

19 Highbury Park, N5 (Highbury & Islington), 020-7704 8099; fax 7354 5697

"Love the decor, love the food" fawn fans of this "authentic" antiques-filled, candlelit eatery in Islington, where "true Turkish cuisine" is coupled with "warm", "family-run service" to ensure an "excellent" experience; but some say the baklava might benefit from "better presentation."

Jade Garden ◐ 20 | 13 | 14 | £20

15 Wardour St., W1 (Leicester Sq./Piccadilly Circus), 020-7437 5065; fax 7429 7851; www.londonjadegarden.co.uk

"Delicious dim sum" and a "huge variety" of "decent" dishes – all at prices that are "pretty good on the pocket" – make this plainly attired Chinatowner "popular" – so "be prepared for long waits and crowded seating"; the other serpent in the garden is "rather rude" staff.

Jenny Lo's Tea House ⊠⊭ 20 10 18 £17
14 Eccleston St., SW1 (Victoria), 020-7259 0399
"Fast, fun and inexpensive" is the lo-down at this "casual cafeteria" with a "noisy" "communal table setting", owned by the daughter of Ken Lo; the "simple, but delicious" Chinese teahouse menu works for "a quick bite" at "cheap" prices – something "almost unheard of in Belgravia."

Jim Thompson's 14 19 13 £28
141 The Broadway, SW19 (Wimbledon), 020-8540 5540; fax 8540 8728
408 Upper Richmond Rd., SW15 (East Putney), 020-8788 3737; fax 8788 3738 ◐
617 King's Rd., SW6 (Fulham Broadway), 020-7731 0999; fax 7731 2835 ◐
889 Green Lanes, N21 (Southgate/Wood Green), 020-8360 0005; fax 8364 3006
The "colourful" "bazaar"-like setting jammed with artefacts (some for sale) adds an "exotic" touch to this chain of Southeast Asians named after an American silk trade pioneer; but whilst the experience is "dazzling to the eye, it's bland to the palate" carp connoisseurs who call the cuisine "about as Thai as jellied eels and mash."

JIN KICHI 27 11 17 £33
73 Heath St., NW3 (Hampstead), 020-7794 6158; fax 7794 6158; www.jinkichi.com
Sure, "it's a real dive", but "getting a booking is easier said than done" at this Hampstead "hole-in-the-wall", on account of "fantastic" sushi and "great grilled" Japanese "dishes you can't find anywhere else" (especially for such "excellent value"); "service is efficient" – but "it would be hard not to be as you're always within an outstretched arm from a member of staff."

Joe Allen ◐ 16 17 18 £33
13 Exeter St., WC2 (Covent Garden), 020-7836 0651; fax 7497 2148
Still a popular "hangout for actors" "after the curtain comes down", this "eccentric", "unpretentious cellar restaurant" just off the Strand serves "solid American cooking in a New York–style atmosphere" (it's "an offshoot of the Manhattan original"); even if the edibles "are no contender for stardom" and the "service sometimes requires a little pushing", it remains "the perfect place" "pre/post theatre", "seeped as it is in West End nostalgia."

Joe's ▽ 13 14 14 £33
126 Draycott Ave., SW3 (South Kensington), 020-7225 2217; fax 7584 1133
When one needs "to break up the shopping" or have an "easy family" "weekend brunch", this "nice little cafe" fits

the bill with a variety of salads and "Modern British dishes catering to all needs and dietary requirements"; but foes fume this "fading star" is "not worthy of its prime location" at Brompton Cross.

Joe's Restaurant Bar ☒ 21 | 17 | 18 | £31

Joseph, 16 Sloane St., SW1 (Knightsbridge), 020-7235 9869; fax 7235 3218

"Be dressed to the nines – but in a casually cool way, of course" – at this "chic" Knightsbridge address, which after over 20 years is "still going strong", attracting "ladies who lunch and their admirers" with a "health conscious" Modern British menu of "simple, elegantly presented options" (including "lots of choice for South Beach dieters"); many of the "professional" servers are "beautiful people" too.

Joy King Lau ◐ 21 | 11 | 14 | £26

3 Leicester St., WC2 (Leicester Sq./Piccadilly Circus), 020-7437 1133; fax 7437 2629

"Don't let the look scare you off – the food's really good" at this functional, multifloor Chinatowner, which has been "pretty busy" "over a long period of years" (at least 30); some are "underwhelmed" by the "uncheerful" scene – certainly, no joy emanates from "silent, brisk staff"; yet all concede "the price is right", especially for the "dim sum, which is what one goes for."

J. SHEEKEY ◐ 25 | 21 | 23 | £50

28-32 St. Martin's Ct., WC2 (Leicester Sq.), 020-7240 2565; fax 7497 0891; www.caprice-holdings.co.uk

"If you love fish, then prepare yourself for a torrid affair" with this "refreshingly unstuffy", "buzzy" Theatreland seafooder where fin fare "fresh off the boat" is turned into "honest", "well-prepared classics", supported by "slick", "unfailingly helpful" service; it's "hard to get a reservation" in one of the five "old-school" oak-panelled rooms, but "easier to book than its sisters, The Ivy" and Le Caprice.

Julie's ◐ 19 | 24 | 19 | £39

135 Portland Rd., W11 (Holland Park), 020-7229 8331; fax 7229 4050; www.juliesrestaurant.com

"Love is in the air" at this "romantic hideaway", one of London's most enduring "first-date choices", thanks to its two "cosy" floors with various nooks and crannies and "fantastic rear patio" spread out over a "charming" Holland Park townhouse; whilst "pleasant" enough, the Modern British cuisine and service don't quite match up – but then, most "don't focus on the food too much" anyway.

Just St. James's 18 | 20 | 15 | £45

12 St. James's St., SW1 (Green Park), 020-7976 2222; fax 7976 2020; www.juststjames.com

In the "beautiful setting of an old bank" in St. James's ("marble everywhere"), this "airy expanse of a restaurant" comprises a "cool" bar, "complete with piano music in the evenings", and a "relaxed" dining area; although a Food score rise validates admirers of the "inventive" Modern British fare, an "erratic" quality in both the cuisine and service have some sighing it's just "too expensive for the experience"; P.S. the downstairs "bordello-style" brasserie, Just Oriental, offers "Asian-influenced" snacks.

Kai Mayfair 25 | 22 | 22 | £52

65 S. Audley St., W1 (Bond St./Marble Arch), 020-7493 8988; fax 7493 1456; www.kaimayfair.com

A "class act" maintain mavens of this "minimalistic" Mayfair Mandarin that "always comes through" with its "perfected Chinese" cuisine (they also "prepare off the menu upon request"), served by "attentive, unobtrusive staff"; admittedly, "the best" comes at "expense-account" bills, but there are "good wines at good prices, if you avoid the reserve list."

Kandoo ◐ ▽ 17 | 13 | 17 | £21

458 Edgware Rd., W2 (Edgware Rd.), 020-7724 2428; fax 7724 6769

It "doesn't look the business from the outside, but it's a different matter" inside this "warm" Edgware Road eatery where the "largely lamb-based" Persian "menu is quite limited, but the portions are large"; being "BYO makes it cheap" to boot; P.S. the name refers to the clay bread oven in the window and not the "brand of children's loo paper."

Kastoori ▽ 25 | 8 | 18 | £18

188 Upper Tooting Rd., SW17 (Tooting Bec/Tooting Broadway), 020-8767 7027

"Worth travelling miles for" fawn fans of this "fantastic-value" Tooting Indian–East African with "great-flavoured" vegetarian fare known to have "converted carnivores"; sure, "ambience is lacking" in the "cramped" premises, but that doesn't deter those who "can't stop going."

Kensington Place ◐ 20 | 16 | 17 | £40

201-209 Kensington Church St., W8 (Notting Hill Gate), 020-7727 3184; fax 7229 2025; www.egami.co.uk

Approaching its 20th anniversary, it might be "an ageing rock star", but this "bright, open" Notting Hill Gate venue "maintains a zest that keeps one happy", with a "fabulous, buzzy atmosphere", a "chance to ogle celebrity guests" and "delicious" Modern British cooking with "an ever-changing list of specials"; "with the big windows onto the street, it's a bit of a fishbowl" though – and vocal echoes are nigh "unbearable" ("noisiest restaurant in town").

Kettners ◐ 13 | 20 | 18 | £26

29 Romilly St., W1 (Leicester Sq.), 020-7734 6112; fax 7287 6499; www.pizzaexpress.com/kettners

While it occupies an "opulent" 1867 townhouse, this place is primarily "a poshed-up Pizza Express" (and actually "a chain affiliate"), serving an Eclectic all-day menu of "basic chophouse-cum-pizzeria" staples at "reasonable prices", accompanied by "nice live piano music"; whilst it's "a retreat from the hubbub of Soho", the "predictable" fare has regulars recommending "you're better off grabbing a couch" and "a bottle of champers" in the "plushy" champagne bar.

Kew Grill ▽ 22 | 20 | 18 | £39

10B Kew Green, Kew (Kew Gardens), 020-8948 4433; fax 8605 3532; www.awtonline.co.uk

"Brilliant (for a grill)" grin groupies of this "warm, intimate" yearling "on the way to Kew Gardens" from celebrity chef Antony Worrall Thompson and "Jay, his hard-working wife"; the Traditional British menu of "excellent, simple organic dishes" is "great for carnivores", and even if it's "not a destination restaurant", most agree it "stands out in an underserved area."

Khan's ◐ 21 | 10 | 13 | £18

13-15 Westbourne Grove, W2 (Bayswater/Queensway), 020-7727 5420; fax 7229 1835; www.khansrestaurant.com

"Exquisitely tacky decor" – "cheesy, but entertaining" – and "divine dishes" make this "crowded" Bayswater Indian "always bustling, no matter what day or time it is"; but even if "staff are not the most helpful of people", most "never leave unsatisfied", especially as this "old-fashioned curry house" has "prices that give you more poori for the pound."

Khan's of Kensington ◐ 20 | 13 | 19 | £21

3 Harrington Rd., SW7 (South Kensington), 020-7584 4114; fax 7581 2900

Attracting an "eclectic crowd", this South Kensington standby is commended for its "reliably tasty" menu, which "specialises in spicy tandoor creations", and "fast, fast, fast" service; however, dissenters dismiss it as "definitely one of those tourist places."

Kiku 22 | 13 | 18 | £40

17 Half Moon St., W1 (Green Park), 020-7499 4208; fax 7409 3359; www.kikurestaurant.co.uk

With its "fresh-like-in-Japan" offerings, this Mayfair Japanese satisfies many a raw-fish fix; your "credit card will be crying", "but when's the last time you had really, really good sushi and got it cheap?"; the savvy ease the squeeze by opting for the "excellent-value lunch sets" (it's "better at daytime", anyway, as the "uncluttered" decor can seem "sterile" at dinner).

Koi 20 | 15 | 18 | £40

1E Palace Gate, W8 (Gloucester Rd./High St. Kensington), 020-7581 8778; fax 7589 2788

"The chefs are always happy to talk" at this "cheerful Japanese diner" that's "good after a concert at the Royal Albert Hall" nearby; the "really competent sushi" and other "authentic" cuisine is "pretty pricey", and as the decor "doesn't put on airs", some prefer the "efficient takeaway."

Kulu Kulu Sushi ⊠ 19 | 11 | 15 | £20

76 Brewer St., W1 (Piccadilly Circus), 020-7734 7316; fax 7734 6507
51-53 Shelton St., WC2 (Covent Garden), 020-7240 5687; fax 7240 5687
39 Thurloe Pl., SW7 (South Kensington), 020-7589 2225; fax 7589 2225

"Be prepared to queue and squeeze into your seat – once you get one" at this "down-to-earth" Japanese trio whose fans "forget the decor" and focus on "fresh, delicately prepared" food, presented "conveyor belt–style" at a "very affordable price"; however, the "hot dishes are less outstanding" and the service tends toward the "harried."

La Bouchée 19 | 16 | 16 | £33

56 Old Brompton Rd., SW7 (South Kensington), 020-7589 1929; fax 7584 8625

"Whilst it's the size of a large closet, the atmosphere is warm" at this "Parisian bistro hidden" in South Ken, where a "stylish, eccentric crowd" feeds on "uncomplicated" "Classic French cuisine", including "the best coq au vin this side of the Channel"; if the "tables are far too close together" and staff "a little rude", that all adds to the "authentic", "bustling bourgeois" feel of this "good first-date" place.

La Brasserie 15 | 16 | 14 | £32

272 Brompton Rd., SW3 (South Kensington), 020-7581 3089; fax 7581 1435

Boasting a "huge following of long-standing regulars", this "timeless" Brompton Cross venue "infuses in you the truly French feel" of a "traditional brasserie" where the food is "not haute cuisine, of course", but "hearty" enough; the "slightly sniffy" staff augments the "authenticity."

Ladbroke Arms 19 | 16 | 14 | £28

54 Ladbroke Rd., W11 (Notting Hill Gate), 020-7727 6648; www.capitalpubcompany.co.uk

"Don't want anyone else to go there – it's mine, all mine" say selfish supporters of this "cosy" but "smart" spot that "sets the gastro-pub standard" with a "simple, surprisingly good" Modern European menu and a "lovely patio for alfresco dining"; a "well-heeled crowd" appreciate that it's "away from the commotion on Notting Hill Gate" – perhaps too far away, the lachrymose lament ("you could go to your grave waiting to be served").

La Famiglia 22 | 16 | 21 | £41

7 Langton St., SW10 (Fulham Broadway/Sloane Sq.), 020-7351 0761; fax 7351 2409; www.lafamiglialondon.com

"Preserving a winning formula for years", this "classic Tuscan trattoria" in the "unlikely location" of a "bright, loud" "terraced house" in Chelsea is something of a "hot spot", drawing "stars" and "the politically connected" with a "wide-ranging" menu of "terrific", "honest" cooking and "friendly" staff who "make you feel part of the *famiglia*"; P.S. "if the weather permits, eat outside."

La Fontana ∇ 20 | 12 | 17 | £41

101 Pimlico Rd., SW1 (Sloane Sq.), 020-7730 6630; fax 7730 5577

An "oldie, but goldie", this low-key, 42-year-old Pimlico Italian – now helmed by the original owner's daughter, Joanna Pavesi – continues to enjoy a reputation for "reliable, good food", "particularly during the truffle season" when the "white shavings" are "to die for"; but "you will also want to die when you see the bill."

La Fromagerie Café 23 | 20 | 17 | £22

2-4 Moxon St., W1 (Baker St.), 020-7935 0341; fax 7935 0341; www.lafromagerie.co.uk

Although there "are way too few seats" at this cafe in Marylebone, "if you can get [one], what they offer is good" on the Franco-Italian menu, which includes "lovely salads, gorgeous desserts and, of course, cheese to die for"; despite "disorganised" service, it makes for a "charming" respite; P.S. the ground-floor deli, featuring a glassed-in room full of *fromagerie*, is "a gourmand's paradise."

La Genova ☒ – | – | – | M

32 N. Audley St., W1 (Bond St.), 020-7629 5916; www.lagenovarestaurant.com

An "excellent old-style Italian with moderate prices (by London standards)", this "beautiful" Mayfair veteran offers "ample servings of market-fresh produce" cooked "with flair" and ambience "full of *bonhomie* from an owner who insists on talking to" everyone; P.S. it can "be swamped by Americans due to its location" "near the U.S. embassy."

LANES 24 | 24 | 27 | £59

Four Seasons Hotel, Hamilton Pl., W1 (Green Park/Hyde Park Corner), 020-7499 0888; fax 7493 6629; www.fourseasons.com/london

"Spacious" and "businesslike", this dining room "in the Four Seasons on Park Lane" decorated with jewel-toned stained glass and wood panelling is "an unknown star", where diners "never worry about anything", thanks to "superior" "service with a smile" and "impeccable" Asian-influenced Eclectic cuisine, reflecting chef Bernhard Mayer's years of working in the Far East.

Lanesborough Conservatory 21 | 26 | 24 | £56

The Lanesborough, 1 Lanesborough Pl., SW1 (Hyde Park Corner), 020-7333 7254; fax 7259 5606; www.lanesborough.co.uk

"You feel you are in a different country" at this "dreamy" "Anglo-Raj fantasy"-conservatory (complete with palm trees and fountains) on Hyde Park Corner – "the height of refinement" for "business entertaining" or the "ultimate afternoon tea"; although "pricing is a bit over the top", the "exquisite" Eclectic menu and "gracious service" make it "worth the splurge", and will "make you want to linger"; P.S. at weekends, there's "dressy" live "music and dancing" in the evening – "*so* civilised."

Langan's Bistro ☒ 19 | 19 | 21 | £48

26 Devonshire St., W1 (Baker St.), 020-7935 4531; fax 7493 8309; www.langansrestaurants.com

"Quirky to some, cosy to others, but never a disappointment to anyone" declare devotees of this Marylebone "upmarket bistro" (crammed with "engaging art" and upside-down umbrellas) that's "still going strong" after 40 years; though a bit "boring", the "Traditional" British–French "comfort food" is "solid", whilst the "service is grand" – especially "if you are known" to them.

Langan's Brasserie ◐☒ 19 | 19 | 19 | £47

Stratton House, Stratton St., W1 (Green Park), 020-7491 8822; fax 7493 8309; www.langansrestaurants.co.uk

"You always hope you'll spot a celeb" amongst the "upscale crowd" at this "entertaining", "bustling" Mayfair "dining institution" that's "still loads of fun" after 30 years; whilst there's "nothing cutting-edge" about the "Classic Anglo-French fare", it's "easy to find something you like on the large menu"; and if a handful think it's "resting on old laurels" and a magnet for "wideboys and dodgy dealers", even they concede it has the good "grace of staying open late" – "a big plus, especially after the theatre."

Lansdowne, The 20 | 16 | 14 | £28

90 Gloucester Ave., NW1 (Chalk Farm), 020-7483 0409; fax 7586 1723

"Trendy, scruffy thirtysomethings with money hang out" at this "artistically" "shabby" "Primrose Hill favourite gastro-pub", with an "informal downstairs" bar serving "great wood-fired pizzas" and the "more elegant, yet still casual upstairs dining room" for "excellent" Eclectic–Modern European fare; "slightly dippy service" does not deter the "interesting folk."

La Piragua – | – | – | M

176 Upper St., N1 (Highbury & Islington), 020-7354 2843; fax 7354 2843; www.lapiragua.co.uk

"Huge" "steaks that make you feel like you are back in South America" – and may "be the cheapest in town" – star at this Islington "authentic" Colombian; it's "great for hungry men after football games" at nearby Highbury, but perhaps "not for a romantic evening out", given the somewhat "weird" decor (e.g. "paintings of fat, naked women on the walls").

La Porchetta Pizzeria 18 | 10 | 16 | £16

33 Boswell St., WC1 (Holborn), 020-7242 2434 ☒
265 Muswell Hill Broadway, N10 (Highgate), 020-8883 1500 ◐
147 Stroud Green Rd., N4 (Finsbury Park), 020-7281 2892; fax 7837 6200 ◐
141-142 Upper St., N1 (Angel/Highbury & Islington), 020-7288 2488 ◐
84-86 Rosebury Ave., EC1 (Angel), 020-7837-6060; fax 7837 6200
This "perennially popular" pizza chain is "overwhelmed by diners" – especially at "raucous birthday parties" – drawn by "huge" "thin-crust pizzas" with "unusual" toppings and other "hearty Italian" fare that is "incredibly inexpensive, by London standards"; on the downside, some of the "flirty staff" are "not very good with English" and the "cold decor" may make it "better to do takeaway."

La Porte des Indes ◐ 22 | 23 | 21 | £42

32 Bryanston St., W1 (Marble Arch), 020-7224 0055; fax 7224 1144; www.laportedesindes.com
"A real theme park of a restaurant" – with "striking" "decor out of *Arabian Nights*", "fantastical palm trees" and a "waterfall to add to its exoticism" – this Blue Elephant sibling near Marble Arch offers an "out-of-the-ordinary Indian fare" with "French twists", and whilst some feel the food "doesn't warrant the premium it charges" ("you pay a little too much for the glitz"), the "great value buffet lunches" make amends – as does "intelligent service."

LA POULE AU POT 23 | 22 | 21 | £40

231 Ebury St., SW1 (Sloane Sq.), 020-7730 7763; fax 7259 9651
There's "no denying the authentic bistro" feel of this "*très charmant*" Pimlico Green stalwart whose "gratifying" menu includes "everyone's favourite French dish" (like a "killer onion soup"), "from hearty country to upscale Parisian"; even if "service can be hit-and-miss in a shoulder-shrugging, Gallic kind of way", that doesn't detract from this "cosy marvel" that's "perfect for seduction", particularly on the highly "pleasant" patio.

La Rueda ◐ 17 | 13 | 15 | £26

102 Wigmore St., W1 (Bond St.), 020-7486 1718; fax 7486 1718
642 King's Rd., SW6 (Fulham Broadway), 020-7384 2684; fax 7384 2684
66-68 Clapham High St., SW4 (Clapham Common/ Clapham North), 020-7627 2173; fax 7627 2173
www.larueda.co.uk
Expect a big "*hola*" from "cheeky waiters" at this "old-school" Spanish trio that gets "wild" on nights when there's "some dancing" to augment the "tummy-filling" tapas and "a little sangria"; loyalists love the "lively" scene, but *enemigos* argue it's "best for big parties who get too drunk to notice" the "production-line food."

Latium ☒ ▽ 25 | 16 | 24 | £44

21 Berners St., W1 (Goodge St.), 020-7323 9123; fax 7323 3205; www.latiumrestaurant.com

"Bravo" bellow boosters for this Bloomsbury bambino, only three years old, but already a source for "satisfying portions" of "impeccable", "simple modern Italian food" and a "tempting wine list" with "a wide range of prices" ("let the manager, who is an excellent sommelier, guide you"); the "minimalist decor unfortunately makes it louder than it should be, given its size", but there's "always a warm welcome" from the "enthusiastic staff."

LA TROMPETTE 27 | 21 | 25 | £47

5-7 Devonshire Rd., W4 (Turnham Green), 020-8747 1836; fax 8995 8097; www.latrompette.co.uk

"How lucky Chiswick is to have" this "special" sibling of Chez Bruce and The Glasshouse; the *trompettes* sound for the "fantastic" New French menu, "interesting wine list", "first-class staff" and "cool" if close digs ("truly an intimate dining experience"); and so, despite a "£15 cab ride to get there" most agree it's "a place worth visiting time and again" for "West End quality at suburban prices"; N.B. the post-*Survey* arrival of a new chef may outdate the Food score.

La Trouvaille 22 | 17 | 22 | £37

12A Newburgh St., W1 (Oxford Circus), 020-7287 8488; fax 7434 4170 ☒

353 Upper St., N1 (Angel), 020-7704 8323; fax 7359 6671

www.latrouvaille.co.uk

"Like escaping to a little boîte in the backstreets of Paris", this "Soho treat" and its brasserie-style Islington sibling are "cosy", "rustic" venues for French cooking that combines "bourgeois ingredients with contemporary" techniques ("it's amazing what they can do with mutton"); and even if the "dishes are small, they will not leave you hungry"; "staff is knowledgeable", *aussi.*

Launceston Place 20 | 19 | 22 | £49

1A Launceston Pl., W8 (Gloucester Rd.), 020-7937 6912; fax 7938 2412; www.egami.co.uk

"Unfussy" and "unflashy", this "intimate" Kensington townhouse – with a "wonderful warren of rooms" "flowing into each other" – is "favoured by an older generation" for its "fresh" Modern British fare that offers "no sensations, but no disappointments either", complemented by "gracious servers" with "a sense of humour"; true, the "tables are packed tight, but it's not noisy, thanks to the locals' restraint."

L'Aventure ☒ 23 | 21 | 21 | £44

3 Blenheim Terrace, NW8 (St. John's Wood), 020-7624 6232; fax 7625 5548

"Delicious, authentic" "Classically French" cuisine (on "handwritten menus"), a "warm welcome" and an ambience just right for a "romantic" adventure sum up this "delightfully small" "gem" in an "unexpected location" near Abbey Road; and if a few find the "service a little erratic", *la majorité* declare that eating here is "what dining is all about."

Le Boudin Blanc 22 | 17 | 19 | £38

Shepherd's Mkt., 5 Trebeck St., W1 (Green Park), 020-7499 3292; fax 7495 6973; www.boudinblanc.co.uk

A "*frantique*" bi-level "bastion of Gallic cuisine and spirit", this Shepherd's Market venue ("always noisy, upstairs or down") is "perfect if you miss Paris", thanks to its "well-prepared, hearty" Classic French cooking and "attentive-without-being-annoying service" (despite the occasional "*insouciant*" exception); sure, the "close seating is not for the claustrophobic", but such types can gravitate to the "great summer terrace."

Le Café du Jardin ◐ 19 | 18 | 18 | £34

28 Wellington St., WC2 (Covent Garden), 020-7836 8769; fax 7836 4123; www.lecafedujardin.com

Something of a "trendy media hangout", this "noisy" conservatory-like cafe is "lovely pre- and post-theatre" thanks to its "sensible service", "reliable" Modern European menu ("nothing adventurous", but "good value") and, of course, its "location smack in the middle" of Covent Jardin; the "alfresco seating would be splendid if not for the traffic."

Le Café du Marché ⊠ 21 | 18 | 20 | £45

22 Charterhouse Sq., EC1 (Barbican), 020-7608 1609; fax 7251 8575

"Remaining delightfully true to its French roots", this "rustic", "heart-meltingly romantic" bistro "up a cobbled courtyard" "next to Smithfield Market" serves "an authentic slice of rural" Classic Gallic cooking and a "sensational cheese board"; "the staff are helpful – and let's not forget the live music" nightly.

LE CAPRICE ◐ 24 | 21 | 23 | £53

Arlington House, Arlington St., SW1 (Green Park), 020-7629 2239; fax 7493 9040; www.caprice-holdings.co.uk

"Charm seeps through everything" at this "classy", "chic" St. James's institution that's "so popular, you have to beg for a reservation"; but once in, "no matter who you are, you are made to feel special" – even when the "chairs are chokka with celebrities"; the "amazing", "consistent" Modern British–European fare is "not as expensive as one might think", and whist capricious critics think this vet "could use some modernising", the majority maintain "it lives up to the myth."

Le Cercle ⊠ 21 | 20 | 19 | £45

1 Wilbraham Pl., SW1 (Sloane Sq.), 020-7901 9999; fax 7901 9111

"Inventive" "tapas à la français" are the "main attraction" at this "Club Gascon sibling" near Sloane Square with a "cosy atmosphere" ("ask for the charming booths along the sides of the room"); the "small-servings concept" allows "a voyage around regional France" and "works for a date when flirting and eating off each other's plates"; just be aware that "what seems a bargain is not" – those *petit* portions add up – and staff "need some humility."

Le Colombier 20 | 18 | 19 | £45

145 Dovehouse St., SW3 (South Kensington), 020-7351 1155; fax 7351 5124

A "smart clientele" of "all ages" gets "catered to" at this "romantic", "seriously French" bistro in a "charming" "Chelsea backwater"; whilst "not as cheap as it was", the "old-fashioned" "bourgeois cuisine" "far exceeds the standard" and the "service is warm" (though perhaps it "could be more friendly to non-regulars"); P.S. the terrace at the front "is the best place to sit."

Ledbury, The – | – | – | E

127 Ledbury Rd., W11 (Westbourne Park), 020-7792 9090; www.theledbury.com

At their stylishly elegant Notting Hill newcomer, restaurateur Nigel Platts-Martin and top toque Philip Howard (The Square) have installed a team with some serious credentials: in the kitchen, a young Australian chef also from The Square produces a sophisticated New French menu, a sommelier from Zuma oversees the cellar and a manager from The Connaught handles the front of house; it's a smallish space, but blessed with a large terrace.

Le Deuxième ◐ 21 | 17 | 20 | £35

65A Long Acre, WC2 (Covent Garden), 020-7379 0033; fax 7379 0066; www.ledeuxieme.com

"Achieving success" (and a rise in the ratings), this "cleanly designed" Covent Garden "spin-off of Le Café du Jardin" "caters to all tastes" with a "carefully crafted" Modern European menu that includes "lovely" pre- and post- "theatre prix fixes"; thanks to the manager's ministrations, staff now does a "prompt", "thorough" job.

Lee Ho Fook ◐ 20 | 13 | 16 | £25

15-16 Gerrard St., W1 (Leicester Sq./Piccadilly Circus), 020-7494 1200; fax 7494 1700

This "homey" Chinatown Chinese "has been around for donkey's years" (46, actually), and although it "badly needs a redo", folks remain gung-ho over its "wide selection" of dim sum and "smashing" mains at "affordable" prices; "service is brusque, but fast."

LE GAVROCHE ⊠ 28 | 24 | 27 | £87

43 Upper Brook St., W1 (Marble Arch), 020-7408 0881; fax 7491 4387; www.le-gavroche.co.uk

Although she's pushing 40, Mayfair's "grande dame of the culinary scene" "never misses a beat" warble "wellcosseted" fans of Michel Roux Jr.'s "leave-your-diet-at-the-door" Classic "French haute cuisine", "brilliant wines", "extremely elegant" (if "slightly staid") surrounds and the "graciousness" of staff that "seamlessly pull together all aspects of the meal"; the experience is "expensive, but not insane" when you consider it's "a symphony fit for royalty"; N.B. *messieurs*: jackets, *s'il vous plaît.*

LE MANOIR AUX QUAT'SAISONS 28 | 26 | 26 | £85

Le Manoir aux Quat'Saisons, Church Rd., Great Milton, Oxfordshire, 01844 278881; fax 01844 278847; www.manoir.com

In the "matchless setting" of a "refined rustic" 15th-century Cotswold manor house, complete with "lovely gardens for a stroll", chef Raymond Blanc's "superb" New French menu offers "phenomenal dining", supported by "sophisticated service" that's "Gallic to the core"; it's all like "a slice of heaven, and you certainly pay the moon" – though children "under 12 have their own surprisingly cheap menu – what a great idea!"; P.S. it also has 32 "charming" bedrooms "if you can't bear eating and leaving."

Le Mercury ◐ 16 | 15 | 16 | £22

140A Upper St., N1 (Angel/Highbury & Islington), 020-7354 4088; fax 7359 7186

Offering "a throwback to the bistro age", this "cute" Islingtonian is "a real find" for "a candlelit", "romantic evening" with "good and simple" New French fare at "bargainous prices" – making it "popular" with many "bored with home cooking"; however, some surveyors' temperatures are rising over the rather "variable service."

Lemonia ◐ 20 | 16 | 19 | £28

89 Regent's Park Rd., NW1 (Chalk Farm), 020-7586 7454; fax 7483 2630

"A true Primrose Hill institution", and "great celeb-spotting haunt" to boot, this "thriving" taverna gets "more cramped than an island-hopping" boat in summer, what with all the fans of its "wholesome", "traditional Greek food" and "comical, cheerful staff" who "cope under the intense pressure"; P.S. "get matey with the chief and your table-waiting time comes down significantly."

Le Palais du Jardin ◐ 19 | 18 | 16 | £39

136 Long Acre, WC2 (Leicester Sq.), 020-7379 5353; fax 7379 1846

There's "always a party going on – sometimes that's good, sometimes bad" – at this "cavernous" Covent Garden brasserie with a "broad selection of seafood" on a "tasty", "albeit slightly pricey" Classic French menu; antagonists argue "its appeal eludes" them ("cramped space", "average service"), but most agree it's "convenient to the theatre" and "a reliable late-night" option.

Le Petit Max 23 | 14 | 20 | £35

Riverside Plaza, Chatfield Rd., SW11 (Clapham Junction), 020-7223 0999; fax 7223 2558

Celebrity chef-owner Max Renzland's latest venture, "hidden in Battersea", registers maximum impact with its "ever-changing", "high-quality French Bistro cuisine" that is "well cooked and charmingly served"; converts confide they "could eat here every week, and never tire of the food", especially given the relatively "reasonable prices."

Le Pont de la Tour ◐ 21 | 22 | 19 | £59

Butlers Wharf, 36D Shad Thames, SE1 (London Bridge/ Tower Hill), 020-7403 8403; fax 7403 0267; www.conran.com

An "awesome setting" allows for "unbeatable views of Tower Bridge" ("watched it raised for boats three times!") at this "stylish" Conran Group venue; the "broad, ambitious" Classic French menu is long on "swimmingly good seafood", and whilst some snipe about the "expense-account prices" and "service that varies from visit to visit", the satisfied say it's "a safe play for a date or business."

L'Escargot ◐ ⊠ 23 | 21 | 21 | £48

48 Greek St., W1 (Leicester Sq./Tottenham Court Rd.), 020-7437 6828; fax 7437 0790; www.whitestarline.org.uk

In the heart of Soho, this "great old townhouse" attracts "a mix of clientele – theatregoers, drag queens" – to its "intimate" ground-floor room with "mirrors everywhere" and its "classy" Picasso room upstairs that is "filled with paintings"; the "consistently excellent" New French menu is supported by an "endless wine list" and "attentive servers" who find "nothing too much trouble."

Le Soufflé ⊠ 23 | 20 | 23 | £53

Hotel InterContinental, 1 Hamilton Pl., W1 (Hyde Park Corner), 020-7318 8577; fax 7491 0926; www.intercontinental.com

"When it's firing on all cylinders, which is often, the experience can be sublime" at this "quiet" hotel dining room on Hyde Park Corner; nightly piano music accompanies an "excellent" New French menu, including the eponymous egg whites and a "fine cheese selection", and "smooth service"; of course it's "old-fashioned" and the "price tag's a bit steep."

L'Estaminet ⊠ 21 | 17 | 19 | £38

14 Garrick St., WC2 (Covent Garden/Leicester Sq.), 020-7379 1432; fax 7379 1530

"A hidden gem waiting to be discovered" agree admirers of this "quietly romantic" Covent Garden basement with "excellent" Classic French cooking – "more old-style than nouvelle" – and a cheese selection "to die for"; "experienced servers" are on hand to ensure "this little bistro hits the spot if you have got a hankering" for a "traditional Gallic" experience.

Les Trois Garçons ☒ 20 | 25 | 18 | £47

1 Club Row, E1 (Liverpool St.), 020-7613 1924; fax 7012 1236; www.lestroisgarcons.com

Imagine "yourself in an antiques shop–zoo-taxidermist haven", with "stuffed animal heads around the room" and "handbags dangling from the ceiling", and you'll get a sense of this "fantastically camp" "converted pub"; though "interesting", the "steeply priced" Classic French fare is "not as original as the decor", but enthusiastic Eastenders agree this "eccentric" site is "worth it for the wow factor."

Le Suquet ◐ 21 | 15 | 17 | £43

104 Draycott Ave., SW3 (South Kensington), 020-7581 1785; fax 7225 0838

"Underneath the rough setting lies an absolute diamond", according to *amis* of this "cramped" Chelsea venue that "never seems to change" (in fact, it "looks exactly as it did in the early '70s"); it scores with "fresh, simply cooked" "seafood to die for" ("trust your charming French waiter" to recommend); even if it's "somewhat expensive for semi-casual dining", most adore this "taste of Cannes in London."

L'Etranger 24 | 20 | 19 | £49

36 Gloucester Rd., SW7 (Gloucester Rd.), 020-7584 1118; fax 7584 8886; www.etranger.co.uk

Those seeking an "exquisite" "fusion of French and Asian" fare (including "the best blackened cod you can imagine") are no strangers to this "hip place for foodies" near Albert Hall; the "cosy", if "rather sparse" dining room has "just enough buzz to feel good", and "service is charming"; although "it's a tad expensive", why not go the whole hog "afterwards and head down to the club downstairs."

Le Vacherin – | – | – | E

76-77 South Parade, W4 (Chiswick Park), 020-8742 2121; fax 8742 0799; www.levacherin.co.uk

"A good find for Chiswick locals", this young, "modern-looking bistro" offers "a real taste of France" with its "well-prepared and -presented food" and Southwestern wine list; but patience is required, as the service can be "slow"; P.S. they offer "occasional, very good special events", like wine tastings and exhibitions.

Levant ◐ 20 | 23 | 16 | £39

Jason Ct., 76 Wigmore St., W1 (Bond St.), 020-7224 1111; fax 7486 1216; www.levant.co.uk

You're in Marylebone, but the "exotic decor transports you to the Middle East" at this "sexy", "cool" Lebanese, whose "varied", "terrific" menu has Mediterranean and North African influences, along with "wonderful cocktails"; "slightly overpriced", perhaps, but it's "great for group outings" – especially when the "belly dancer performs: quite a surprise at the company Christmas lunch."

Levantine ◐ ▽ 18 | 19 | 17 | £27

26 London St., W2 (Paddington), 020-7262 1111; fax 7402 4039; www.levant.co.uk

"Perfect for a night out with the girls" or guys, this Levant sibling features artefact-filled, "Middle Eastern decor" and "live belly dancing between the tables"; the "very good Lebanese food" is "not the cheapest around", however, and some feel the "lack of options in this area" around Paddington Station make "it seem better than it really is"; P.S. "must do the trip down to the fab loos."

Light House ▽ 16 | 17 | 20 | £38

75-77 Ridgeway, SW19 (Wimbledon), 020-8944 6338; fax 8946 4440

"Really nice", "smiley" staff make this low-key Wimbledon Village haunt a "pleasant, comfortable place to dine" on its "ever-changing" Eclectic cuisine; but some just don't see the light, suggesting the "fusion of dishes is like trying to marry camels with the ocean – a cool idea, but risky."

Lilly's ▽ 22 | 20 | 22 | £28

75 Wapping High St., E1 (Wapping), 020-7702 2040; fax 7702 4828; www.lillysrestaurant.co.uk

"Bringing a bit of glam to Wapping", this "neighbourhood find" – modern and bright, with a "NY brasserie feel" – offers "generous portions" of "simply prepared" Modern British grills; N.B. its owner was a founder of the Cafe Med chain.

L'Incontro ◐ ▽ 19 | 20 | 19 | £47

87 Pimlico Rd., SW1 (Sloane Sq.), 020-7730 3663; fax 7730 5062; www.lincontro-restaurant.com

The "smart surroundings" of this "contemporary" Pimlico setting include "wonderful" black-and-white photographs lining the walls and a private, "great downstairs room with David Linley panelling"; whilst most applaud the "creative" Italian cooking (the "seafood can not be beaten"), those contro claim "the kitchen, while capable of excellence, sometimes appears to be going through the motions."

Little Bay ◐ 19 | 15 | 18 | £17

171 Farringdon Rd., EC1 (Farringdon), 020-7278 1234; fax 7278 5368

228 Belsize Rd., NW6 (Kilburn Park), 020-7372 4699; fax 7223 6131 ⊄

228 York Rd., SW11 (Clapham Junction), 020-7223 4080; fax 7223 6131

www.little-bay.co.uk

"About as cheap and cheerful as London restaurants come", and "fantastically bohemian" to boot, this "idiosyncratic" trio is "great for large parties", and whilst the "interesting" Modern European–Med is "no gastronomic tour-de-force", all agree it is "astonishingly good value"; "no matter how busy" it gets, the "charming" service "always manages to squeeze you in."

Little Italy ◐ 20 | 15 | 21 | £29

21 Frith St., W1 (Leicester Sq./Tottenham Court Rd.), 020-7734 4737; fax 7734 1777

In "cosy" Soho quarters, this "little Italian" offers a "great ambience", "charming staff" and "simple, delicious" "comfort food"; but "they do pump up the music after 11 PM" when the place turns into a "late-night party scene"; N.B. a post-*Survey* refurb may impact the Decor score.

Livebait 17 | 13 | 16 | £30

21 Wellington St., WC2 (Covent Garden), 020-7836 7161; fax 7836 7141

43 The Cut, SE1 (Waterloo), 020-7928 7211; fax 7928 2279

www.santeonline.co.uk

"The formula can't be beat" profess fans of this "bustling, noisy" pair in Covent Garden and Waterloo, known for "no unnecessary frills", either in the "basic white-tile decor" ("like eating in a gentleman's urinal") or the "simply, freshly prepared seafood" at "quite a reasonable price"; but critics carp it all feels "formulaic" now – "the menu appears to have been passed from an inspired chef to an accountant."

LMNT ▽ 19 | 23 | 22 | £21

316 Queensbridge Rd., E8 (Dalston Kingsland B.R.), 020-7249 6727; fax 7249 6538; www.lmnt.co.uk

From "the depths of E8" comes this "temple of Egyptian kitsch (think Tutankhamen fireplaces, erotic tiling in the toilets)" in an "unassuming converted pub", and even if the "amazing surroundings" dominate proceedings, it's good to know there's also "smiley service", "tasty" New French cooking and "wallet-friendly" prices; P.S. "book a table in the urn and enjoy."

Lobster Pot, The ⊠ – | – | – | E

3 Kennington Ln., SE11 (Kennington), 020-7582 5556; fax 7582 9751; www.lobsterpotrestaurant.co.uk

With a "kitschy seaside" setting – complete with recorded seagulls calling and "ship horns sounding all the time" – this old salt "off the beaten track" in Kennington serves up Classic French fish dishes, including a platter of "serious shellfish" for those "brave enough to try"; however, the less culinarily convinced "go for the fun decor, not the food."

LOCANDA LOCATELLI 24 | 20 | 22 | £60

Hyatt Regency London – The Churchill, 8 Seymour St., W1 (Marble Arch), 020-7935 9088; fax 7935 1149; www.locandalocatelli.com

"If you are into elegant, upscale Northern" Italian cuisine with "funky twists", it'll be "hard to find any fault" with the "otherworldly" offerings from TV chef Giorgio Locatelli (who "himself is in the kitchen with his wife at front of house"); some suggest, however, that this "stylishly" "clinical" Marylebone locale is "becoming a little arrogant", citing a "tortuous reservation system" and service that veers from "cold" to "incredibly accommodating."

Locanda Ottoemezzo ☒ 24 | 17 | 22 | £39

2-4 Thackeray St., W8 (High St. Kensington), 020-7937 2200; fax 7937 9871

"It's hard to remember you're in London and not Italy", given the "arty atmosphere" (adorned with Fellini film posters) and "excellent, homestyle Italian" cucina at this "cosy" corner, aka the "best-kept secret" in Kensington; the "menu's not very long, but always worth the bill"; in short, "it's like going for dinner at your best friend's" – though he recommends you ring him for a reservation on weekends.

Lola's ▽ 20 | 16 | 18 | £45

The Mall Bldg., 359 Upper St., N1 (Angel), 020-7359 1932; fax 7359 2209; www.lolas.co.uk

In an "old tram shed", this "interesting" Islingtonian attracts local "luvvies aplenty" – "Sadler's Wells is just a short walk away" – for its "high-quality" Modern European cooking, including a notably "cheap set lunch"; but the consensus is that a "slower pace of changing chefs would be useful", since it often makes the "nice" staff "clueless as to what's on the menu."

Lonsdale, The ◐ 19 | 24 | 17 | £32

48 Lonsdale Rd., W11 (Ladbroke Grove/Notting Hill Gate), 020-7727 4080; fax 7727 6030; www.thelonsdale.co.uk

"Frequented by Brit-pop stars", the "scene is fantastically cool"/"achingly trendy" at this "very loud" Notting Hill pub ("don't go for conversation"); and whilst "the trust-fund crowd" are "here to be seen, not to be fed", the Eclectic menu of global "grazing plates" is "surprisingly good" (with a higher Food score); just expect to "suffer from bar goers' bums in your face when trying to eat."

L'ORANGER ☒ 26 | 23 | 24 | £63

5 St. James's St., SW1 (Green Park), 020-7839 3774; fax 7839 4330

"A smooth, successful operation" opine advocates of this "understatedly" "classy", "intimate space" where "fine dining in the true French style" means a "sophisticated, subtle" Provençal menu, plus "great cheese board", and "sublime service"; it's all "a touch formal" and, "reflecting its location" in St. James's, "the prices tend to make the eyebrows climb above the hairline", but overall enthusiasm reigns for this "elegant", "extraordinary eating adventure."

Lou Pescadou ◐ ▽ 21 | 16 | 21 | £38

241 Old Brompton Rd., SW5 (Earl's Ct.), 020-7370 1057; fax 7244 7545

Entering its third decade, this "sentimental fave" remains "a treat in a nice neighbourhood" (Earl's Court) for "excellent French" fish and other Classics, served by "welcoming", "campy" staff; a few finicky folks fuss it's "rather expensive for" its "casual" surroundings – i.e. "tables are so close it's hard to get in and out without a 'sorry.'"

Lucio 23 | 19 | 22 | £46

257-259 Fulham Rd., SW3 (South Kensington), 020-7823 3007; fax 7823 3009

A "great addition to the [Chelsea] scene" say converts to "caring owner" Lucio Altana's (ex San Lorenzo) "trendy" but "relaxed" venue, with "real Italian" cooking that's "more interesting than the standard fare" and "reasonably spaced tables – you can actually talk!"

Lucky 7 ◐⊄ 18 | 18 | 14 | £17

127 Westbourne Park Rd., W2 (Royal Oak/Westbourne Park), 020-7727 6771; fax 7727 6798

"As close to an American diner as you'll ever get" in London, Tom Conran's "tiny" venue "in the wilds of Notting Hill" nails it with "funky, '50s"-style decor and "awesome" U.S.-Mexican "comfort food" to "pig out" on; now, "if only they had more room", the unlucky wouldn't have "to share a table at busy times."

Luigi's of Covent Garden ◐☒ 20 | 16 | 19 | £36

15 Tavistock St., WC2 (Covent Garden), 020-7240 1789; fax 7497 0075; www.luigisofcoventgarden.com

"You can always count on" this "long-serving", "popular" Covent Garden trattoria that offers "solid" "Italian home cooking" along with a chance to "rub heads with the after-theatre crowd, including actors"; the "matter-of-fact service warms up with repeat visits", but that doesn't mollify malcontents who feel the "old-fashioned" digs "could do with a face-lift."

Lundum's 25 | 23 | 23 | £43

117-119 Old Brompton Rd., SW7 (Gloucester Rd./ South Kensington), 020-7373 7774; fax 7373 4472; www.lundums.com

"Who'd ever think: Danish food in London?" – well, plenty would, if it's this South Ken Scandinavian, a "slick, polished and professional" scene, from the "authentic, appetising" menu, featuring "exquisite fish", to the "cool, elegant" (and, of course, white) digs to the "most charming service"; the "cosy" "Library Lounge is perfect for a drink before your meal"; all in all, a "grown-up" gastronomic experience.

Made in Italy ◐ 21 | 14 | 12 | £25

249 King's Rd., SW3 (Sloane Sq./South Kensington), 020-7352 1880

"Sitting on the roof terrace in summer is a rare treat" at this "casual, cramped" King's Road trattoria where the highlight of the "authentic Southern Italian" menu is "the smoky, delicious" brick-oven pizza; snipers aim their fire at "sloppy waiters" who are "always rushed off their feet."

Maggie Jones's 21 | 20 | 20 | £34

6 Old Court Pl., W8 (High St. Kensington), 020-7937 6462; fax 7376 0510

"Rustic" and "charming", this old-timer has "the feel of a country inn" (even though it's "tucked away" in Kensington); its "hearty" Traditional British "comfort food", though "not sophisticated", is "truly satisfying"; most find the "friendly staff eager to please", although a handful say the "service is not up to scratch."

Maggiores 20 | 21 | 21 | £38

33 King St., WC2 (Covent Garden/Leicester Sq.), 020-7379 9696; fax 7379 6767; www.maggiores.uk.com

With "flowers blooming overhead", a "log fire and fairy lights", this" "stunningly romantic" Covent Garden venue is "a must for any couple"; reviewers have a "warm spot" for its "fresh, tasty" Franco-Italian fare; other pluses are the "great wine list", "accommodating" staff and "pre-theatre menu that includes a [complimentary] cocktail."

Ma Goa ∇ 27 | 18 | 20 | £28

242-244 Upper Richmond Rd., SW15 (East Putney), 020-8780 1767; www.ma-goa.com

"Authentic, beautifully cooked" Goan dishes and a "lovely, sociable atmosphere" are the hallmarks of this "family-run" Putney Indian, which has been "recently redecorated" in a modern style; however, a handful huff it's "a bit pricey for a curry restaurant" and "recommend the takeaway."

Malabar ◐ 23 | 15 | 20 | £25

27 Uxbridge St., W8 (Notting Hill Gate), 020-7727 8800; www.malabar-restaurant.co.uk

"You don't have to dress up" for this "unpretentious" Indian set in a "trendy area of Notting Hill" that's "low-key, high spirit" and a "nifty" option for "fresh, inventive" curries of "outstanding flavours" at "reasonable prices", smoothed along by "smiling waiters."

Malabar Junction ◐ 20 | 16 | 18 | £23

107 Great Russell St., WC1 (Tottenham Court Rd.), 020-7580 5230; fax 7436 9942

"Good for a spot of curry after a day at the British Museum" nearby, this "pleasant, gardenlike" setting with a "glass conservatory ceiling" is a "soothing" environment for "delicious Keralan fare" (including "interesting coconut-based dishes") from a "creative" menu; but some find the "decor tired and dated", and service "rather diffident."

Malmaison Hotel Bar & Brasserie ∇ 16 | 19 | 17 | £38

Malmaison Hotel, 18-21 Charterhouse Sq., EC1 (Barbican/Farringdon), 020-7012 3700; fax 7012 3702; www.malmaison.com

"In the middle of Charterhouse Square", this red-brick Victorian hotel harbours a "hip" basement dining room that's as good for "a romantic tête-à-tête as for a group dinner"; the French Brasserie fare is "pleasant", albeit "average", but service ranges from "professional" to "inexperienced"; P.S. there's also a "credible cocktail bar."

Mandalay ⊠ 22 | 7 | 21 | £19

444 Edgware Rd., W2 (Edgware Rd.), 020-7258 3696; fax 7258 3696

This "fun little hole-in-the-wall" on Edgware Road might look "like a greasy spoon", but the "simple surroundings" belie the "unbeatable", "unusual" Burmese dishes at "excellent value"; this "best-kept secret" is owned by two "cordial" brothers, who run an "intoxicatingly happy" team of servers.

Mandarin Kitchen ◐ 24 | 11 | 16 | £32

14-16 Queensway, W2 (Bayswater/Queensway), 020-7727 9012; fax 7727 9468

Signature dishes like "knock-your-socks-off Peking duck" and "out-of-this-world lobster noodles" ensure that this "hectic" Queensway stalwart Chinese is "always packed", and whilst many overlook the "bizarre, '70s-style decor (that's almost fashionable again)", the "only problem is that staff persist at turning the table once you've finished."

Mango Tree 21 | 20 | 19 | £40

46 Grosvenor Pl., SW1 (Victoria), 020-7823 1888; fax 7838 9275; www.mangotree.org.uk

"Not far from Victoria Station", this "sleek", "minimalist" venue – "a bit stark" say some – comes "recommended" for "generous portions" of "outstanding", "perfectly prepared Thai" fare, served by "efficient" staff; a few gripe about "overpowering noise levels" at busy times, but in the main, most say they "will be returning", especially "if in the area."

Manicomio 18 | 16 | 17 | £33

85 Duke of York Sq., SW3 (Sloane Sq.), 020-7730 3366; fax 7730 3377

Making an "enjoyable" sojourn in the Duke of York's barracks development, this easy-going Italian eatery – with an adjoining cafe/deli –offers a "fresh, interesting" Italian menu and is "good for people-watching", particularily on the popular patio; a few feel it's "somewhat overpriced for the quantity and quality", with "variable service."

Manzi's ◐⊠ 21 | 15 | 18 | £36

1-2 Leicester St., WC2 (Leicester Sq./Piccadilly Circus), 020-7734 0224; fax 7437 4864; www.manzis.co.uk

It's "well worth the squeeze" at this "old-world" Chinatown institution known for its "fresh", "classic" seafood, like the "delicious sole" and "nifty fish 'n' chips"; some feel it's "lost its loving feeling" – staff can be "a bit surly at times" – but this "relaxed" spot remains "extremely popular", especially for an "excellent pre-theatre" meal.

Mao Tai ◐ 21 | 17 | 19 | £36

58 New King's Rd., SW6 (Parsons Green), 020-7731 2520; fax 7471 8992
96 Draycott Ave., SW3 (South Kensington), 020-7225 2500; fax 7225 1965
www.maotai.co.uk

It's "hard to go back to other Chinese places" after the "upmarket Szechuan" cooking – which offers "more than just the stock Western favourites" – at this "easy-going", yet "sophisticated" duo in Brompton Cross and Parsons Green; even if "they're expensive for what you get, they're reasonable for the locations", and there's always "home delivery."

Mark's Club ⊠ 23 | 24 | 26 | £74

Private club; inquiries: 020-7499 2936

"Imagine Gosford Park in a Mayfair townhouse" and you have this "comfortable", "intimate" private dining club from legendary Mark Birley that's "keeping alive a lifestyle long dead"; "perfect", "accommodating" service and "lovely" Traditional British cuisine make for a "dining experience" that, surveyors say, is "wonderful for romance or an important deal closing."

Maroush ◐ 22 | 12 | 16 | £25

21 Edgware Rd., W2 (Marble Arch), 020-7723 0773; fax 7723 3161
68 Edgware Rd., W2 (Marble Arch), 020-7224 9339; fax 7723 3161
1-3 Connaught St., W2 (Marble Arch), 020-7262 0222
4 Vere St., W1 (Bond St.), 020-7493 5050; fax 7723 3161
62 Seymour St., W1 (Marble Arch), 020-7724 5024; fax 7723 3161
38 Beauchamp Pl., SW3 (Knightsbridge), 020-7581 5434; fax 7723 3161
www.maroush.com

Most "leave thoroughly satisfied" from this "tried-and-true" West End chain whose "warm hosts" provide "dependably good, decently priced" Lebanese fare; the often-"tacky decor" that "needs updating" is of no concern "at 3 AM when the clubs are closing" and all that matters is pacifying the "post–night out munchies."

Masala Zone 20 | 16 | 16 | £19

9 Marshall St., W1 (Oxford Circus/Piccadilly Circus), 020-7287 9966; fax 7287 8555
147 Earl's Court Rd., SW5 (Earl's Court), 020-7373 0220; fax 7373 0990
80 Upper St., N1 (Angel), 020-7359 3399; fax 7359 6560
www.realindianfood.com

"Bustling with arty types and students", this "cheap and cheerful" trio offers a menu of "fast" Indian fare that's "so good, you always over-order"; even though the decor is "a bit cold" and "service can vary", all concede the "food makes up for it"; P.S. "go for the grand Thali [set dinner] with all the trimmings."

Mash ⊠ ∇ 13 | 16 | 14 | £27

19-21 Great Portland St., W1 (Oxford Circus), 020-7637 5555; www.mashbarandrestaurant.co.uk

"Lounge ambience meets hipster funk" at Oliver Peyton's "trendy" eatery near Oxford Street, comprising an upstairs restaurant with a "cafeteria feel" and "dependable", if "overpriced" Modern European fare, and a "fun downstairs" bar benefiting from "people-watching and homemade beer" from the on-site micro-brewery.

Matsuri 22 | 16 | 20 | £49

71 High Holborn, WC1 (Holborn), 020-7430 1970; fax 7430 1971 ⊠
15 Bury St., SW1 (Green Park), 020-7839 1101; fax 7930 7010
www.matsuri-restaurant.com

There's "something for everyone, Japanese-style" – like the "freshest sushi", "delicious teppanyaki" and "excellent sakes" – at this "upscale" Holborn and St James's duo; even if the "pared-down decor" looks "anodyne" and some prices are "stupidly high", they are "definite business-lunch spots" with "rapid, friendly service"; P.S. "do not miss the famous ice cream bomb for dessert."

Maze – | – | – | VE

10-13 Grosvenor Sq., W1 (Bond St.), 020-7107 0000; fax 7107 0001; www.gordonramsay.com

No stone gathers moss under Gordon Ramsay's energetic feet, and the restless restaurateur's latest venture is a glossy, elegant L-shaped dining room and bar in Grosvenor Square, designed by David Rockwell; head chef Jason Atherton (ex Verre in Dubai) "beautifully prepares" "Asian-French-meets-tapas-bar cuisine", making clever use of a charcoal robata grill, wood oven and plancha.

Medcalf – | – | – | M

40 Exmouth Market, EC1 (Angel), 020-7833 3533; fax 7833 1321; www.medcalfbar.co.uk

"They know what they are doing when it comes to meat" at this former butcher's shop in Exmouth Market, which attracts "a foodie clientele" with a "reasonably priced", "focused menu" of "inspiring, good quality British food", plus a "great wine list with some tremendous Riojas"; a DJ keeps things "very cool post-dinner" on the weekends.

Mediterraneo ◐ 21 | 16 | 18 | £35

37 Kensington Park Rd., W11 (Ladbroke Grove), 020-7792 3131; fax 7243 3630

"Like classic Chanel, it'll never go out of style" say lovers of this "super little trattoria" in "crowded", "casual" digs near Portobello Market where "all ages feel comfortable" and the "well-prepared Italian grub" makes up for not being able "to get a reservation without planning days ahead"; but opinions are split over the "hit-and-miss service" ("warm" and "easy-going" vs. brusque" and "rude").

Mela ◐ 23 | 17 | 22 | £23

152-156 Shaftesbury Ave., WC2 (Leicester Sq.), 020-7836 8635; fax 7379 0527; www.melarestaurant.co.uk

"Simple, bright decor" sets the stage at this "unpretentious" Theatreland Indian offering an "interesting" array of "good-value", "avant-garde" fare "prepared with a delicate hand", including a "fantastic selection of vegetarian dishes" and a "great lunch deal" for under a fiver; "attentive", "personal" service completes this "cheerful" picture.

Memories of China 22 | 18 | 19 | £41

353 Kensington High St., W8 (High St. Kensington), 020-7603 6951; fax 7603 0848

65-69 Ebury St., SW1 (Victoria), 020-7730 7734; fax 7730 2992 ◐

"You can never go wrong here" claim converts to this "upscale Chinese" duo in Belgravia (the stalwart original) and Kensington, "solid" choices for "refined", "reliable" multiregional fare and "courteous" service; still, sceptics say there's "no wow factor", except at the "pricey" bill.

Meson Don Felipe ☒ 21 | 17 | 17 | £23

53 The Cut, SE1 (Southwark/Waterloo), 020-7928 3237; fax 7736 9857

For "atmospheric tapas without stratospheric prices" try this "cramped" Spaniard near Waterloo, where the food is "always of a high standard" and there's a "great selection of Spanish wines too"; as it gets "busier and busier", service "can get stressed" – but no worries, as the "flamenco guitarist teetering on top of a cupboard" distracts diners.

Metrogusto 20 | 18 | 22 | £40

11-13 Theberton St., N1 (Angel/Highbury & Islington), 020-7226 9400; fax 7226 9400; www.metrogusto.co.uk

"Inventive" Italian in "interesting combinations", an "excellent wine list" and an "inviting" art-filled room make this "classy" Islingtonian "what a neighbourhood restaurant should be"; a few flinch at "high prices", still save a kindly word for the "incredibly friendly" owner, Ambro Ianeselli.

Meza ◐☒ 15 | 17 | 13 | £37

100 Wardour St., W1 (Leicester Sq.), 020-7314 4002; fax 7314 4040; www.conran.com

The Conran Group has transformed Soho's Mezzonine into this "lively" Iberian coupling regional cuisine with "amazing cocktails" and sherries; a 1 AM license (3 AM on weekends) makes it "great when it's late", but sceptics scold food that's "far from authentic" and tapas that are "very small indeed."

Michael Moore ☒ – | – | – | E

19 Blandford St., W1 (Baker St./Bond St.), 020-7224 1898; fax 7224 0970; www.michaelmoorerestaurant.com

"Charming chef"-owner Michael Moore maintains "a loyal following" at this "tiny", clean-lined Marylebone eatery;

his "interesting", "constantly changing menu" of Eclectic dishes "from around the world" keeps converts "coming back", and the man himself often "comes out at the end of the meal for a chat"; N.B. there's seating for 10 outside on clement days.

Michiaki ☒ | – | – | – | E

40-42 Baker St., W1 (Baker Street), 020-7486 3898; www.michiaki.co.uk

After moving their Royal China one block down Baker Street, the owners transformed its airy, glass-fronted space into this sleek upscale Japanese with granite floors and symmetrical rows of timber tables; Naoki Hoshino, former head chef at Suntory Ltd., presides over a diverse menu that's supported by a sushi counter, teppanyaki table and succinct wine list.

Mildreds ☒ ▽ 24 | 16 | 18 | £21

45 Lexington St., W1 (Oxford Circus/Piccadilly Circus), 020-7439 2392; fax 7439 2392; www.mildreds.co.uk

"As good as it gets" – so "tasty" it might just "convert a carnivore" – say some about this Soho "staple" serving "creative", "varied" vegetarian fare in a "small, busy" setting; it may "take hours to get a table" (there are "no bookings"), but regulars are ready to "sit on top of people" for "excellent" "comfort food" at "great prices."

Mimmo d'Ischia ◐☒ 22 | 15 | 20 | £44

61 Elizabeth St., SW1 (Sloane Sq./Victoria), 020-7730 5406; fax 7730 9439; www.mimmodischia.co.uk

"Mimmo himself greets you like a friend" at this "old-school" Belgravia Italian – "soldiering on" well into its fourth decade – where "harried" servers ferry "enormous portions" of "authentic, if pricey" fare to "cramped" tables; though some feel the "decor needs to be updated", this "lovely" "landmark" eatery "gets a lot of repeat business."

Mint Leaf 19 | 23 | 18 | £45

Corner of Haymarket & Suffolk Pl., SW1 (Piccadilly Circus), 020-7930 9020; fax 7930 6205; www.mintleafrestaurant.com

With a "sexy", "cool" setting that takes a leaf out of a "Hakkasan-esque" book, this "stylish, sophisticated" Indian in a former Trafalgar Square bank is in mint condition for "impressing friends from out of town" (and indeed, prices for the "inventive, tasteful" cuisine are geared to "client entertainment"); the huge, partitioned space is "great for groups", whilst the popular bar does "fantastic" cocktails.

Mirabelle ◐ 23 | 22 | 22 | £59

56 Curzon St., W1 (Green Park), 020-7499 4636; fax 7499 5449; www.whitestarline.org.uk

"The place for romance" or "to eavesdrop for stock tips", Marco Pierre White's "beautiful dining room" and bar (complete with "glittery" disco ball) in a "plush" Mayfair basement harbours high-"quality Classic French cooking", an "incredible wine list" and "faultless service"; even so, some critics say it's "all show, no go" at this "long-runner" that's been "resting too long on its laurels" – though the Sunday set-price lunch remains the "bargain of the century."

Mitsukoshi ▽ 20 | 10 | 15 | £43

14-20 Lower Regent St., SW1 (Piccadilly Circus), 020-7930 0317; fax 7839 1167; www.mitsukoshi-restaurant.co.uk

"For half-decent Japanese at non-killer prices", try this Piccadilly Circus site set in an Asian department store and serving "superlative" sushi and sashimi alongside other "traditional" dishes; the "downside"? – it "looks like a school classroom", leading some to conclude: "daytime only."

Miyama ▽ 20 | 12 | 18 | £43

38 Clarges St., W1 (Green Park), 020-7499 2443; fax 7493 1573

"No frills, merely serious food" is the lure at this "relatively secret" Mayfair Japanese where "friendly" staff ferry a "wide range" of dishes to regulars who hope this one "remains a relative secret"; P.S. there's a "value-for-the-money" set lunch that's "good for business" folk.

Mju ☒ 22 | 19 | 19 | £50

Millennium Knightsbridge Hotel, 17 Sloane St., SW1 (Knightsbridge), 020-7201 6330; fax 7201 6353; www.mill-cop.com

"Innovative Pacific Rim food" with French influences "tantalises the palate" at this "spacious" dining room inside the Millennium Knightsbridge Hotel where "eye-catching" dishes are matched with wines by a "knowledgeable sommelier"; still, pessimists point to service that's "a bit laid-back" and atmosphere that's "a big fat zero."

Momo 19 | 24 | 17 | £40

25 Heddon St., W1 (Piccadilly Circus), 020-7434 4040; fax 7287 0404
Selfridges, 2nd fl., 400 Oxford St., W1 (Bond St.), 020-7318 3620; fax 7318 3228

"If you go for the food you're missing the point" at this "sexy", "exotic" "low-tables-and-candlelight" Moroccan "hidden away off Regent Street", where "everyone's dressed to the nines" and the staff's "more interested in looking good than serving well"; still, the "funky" North African nibbles are enjoyable enough, and you can also "relax" at the next-door cafe or join a "young crowd" in the club below; P.S. the in-store "Selfridges location is excellent for studying the sociology of shopping."

Mon Plaisir ◐☒ 21 | 18 | 19 | £36

21 Monmouth St., WC2 (Covent Garden/Leicester Sq.), 020-7836 7243; fax 7240 4774; www.monplaisir.co.uk

"Quintessentially French, quintessentially indispensable", this 64-year-old Covent Gardener "charms" "those who know it" with a quintet of "cosy, romantic" rooms and "marvellous, old-fashioned" Bistro fare that's "nothing flashy, but never disappoints"; pessimists take no pleasure in what they deem "dated" decor and cuisine ("nostalgia's not always good"), but most say this "old favourite" "keeps it simple and that's why we like it."

Montagu, The — | – | – | E

Hyatt Regency London – The Churchill, 30 Portman Sq., W1 (Marble Arch), 020-7299 2037; fax 7486 1255; www.london.churchill.hyatt.com

Named after the 18th-century aristocrat Edward Montagu who built his home on the site, this bright, all-day dining room looking out over Portman Square has been given a smart revamp with wooden flooring, muted fabrics and a view into the high-tech kitchen; new chef Ben Purton oversees a polished Modern European menu with a sprinkling of Traditional British comfort food.

Montpeliano ◐ 18 | 17 | 18 | £40

13 Montpelier St., SW7 (Knightsbridge), 020-7589 0032; fax 7838 0268

For "classic favourites with few frills, but satisfying results" stop in to this "lively for people-watching" Italian in Knightsbridge that's "worth keeping on your list" for "reliable" food in a "comfortable" (if "noisy") setting; that said, critics say this "unimaginative" "'60s throwback" may be "past its prime."

Monza ⊠ 18 | 15 | 19 | £34

6 Yeoman's Row, SW3 (Knightsbridge/South Kensington), 020-7591 0210; fax 7591 0210

"Well-hidden, and should remain so" say the secretive of this "small, buzzing" Knightsbridge trattoria offering "Italian staples" amid "Formula One theme" decor; the "colourful", "considerate" staff make up for "tight tables" that prove perilous "if you're next to a smoker"; P.S. "secret melon vodka" and "lethal limoncello" make this the "place to start a night out with friends."

MORGAN M 25 | 16 | 21 | £50

489 Liverpool Rd., N7 (Highbury & Islington), 020-7609 3560; fax 8292 5699

Chef-owner Morgan Meunier has "put his heart and soul into the operation" of this "oasis" in a "pokey backstreet" of Islington; his "imaginative", "intense" New French–vegetarian cuisine is "clearly the star", and although some think the eponymous establishment "takes itself too seriously" ("bright, cold" decor, "stuffy" service), most give it a big round of "applause."

MORO ⊠ 25 | 17 | 20 | £37

34-36 Exmouth Mkt., EC1 (Angel/Farringdon), 020-7833 8336; fax 7833 9338; www.moro.co.uk

A "joyful blend" of Spanish–North African–Med flavours makes for "terrific, unpretentious" cooking at this "vibrant" Exmouth Market haunt, where "relaxed, professional service", a "glitterati crowd" and an "incredible Iberian wine and sherry" choice up the ante; although "it's tough to get into" and it could use "some soundproofing", all agree they "know what they're doing here."

Morton's ☒ 21 | 19 | 22 | £59

Private club; inquiries: 020-7518 2982

Yes, "it did take years to reopen", but after an "astonishing transformation" by restaurateur Marlon Abela, this famous Mayfair dining space is now a "sophisticated" private club with a "bright, buzzy" first-floor setting and a "terrific view of Berkeley Square"; "wonderful, but expensive" New French cooking is paired with "first-class service", and there's also a stylish bar as well as an elegant private room that looks into the 2,000-label wine cellar.

Moshi Moshi Sushi 19 | 13 | 16 | £22

Canary Wharf Waitrose, Canada Pl., E14 (Canary Wharf), 020-7512 9201; fax 7512 9685

24 Upper Level, Liverpool St. Station, Broadgate, EC2 (Liverpool St.), 020-7247 3227; fax 7247 3227 ☒

www.moshimoshi.co.uk

"Everything a sushi bar should be" when "you are out and about", this "quick and easy" Japanese duo (weekday-only in the City) serves up "reliable" raw fin fare from "quality ingredients"; nevertheless, a few find the "conveyor belt dishes" rather "middle-of-the-road."

MOSIMANN'S ☒ 25 | 25 | 25 | £66

Private club; inquiries: 020-7235 9625

"Thank goodness it's private, otherwise it would be packed" sigh fans of chef Anton Mosimann's "superb" members' club located in the "hushed ambience of a converted church" in Belgravia; diners are "treated royally" to "impeccable" Eclectic dishes and an "extended wine list"; although a few have their doubts – "menu needs updating", "astoundingly expensive" – most concede this "total experience" is "quality, from beginning to end."

Motcombs 17 | 17 | 19 | £45

26 Motcomb St., SW1 (Knightsbridge/Sloane Sq.), 020-7235 6382; fax 7245 6351; www.motcombs.co.uk

"A fun place to unwind", this "convivial" 38-year-"old staple of Belgravia" boasts a wine bar with "a lot of buzz" (and pavement seating) and a "comfortable" restaurant with "generally good" Eclectic fare; however, service seems somewhat "pleased with itself", and the whole experience is like "dining circa 1975" malcontents mutter.

Mr. Chow ◐ 22 | 20 | 20 | £53

151 Knightsbridge, SW1 (Knightsbridge), 020-7589 7347; fax 7584 5780; www.mrchow.com

"Be on the lookout for celebs" – as well as "sugar daddies with their nieces" – at this "quirky" "Knightsbridge legend" where diners "can always count on" "excellent" Chinese cuisine (although given the "staggeringly expensive" cost, many feel it "should be more memorable for the money") and "diligent" staff who "manage large groups graciously"; true, "food, decor and service" seem in something of a "'70s time warp" – but since that era's hot right now, it actually makes this veteran rather "hip after all these years."

Mr. Kong ◐ 21 | 9 | 17 | £25

21 Lisle St., WC2 (Leicester Sq.), 020-7437 7341

"Surprisingly sturdy Chinese cuisine" in "scruffy surrounds" sums up the scene at this Chinatown stalwart, whose late hours (until 2:45 AM, most days) makes it "perfect for after-theatre" or "before heading out to the clubs"; "staff quality is mixed" and "don't go if you hate drafts", but you "can't beat the price for the quality" of the "no-nonsense" fare.

MVH – | – | – | VE

5 White Hart Ln., SW13 (Barnes Bridge B.R.), 020-8392 1111; fax 8878 1616

There's an "air of experimentation about" chef-owner Michael von Hruschka's "quite bizarre, but extremely tasty" Eclectic menu at this intimate, "highly individual" Barnes venue; visitors will find "lots to talk about", from the "particularly exciting amuse-bouches" to the "really fun" approach of decorating the restaurant and bar areas with, respectively, "the grace and beauty of heaven and the sexy decadence of hell."

Nahm 22 | 21 | 22 | £58

Halkin Hotel, 5 Halkin St., SW1 (Hyde Park Corner), 020-7333 1234; fax 7333 1100; www.halkin.co.uk

Offering "no concessions to Western tastes", Australian chef David Thompson's "unique", "complex" Thai cuisine with "perfectly balanced flavours" makes for "a real treat" at this "spiffy, modern" Belgravia hotel; whilst fans fawn "the only negative is the variable ambience" ("nearly empty at lunch, but buzzy at dinner"), sceptics say nah to what they deem "utterly overrated", "ridiculously overpriced" cuisine.

Naked Turtle ◐ ▽ 16 | 20 | 21 | £32

505 Upper Richmond Rd. W., SW14 (Richmond), 020-8878 1995; fax 8392 1388

"Your waitress doubles as a jazz singer" in the evenings at this East Sheen eatery "with enough quirkiness to justify a visit", and even if the "interesting" Eclectic fare (signature dish: a kangaroo platter) isn't always "cooked reliably", all agree "the place has a great energy and vibe."

Nam Long-Le Shaker ◐ ☒ 18 | 16 | 14 | £33

159 Old Brompton Rd., SW5 (Gloucester Rd./South Kensington), 020-7373 1926; fax 7373 6043

"The atmosphere never disappoints" at this "popular" South Ken stalwart, "still going strong" after two decades with those who "want to hang out with junior investment bankers"; though many insist it's "all about the cocktails" ("drink more than one, and you won't remember all the [new] friends you made"), others cite an "improvement" in the "funky" Vietnamese fare.

Nathalie ⊠ ▽ 20 | 15 | 22 | £45

3 Milner St., SW3 (Sloane Sq./South Kensington), 020-7581 2848; www.nathalie-restaurant.co.uk

Chef-owner Eric Chatroux often "comes to the table to chat" at this "wonderful Chelsea find" where "well-priced wines go with the equally well-executed" New French menu (special praise to the "inexpensive lunchtime tasting plate", a kind of Gallic bento box); however, for critics the "charming service" doesn't compensate for "simply unexciting food and decor" – perhaps they're sulking over the "strictly enforced rule about not being allowed to smoke until pudding."

Nautilus Fish ⊠ ▽ 19 | 6 | 13 | £15

27-29 Fortune Green Rd., NW6 (West Hampstead), 020-7435 2532

It's not the spot for a romantic rendezvous, but "if you fancy fish 'n' chips with your mates", this simple 32-year-old West Hampstead shop "is the place to go" for "fresh" seafood and "suitably mushy peas"; but naysayers note a decline – "now, almost any other plaice will do"; N.B. the Decor score may not reflect a recent refurb.

Neal Street Restaurant ⊠ 22 | 16 | 20 | £44

26 Neal St., WC2 (Covent Garden), 020-7836 8368; fax 7240 3964; www.carluccios.com

A "Covent Garden institution", entrepreneurial chef Antonio Carluccio's "bright flagship" flourishes with a "fabulous", "fresh" Italian menu "specialising in mushrooms" and truffles ("you can find dishes without them, but why bother?") and service that "can be slow or quick, depending on your mood"; "disappointed" dissenters declare it "looks and feels quite tatty", and even converts concede "cheap it definitely ain't"; but for most, "this old favourite is still on the must-do list when the fungi [season] arrives."

New Culture Revolution 15 | 9 | 13 | £15

157-159 Notting Hill Gate, W11 (Notting Hill Gate), 020-7313 9688
75 Southampton Row, WC1 (Holborn), 020-7436 9706
305 King's Rd., SW3 (Sloane Sq.), 020-7352 9281
42 Duncan St., N1 (Angel), 020-7833 9083
43 Parkway, NW1 (Camden Town), 020-7267 2700
www.newculturerevolution.co.uk

"Fast, simple and inexpensive" characterises the culture of this noodle chain around town; "stark" and "bright", it's "not a romantic venue", but with "a lovely selection of non-greasy" Mandarin eats, it's "excellent for a quick, drop-in meal."

New World ◐ 20 | 11 | 14 | £20

1 Gerrard Pl., W1 (Leicester Sq.), 020-7434 2508; fax 7287 8994

"Dim sum trolleys galore" carry an "amazing assortment" at this "cavernous Chinatown institution" whose "large, exotic menu" features "lots of familiar dishes and many new ones"; negatives note there's "nothing new about New World's" menu and certainly a "cheery smile would help" from the "unhurried servers" – but still, "the wait on weekends can be outrageous, so get there early."

Nicole's ☒ 17 | 16 | 17 | £37

Nicole Farhi, 158 New Bond St., W1 (Bond St./Green Park), 020-7499 8408; fax 7409 0381; www.nicolefarhi.com

"Cool, urbane and trendy" – and that's just the "fashionista" crowd on show at the "sophisticated" surrounds of Nicole Farhi's "chic" Bond Street store – a "great place to relax" "on a shopping trip" and "check out the bags of others" whilst munching "solid" Modern European–Med meals.

noble rot. ☒ 18 | 17 | 16 | £44

3-5 Mill St., W1 (Oxford Circus), 020-7629 8877; fax 7629 8878; www.noblerot.com

"An unsung hero" insist admirers of this "grown-up", glass-fronted eatery, "a little off the beaten path" in Mayfair; among its noble aspects are "refreshingly different" Modern European fare on the plate and "some real clever stuff" (e.g. "lots of sweet wines") in the cellar (to be expected, as its name refers to the mould that intensifies grapes' sugar); and even detractors who deride "forgettable eats" and "snooty service" enjoy the Moroccan-style private club downstairs (diners "can go after dinner").

NOBU 27 | 20 | 21 | £67

Metropolitan Hotel, 19 Old Park Ln., W1 (Hyde Park Corner), 020-7447 4747; fax 7447 4749

Nobu Berkeley ☒

15 Berkeley St., W1, 020-7290 9222; fax 7290 9223 www.noburestaurants.com

"Genius" chef-owner Nobu Matsuhisa "uses his skill and style to blow your mind" at his "ever-crowded" Park Lane Japanese-Peruvian haunt for an "ultrahip", "celebrity" crowd; it's just ceded its title as London's Most Popular, perhaps due to "condescending waiters" and "super-minimal decor"; but all applaud the "exquisite" edibles that embody "the real meaning of fusion", so overall this venue is "hugely satisfying to the senses" – if also "numbing to the finances"; N.B. the Berkeley sib opened post-*Survey*.

Noor Jahan ◐ 21 | 13 | 17 | £29

26 Sussex Pl., W2 (Lancaster Gate), 020-7402 2332; fax 7402 5885
2A Bina Gardens, SW5 (South Kensington), 020-7373 6522

"Book ahead", as this "local curry house" in South Ken "always seems to be full" thanks to the "enduring appeal" of "consistent", "refined" Indian fare that "still hits the spot" after 43 years; however, a few feel it's "being overtaken by newer" competitors; P.S. the younger Notting Hill sibling is "a bit more upscale" and less crowded.

NORTH SEA ☒ 23 | 13 | 18 | £16

7-8 Leigh St., WC1 (Kings Cross), 020-7387 5892; fax 7388 9770

"Extremely fresh fish 'n' chips at a very fair price pulls them into this old fave", a "small" Bloomsbury seafooder that's "hard to find", but "worth a detour" for "simply prepared" Traditional British dishes, "friendly service" and some "outstanding special beers"; "there's not much decor" to speak of, but "the food more than makes up for it."

Noto ▽ 22 | 9 | 20 | £16

Harrods, ground fl., 87-125 Brompton Rd., SW1 (Knightsbridge), no phone ☒

399 Edgware Rd., NW9 (Colindale), 020-8200 1189; fax 7588 5656

2-3 Bassishaw Highwalk, EC2 (Bank/Moorgate), 020-7256 9433; fax 7588 5656 ☒

www.noto.co.uk

"Can't beat it for the 30-minute lunch" with "colleagues" say those familiar with these "little gems" in Chinatown and near the Guildhall; even if there's "nothing mind-blowingly different or exciting" on the "authentic" Asian menu (which includes "good, fresh sushi" and "superb curry"), it comes "at a reasonable price"; besides, "the majority of customers are Japanese, which can't be a bad thing"; N.B. the Harrods branch is unrated.

Notting Grill 21 | 19 | 15 | £39

123A Clarendon Rd., W11 (Holland Park/Ladbroke Grove), 020-7229 1500; fax 7229 8889; www.awtonline.co.uk

"If you like meat, look no further" than this "offbeat, funky" Notting Hill premises from celebrity chef Antony Worrall Thompson, where the British chophouse menu "combines robust, modern cooking with old-time, 'retro' favourites"; however, dips in the Food and Service scores suggest "a lack of attention" – particularly in staff, who seem "below standard given the cost"; P.S. "the best place is downstairs, if you don't mind the smokers" (who are banned upstairs).

Notting Hill Brasserie 23 | 23 | 22 | £42

92 Kensington Park Rd., W11 (Notting Hill Gate), 020-7229 4481; fax 7221 1246

"Still undiscovered by the trendies" of Notting Hill, this "cosy", "charming townhouse", with "subtle lighting" and "perfectly spaced tables", is "a real find for an outstanding dining experience" of "top-notch" Modern European cooking delivered by "discreet" service; also worth noting is the "nice touch of live jazz in the evenings" in the "wonderful cocktail bar."

Noura ◐ 23 | 19 | 21 | £35

16 Curzon St., W1 (Green Park), 020-7495 1050; fax 7495 1055
22 Lower Regent St., SW1 (Piccadilly Circus), 020-7839 2020; fax 7839 7700
122 Jermyn St., SW1 (Piccadilly Circus), 020-7839 2020; fax 7839 7700
16 Hobart Pl., SW1 (Victoria), 020-7235 9444; fax 7235 9244
www.noura.co.uk

"Divine, wholesome food", "the kindest waiters in town" and "nice, contemporary decor" characterise this "bustling", burgeoning "Lebanese chain"; although "hardly romantic" as venues, they are "child-friendly" and "perfect for a crowd", allowing "you to share the fabulous dishes" and "nice wines."

Novelli at Auberge du Lac ∇ 24 | 23 | 22 | £58

Auberge du Lac, Welwyn, Hertfordshire, 01707 368888; fax 01707 368898; www.brocket-hall.co.uk

"A beacon of hope for a barren dining landscape" attest admirers of this historic Hertfordshire hunting lodge housing heartthrob chef Jean-Christophe Novelli's Classic French cuisine; the digs are "dated, but elegant", and the food, whilst "a little hit-and-miss", invariably "interesting"; all also agree it's a "super place in summer" with "beautiful" lakeside views; N.B. Novelli also mans the stoves at his namesake private club in the City.

Nyonya 20 | 16 | 19 | £21

2A Kensington Park Rd., W11 (Notting Hill Gate), 020-7243 1800; fax 7243 2006; www.nyonya.co.uk

"Watch the crowd pass by through the curved window", overlooking a Notting Hill crossroads, at this casual noodle bar with an "authentic Malaysian (rare in London town)" and Chinese menu of "imaginative dishes and delicate flavours"; the "uncomfortable" communal seating means it's "not a destination" venue, but most appreciate "they are trying pretty hard" at this "great-value" spot.

Oak, The 18 | 19 | 14 | £25

137 Westbourne Park Rd., W2 (Westbourne Park), 020-7221 3355; fax 7467 0600

Near Westbourne Park, this "cosy" "old pub changed into a restaurant" features "fantastic wood-fired pizzas" and other Italian fare at "good prices"; but the "noise level is ear-splitting" – better "learn sign language to converse" and pass the time, as the food "arrives long after ordering."

Occo – | – | – | E

58 Crawford St., W14 (Edgware Road/Marylebone), 020-7724 4991; fax 7724 4500; www.occo.co.uk

North African furnishings lend an authentic touch to this relaxed newcomer on a Marylebone street corner; the airy dining room and conservatory offer modern Moroccan meals, including a wide tapas selection; there are also two bars – an intimate red fabric-lined lounge space and a private members' room with resident DJ.

Odette's 17 | 18 | 16 | £44

130 Regent's Park Rd., NW1 (Chalk Farm), 020-7586 5486; fax 7722 5388

This "bistro-style restaurant on Primrose Hill's magical high street" is a "romantic" spot ("perfect for anniversaries!") with "loads of mirrors" and a "tasty", "solid" Modern Anglo-French menu "that is what it is, without pretensions"; but a fall in the Food and Service scores supports sceptics who claim the place has "gone downhill", so that it seems rather "overpriced."

Odin's ⊠ 20 | 24 | 23 | £44

27 Devonshire St., W1 (Baker St.), 020-7935 7296; fax 7493 8309; www.langansrestaurants.co.uk

It "may not be as chic as it once was", but as it approaches 40, this "clubby and comfortable" Marylebone stalwart still "maintains high standards" of "reliable", "well-prepared" Traditional English and French cuisine, backed by "a fine collection of art" on the walls and "excellent", "discreet" service; it "may be the best restaurant in London to take your mistress to" – or "people one wishes to impress at not too great a cost."

Oliveto 21 | 14 | 18 | £33

49 Elizabeth St., SW1 (Sloane Sq./Victoria), 020-7730 0074; fax 7823 5377

"Popular with locals", this "casual", "cramped" Belgravian gets "very loud" ("no absorbent chairs/carpeting"), but is "a real treasure" for "high standard", "authentic" Sardinian cooking, like "terrific pizza" and "original" pastas; whilst some feel "its popularity has undermined service", most claim they'll "go back often to" this, "one of few trendy, but low-key places to catch up with friends."

Olivo 20 | 12 | 17 | £39

21 Eccleston St., SW1 (Victoria), 020-7730 2505

"A great asset to Victoria", Oliveto's older sibling – in "plain" premises that seem "incongruous" with the "smart crowd" within – provides "relief to jaded palates" with "sometimes interesting, sometimes odd" "Sardinian specialities" in an "enjoyable atmosphere"; in toto, "*tutto perfecto*!"

1 Lombard Street ⊠ 20 | 20 | 19 | £51

1 Lombard St., EC3 (Bank), 020-7929 6611; fax 7929 6622; www.1lombardstreet.com

"Another old-bank-cum-restaurant", this "imposing" venue is "as good as it gets in the Square Mile" for a "power lunch" or "romantic" evening meal, with an "interesting" New French menu served in "comfortable", "stylish" surrounds; despite "eye-popping" prices and sometimes "slothlike" service, few dispute it's "a safe City fallback" for "solid business dining."

1 Lombard Street Brasserie ☒ 19 | 19 | 16 | £43

1 Lombard St., EC3 (Bank), 020-7929 6611; fax 7929 6622; www.1lombardstreet.com

"A City favourite" as somewhere to "go for lunch, and stay for dinner and drinks", the weekday, "more relaxed" sister of 1 Lombard Street is a "light, airy space" ("the large skylight really makes the room") with a "nice buzz" and a "reliable, if not exciting" Modern European menu; it "can be hard to grab a waiter", and regulars recommend you "get a table by the walls as the middle ones [by the bar] are too noisy."

One-O-One 23 | 16 | 20 | £58

Sheraton Park Tower, 101 William St., SW1 (Knightsbridge), 020-7290 7101; fax 7201 7884

"They know fish" declare devotees of the "distinctly different, flavourful" offerings at this "expensive" but well-located New French in the Sheraton Park Tower; despite the regularly changing art exhibition, however, naysayers are nonplussed by the room – "get thee a decorator!" – and would prefer some one-on-one treatment from staff ("service gets spotty when the restaurant is full", though they promise the lunch prix fixe will take only 60 minutes).

Oriel 14 | 15 | 12 | £27

51 Sloane Sq., SW1 (Sloane Sq.), 020-7730 2804; fax 7730 7966

Its "great location" on Sloane Square – "convenient for a bite after shopping" and "watching the world go by" – makes this Gallic-style ("smoky", "crowded") Chelsea cafe a "trusted faithful" for many; but opponents argue the Modern European "staples", served all day, "leave a lot to be desired" and "the service is the rudest outside of Paris" – "unless you're one of the Rangers (Sloane variety)."

ORIGINAL LAHORE KEBAB HOUSE ◐ 27 | 4 | 12 | £15

148-150 Brent St., NW4 (Hendon Central), 020-8203 6904
2-4 Umberston St., E1 (Aldgate East/Whitechapel), 020-7481 9737; fax 7488 1300

"Be prepared to be packed like sardines, both when waiting and eating" some of the "best subcontinental food in London" at these "fabulous" "favourites" near Commercial Road and in Hendon; the Pakistani plates are "cheap", "authentic" and "for the adventurous" ("asbestos palates" recommended), "definitely outweighing the divish decor and service" (though Umberston Street's post-*Survey* expansion may outdate the ratings).

Original Tagine ▽ 22 | 16 | 18 | £25

7A Dorset St., W1 (Baker St.), 020-7935 1545

For "something a bit different", try this "small, simple space" near Baker Street with its "good-value", "authentic" North

African fare – including "better tangines than in Morocco"; sure, the "sweet service" can be "slow", but few complain about this "charming" spot: "let's keep it a secret."

ORRERY 26 | 23 | 24 | £63

55 Marylebone High St., W1 (Baker St./Regent's Park), 020-7616 8000; fax 7616 8080; www.orrery.co.uk

Considered "the jewel in the Conran crown", this "sleek", "airy" Marylebone eatery ("lots of light at lunchtime") "achieves dining bliss" thanks to André Garrett's "exquisite" New French menu, "terrifically paired with an outstanding wine list" and trumped by a "tantalising cheese trolley"; you're served by "stunningly proactive staff", and whilst it all can "seriously dent your wallet", watching "the rather smart-looking clientele offers entertainment that's worth the price of admission."

Orso ◐ 19 | 15 | 18 | £38

27 Wellington St., WC2 (Covent Garden), 020-7240 5269; fax 7497 2148

"Theatre glitterati-watching is a speciality" at this "lively" Covent Garden Italian ("similar to the NYC eatery") where "witty waiters" deliver "unpretentious" Tuscan fare that's "good, but not top-drawer"; some feel the "subterranean decor" – "off-putting on a sunny day, comforting in winter" – "could do with a face-lift", but appreciation is shown for ambience that's "always friendly, without being too familiar."

OSLO COURT ⊠ 25 | 14 | 26 | £42

Charlbert St., Prince Albert Rd., NW8 (St. John's Wood), 020-7722 8795; fax 7586 7695

"Despite being hidden in a block of flats", this "eccentric" St. John's Wood institution is "packed with generations of diners" getting "stuffed to the gills" on "generous portions" of "excellent" Classic French fare, served by staff so "sweet" "you'll want to eat them up"; sure, it's a mid-20th-century "time warp" but to quote the "loyal locals": "long may it reign over us."

Osteria Antica Bologna ▽ 17 | 14 | 15 | £25

23 Northcote Rd., SW11 (Clapham Junction B.R.), 020-7978 4771; fax 7978 4771; www.osteria.co.uk

"Tucked away on busy Northcote Road", this "cosy", wood-panelled trattoria has admirers applauding its "always interesting", if not "overwhelming" Italian cucina; it's a "useful eatery for the neighbourhood."

OSTERIA BASILICO ◐ 24 | 18 | 19 | £31

29 Kensington Park Rd., W11 (Ladbroke Grove/Notting Hill Gate), 020-7727 9957; fax 7229 7980

"Make a reservation or you'll be out of luck" at this "always bustling", "cheerful" Notting Hill trattoria where the "staff and customers pretend there are not famous people all around"; the "incredible", "robust Italian food" – especially "amazing pizzas and pasta" – comes at "reasonable prices", compensating for the almost "too-close-for-comfort" quarters (though that just makes it all the easier to "hang out with Gwyneth and Chris"); P.S. insiders' tip: it's "better upstairs than down in the basement."

Osteria dell'Arancio ▽ 21 | 18 | 18 | £37

383 King's Rd., SW10 (Sloane Sq./South Kensington), 020-7349 8111; fax 7349 8123; www.osteriadellarancio.co.uk

Adorned with "spectacular", wacky art, this "very un-traditional Italian" newcomer, spread over two floors of a Chelsea townhouse, is a "fun place" where the "waiters have a sense of humour" and you can "go with the kids"; the "weekly changing" four-course prix fixe of Marchigiani regional dishes is "good quality", but offers a "very limited" choice, leading some to suggest "à la carte would be nice."

Ottolenghi 24 | 18 | 16 | £27

63 Ledbury Rd., W11 (Notting Hill Gate), 020-7727 1121
287 Upper St., N1 (Angel), 020-7288 1454; fax 7704 1456
www.ottolenghi.co.uk

"Amazingly flavoursome" Middle Eastern–Med fare is on "mouth-watering display, and tastes even better than it looks" at these "interesting ventures" in "modern" and already "crowded" Notting Hill and Islington sites; although some individuals claim that "sharing a big table with others" "can be annoying", the "good vibe" and "funky" all-white setting make up for it.

Oxo Tower 20 | 24 | 18 | £53

Oxo Tower Wharf, Barge House St., SE1 (Blackfriars/Waterloo), 020-7803 3888; fax 7803 3838; www.harveynichols.com

It's the "unsurpassed view" over the Thames "you're paying for, so make sure you get a window table" at this "upscale" dining room atop a South Bank landmark that's "great for a special occasion"; although the vistas "are more memorable than the food", the Asian-influenced Eclectic cooking is "classy" enough; "patchy" staff behaviour has lowered the Service score, "but it's fine for after-theatre" (the National is nearby).

Oxo Tower Brasserie 19 | 24 | 17 | £42

Oxo Tower Wharf, Barge House St., SE1 (Blackfriars/Waterloo), 020-7803 3888; fax 7803 3838; www.harveynichols.com

A "cheaper alternative to Oxo Tower" along the corridor, but with the same "unbeatable view" of the Thames, this "bustling" South Bank brasserie is "not a place for relaxation", attracting a "fun, flirty" crowd with "loud" "live jazz"; the "ever-evolving" Med–Pacific Rim menu is "a safe bet", and even if "hit-and-miss service" lets the side down, the place is "always a winner" with "out-of-town visitors" and a "favourite for marriage proposals."

Ozer Restaurant & Bar ◐ 20 | 18 | 18 | £28

5 Langham Pl., W1 (Oxford Circus), 020-7323 0505; fax 7323 0111; www.sofra.co.uk

"So much nicer than it looks from the outside", this "dark", "nicely decorated" Turk near Regent Street (from the "same owners as Sofra") is a "great place to pop in for a drink, nibble or full meal" from a "not-too-pricey" modern Ottoman menu where "even the simplest of dishes enjoy a touch of sophistication"; but the enthusiasm of the "crowd at the bar/lounge" means the "red-riddled room roars" at "airport runway levels" some nights.

Pacific Oriental ☒ 16 | 16 | 17 | £34

1 Bishopsgate, EC2 (Bank), 020-7621 9988; fax 7929 7227; www.orientalrestaurantgroup.co.uk

The six-meter-high waterfall creates "soothing" ambience at this split-level "noodle bar–cum-microbrewery" that's "worth a try" for "decent Pan-Asian food" (which "has improved vastly in the last year") or a taste of "their own beer" "in the busy downstairs bar"; but some say "there are better places in the City" – "no real criticism, it just doesn't quite hit the spot."

Painted Heron, The 24 | 19 | 19 | £41

112 Cheyne Walk, SW10 (Sloane Sq.), 020-7351 5232; fax 7351 5213 ☒

205-209 Kennington Ln., SE11 (Kennington), 020-7793 8313; fax 7793 8323

www.thepaintedheron.com

Reviewers paint a pretty rosy picture of the "high-class, inventive Indian" cooking offered by this "secret" eatery on the Embankment and its younger "off-the-beaten-track" sibling that's "such a welcome addition" to Kennington; the "food's much better than the service and decor", but the former is "polite and efficient", and "in warmer times, you can sit outside."

Palmerston, The – | – | – | M

91 Lordship Ln., SE22 (East Dulwich B.R.), 020-8693 1629; fax 8693 9662; www.thepalmerston.co.uk

A "pleasant addition to the area" around East Dulwich, this year-old gastro-pub co-owned by chef Jamie Younger (ex Bibendum) attracts locals with its "warm atmosphere and sophisticated vibe"; the Modern British menu contains some "quite exquisite" dishes, along with a "wine list that caters to all palates"; the wood-panelled walls and floor lend a warm feel.

Parsee ☒ ▽ 19 | 6 | 19 | £29

34 Highgate Hill, N19 (Archway), 020-7272 9091; fax 7687 1139; www.theparsee.co.uk

This Highgate Villager from chef Cyrus Todiwala (of Café Spice Namasté fame) offers "a totally new perspective on

Indian food" via an "authentic" Parsee menu that blends Persian and Gujarat aspects, producing "original" flavours – "even the chutney lived in the memory"; a few don't see "what all the fuss is about", but most say it's "a must-try" – though it's certainly a "shame about the takeaway decor."

Pasha ◐ 20 | 17 | 17 | £28

301 Upper St., N1 (Angel/Highbury & Islington), 020-7226 1454; fax 7226 1617

"A more polished, sophisticated version of the Turkish restaurants in the vicinity", this family-run Islington eatery is "well known" for "well-presented", "suave cooking" that "comes quickly" and "at a fair price"; "you come away feeling you are friends with the staff" and it's also "a great place after a play at the Almeida."

Pasha ◐ 18 | 24 | 19 | £39

1 Gloucester Rd., SW7 (Gloucester Rd.), 020-7589 7969; fax 7581 9996; www.pasha-restaurant.co.uk

"Cosy little booths" "set the mood for romance" at this "intimate", "exotic" Moroccan-themed South Kensington venue (owned by The Ivy's parent company); negative nabobs note nothing else quite "lives up to the decor", but if the "North African food is not the best in London, it's very tasty all the same" and comes in "portions huge" enough to please any pasha.

Passione ⊠ 24 | 14 | 21 | £44

10 Charlotte St., W1 (Goodge St.), 020-7636 2833; fax 7636 2889; www.passione.co.uk

It may reside in "cramped quarters", but the modest "surroundings belie" the "careful preparations" of chef Gennaro Contaldo, whose "outstanding" cucina – focusing on fungi and other "foods in season" – is so "genuine" it reminds the well-travelled of "local Italian restaurants, albeit at three times the price"; "service is attentive and respectful", so no surprise the passione hail this as "one of the gems of Charlotte Street."

PATARA 25 | 20 | 22 | £37

3-7 Maddox St., W1 (Oxford Circus), 020-7499 6008; fax 7499 6007
15 Greek St., W1 (Leicester Sq./Tottenham Court Rd.), 020-7437 1071; fax 7437 1089
181 Fulham Rd., SW3 (South Kensington), 020-7351 5692; fax 7351 5692
9 Beauchamp Pl., SW3 (Knightsbridge/South Kensington), 020-7581 8820; fax 7581 2155
www.patarathailand.com

"Taste buds are continually tantalised" by the "innovative", "exotic" eats at these Southeast Asians where "each course is like eating the cover shot of *Gourmet* magazine"; the opening of the new Greek Street flagship has boosted the Decor score, and ratings have also risen for the "beautiful, accommodating staff"; the less-convinced carp there's "not much bang-for-the-kok" here, but to most this quartet is simply "Thai-rific."

Paternoster Chop House ⊠ ▽ 18 | 17 | 18 | £41

Warwick Ct., Paternoster Sq., EC4 (St. Paul's), 020-7029 9400; fax 7029 9409; www.conran.com

"Far less fancy than you might think and all the better for it", this chophouse near St. Paul's Cathedral offers gutsy, "good old-fashioned English" "cuts of meat and seafood"; nearly all offer a prayer of thanks for a "newcomer" in "a part of town lacking dining options"; but whilst devotees devour the menu's twists on "the 'beast of the day' and other animals that have grown up on wild heather", nonbelievers are negative about the "erratic" eats and service, calling the experience "expensive for what it is."

Patisserie Valerie 20 | 13 | 14 | £16

162 Piccadilly, W1 (Green Park), 020-7491 1717
27 Kensington Church St., W8 (High St. Kensington), 020-7937 9574; fax 7937 9574
105 Marylebone High St., W1 (Baker St./Bond St.), 020-7935 6240; fax 7935 6543
44 Old Compton St., W1 (Leicester Sq.), 020-7437 3466; fax 7734 6133
8 Russell St., WC2 (Covent Garden), 020-7240 0064; fax 7240 0064
81 Duke of York Sq., King's Rd., SW3 (Sloane Sq.), 020-7730 7094; fax 7730 7094
215 Brompton Rd., SW3 (Knightsbridge), 020-7823 9971; fax 7589 4993
17 Motcomb St., SW1 (Knightsbridge), 020-7245 6161; fax 7245 6161
www.patisserie-valerie.co.uk

It's so "authentic, you can almost hear the accordions" at this all-day "classic French Bistro" chain that's "always a good standby" for "meeting, greeting and people-watching", whether it be with "a date, children or your grandmother"; the "hearty", "reliable" menu extends to lots of "sweet gooey things" ("fun, fab and fattening!"), but some cynics warn "service can be patchy" at "overcrowded times"; P.S. the original Soho "institution" celebrates its 80th *anniversaire* this year.

Patterson's ⊠ 23 | 16 | 21 | £47

4 Mill St., W1 (Oxford Circus), 020-7499 1308; fax 7491 2122; www.pattersonsrestaurant.com

"Not many people know about" this understated New French "professionally" run by an eponymous "father-and-son team", but an "interesting", "well-executed" menu, coupled with "polite, personable" staff, puts the place "on the map" in Mayfair; still, some find it "rather staid", so they're "not in a rush to go back."

Pearl 23 | 25 | 23 | £57

Renaissance Chancery Court Hotel, 252 High Holborn, WC1 (Holborn), 020-7829 7000; fax 7829 9889; www.pearl-restaurant.com

"Pleasing" pearly decor provides a "spectacular" shell for chef Jun Tanaka's "unqualifiedly superb", "beautifully presented" New French cuisine at this newcomer in a "fine" Holborn hotel; if "perhaps a bit over-attentive at times", the "service is friendly"; and "although a touch too formal" for every day, it's "perfect for client dinners" and "special occasions" – and, whilst "pricey", "not that expensive for such an amazing level."

Pellicano 23 | 17 | 21 | £38

19-21 Elystan St., SW3 (South Kensington), 020-7589 3718; fax 7584 1789

"The residents keep their secrets well", but word's getting out about this "quiet local" "in the heart of Chelsea" that's just about "as good as a neighbourhood Italian gets", with cucina that reaches "a consistently high standard" and "attentive staff" who are "friendly with children"; there's also a quite "good-value lunch menu" whisper the "well-established clientele."

Pengelley's – | – | – | VE

164 Sloane St., SW1 (Knightsbridge), 020-7750 5000; fax 7750 5001; www.pengelleys.com

Equipped with backing from Gordon Ramsay's restaurant group, toque Ian Pengelley (ex e&o) has taken over two floors of the former Monte's site in Knightsbridge; the result is this classy, oak-panelled dining room flooded with natural light, serving high-end Pan-Asian specialties reflecting the chef's culinary training in China, Thailand and Singapore; upstairs is a separate bar with dance floor and a 1 AM license.

PEPPER TREE 24 | 15 | 19 | £15

19 Clapham Common Southside, SW4 (Clapham Common), 020-7622 1758; fax 7720 7531; www.thepeppertree.co.uk

With "benches and [long wood] tables à la school canteen", the "communal seating" creates a "convivial atmosphere" at this "cheerful", "cosy" corner in Clapham Common, celebrated for "cheap curries" and other "consistently excellent" Thai "classics"; whilst it's usually "quick and easy", there's no reserving – so "arrive after 8 PM and you will have to stand in a queue – possibly outside!"

Pescatori ⊠ 19 | 15 | 18 | £38

11 Dover St., W1 (Green Park), 020-7493 2652; fax 7499 3180
57 Charlotte St., W1 (Goodge St.), 020-7580 3289; fax 7580 0539
www.pescatori.co.uk

They may "look like nothing fancy", but these "pleasant" trattorias in Mayfair and Fitzrovia offer a "great front-of-house welcome" and a "delicately cooked" Med menu that's "mainly fish, but they cope with meat eaters just as well"; service is generally "observant without being imposing", but wallet-watchers warn "prices are going up."

Petersham, The ▽ 21 | 24 | 23 | £47

The Petersham Hotel, Nightingale Ln. (Richmond), 020-8940 7471; fax 8939 1002; www.petershamhotel.co.uk

In a "stunning location on the Thames" at Richmond, this "lovely dining room" features "wonderful" servers and a "consistently good", French-influenced Modern British menu to "complement the view"; some sigh the scene's "a bit stiff" (and so are the prices), but relax – it's perfectly positioned "for a good walk afterwards"; P.S. there's a vaulted "wine cellar you can dine in" for private parties.

PÉTRUS ☒ 27 | 25 | 26 | £83

Berkeley Hotel, Wilton Pl., SW1 (Hyde Park Corner), 020-7235 1200; www.petrus-restaurant.com

"They say fine wines do not travel well – not so this Pétrus" rave reviewers who find this relocated New French's "fancier premises" in Belgravia "a big improvement"; true, "a certain solemnity has set in", but the combo of chef/co-owner Marcus Wareing's "splendid, innovative" cuisine, "first-class service" ("felt like a queen for the night") and David Collins' claret-coloured, "clubby" decor make it "close to perfection" – even if the "over-the-top trimmings" translate to "over-the-top prices."

Phoenix Palace ◐ 23 | 14 | 16 | £25

3-5 Glentworth St., NW1 (Baker St.), 020-7486 3515

"One of the best places for authentic food without having to go to Chinatown", this "expansive" Marylebone venue works well "if you know what you're after" on the Chinese menu that's "far above average" (and "far better than the functional premises would suggest"); foes are "not so sure about the service" – which ranges from "pushy" to "slow."

PIED À TERRE ☒ 27 | – | 24 | £64

34 Charlotte St., W1 (Goodge St.), 020-7242 7426

Closed by a "devastating fire" in late 2004, this "fantastic" Fitzrovian is slated for a September rebirth – "hopefully with a warmer, more cosy atmosphere" plead patrons tired of the old "cold decor"; happily, all else is near-"flawless", and unchanged – from chef Shane Osborn's "sumptuous", "masterful" New French fare to the "impeccable"-"but-unintimidating" service under manager David Moore; "expensive", yes, but worth it to "treat yourself."

Pig's Ear ▽ 17 | 17 | 14 | £26

35 Old Church St., SW3 (Sloane Sq.), 020-7352 2908; fax 7352 9321; www.thepigsear.co.uk

"Perfect for a rainy Sunday", this new, "nice and cosy" gastro-pub charms Chelsea with its "good ales", "eclectic" and "tasty" New French fare (including the eponymous pig's ears – which are "not as bad as they sound") and "knowledgeable staff"; if the downstairs bar is "always too busy", the "upstairs dining room provides a quiet oasis."

Ping Pong ⊠ – | – | – | M

44-45 Marlborough St., W1 (Oxford Circus), 020-7851 6969; www.pingpongdimsum.com

The brainchild of a former Nobu manager, this earth-toned, spacious Soho debutante specialises in dim sum, with an extensive selection of inexpensive victuals complemented by Chinese noodle and rice dishes (with several lunch choices for less than a tenner) and an innovative cocktail list; counter areas where you can watch the chefs at work and round communal tables are already making it a popular party spot; N.B. no reservations.

PIZZA EXPRESS 16 | 14 | 15 | £17

137 Notting Hill Gate, W11 (Notting Hill Gate), 020-7229 6000 ◐
29 Wardour St., W10 (Leicester Sq./Piccadilly Circus), 020-7437 7215; fax 7494 2582 ◐
35 Earl's Court Rd., W8 (Earl's Ct.), 020-7937 0761 ◐
9-12 Bow St., WC2 (Covent Garden), 020-7240 3443; fax 7497 0131 ◐
46-54 Battersea Bridge Rd., SW11 (Earl's Ct./Sloane Sq.), 020-7924 2774
363 Fulham Rd., SW10 (Fulham Broadway/South Kensington), 020-7352 5300 ◐
895-896 Fulham Rd., SW6 (Parsons Green), 020-7731 3117; fax 7371 7884 ◐
The Pheasantry, 152-154 King's Rd., SW3 (Sloane Sq.), 020-7351 5031; fax 7349 9844 ◐
7 Beauchamp Pl., SW3 (Knightsbridge), 020-7589 2355; fax 7589 5159 ◐
125 Alban Gate, London Wall, EC2 (Moorgate/St. Paul's), 020-7600 8880; fax 7600 8128
www.pizzaexpress.com
Additional locations throughout London

"Lovely new additions to the old faithful menu" give "even more reason to go" to these "ubiquitous" pizzerias around town, offering "no-frills, good-quality" Italian eats in a "pleasant" environment with sweetly "casual" service; sure, "you can get better elsewhere", but for a "reliable pizza fix" that's "cheap to boot", "look no further."

Pizza Metro 20 | 10 | 19 | £22

64 Battersea Rise, SW11 (Clapham Common/ Clapham Junction B.R.), 020-7228 3812; fax 7738 0987; www.pizzametropizza.com

For over a decade, this "noisy" "little piece of Naples in the heart of Battersea" has dolled out the namesake dish, plus pastas, from an undemanding Italian menu; whilst it's still great to "go in a group and get a pizza that is a metre in length", a Food score fall supports sighs that it's "a shadow of its former self" since the "original owner who made it famous sold" out a couple of years ago.

Pizza on the Park ◐ 16 | 13 | 14 | £24

11 Knightsbridge, SW1 (Hyde Park Corner), 020-7235 5273; fax 7235 6853; www.pizzaonthepark.co.uk

"Decent pizza and great jazz" (in the downstairs Music Room), plus "nice views across Knightsbridge to Hyde Park", make this "cavernous" Italian a source for a "satisfying, straightforward" evening; critics "can't see why you would make it a special trip" to this "most upscale [member] of the Pizza Express chain", since the higher "prices are based on location rather than quality", but for most the "music and marinara" formula is "fun" enough.

Pizza Pomodoro ◐ 15 | 13 | 15 | £22

51 Beauchamp Pl., SW3 (Knightsbridge), 020-7589 1278; fax 7247 4001

7-8 Bishopsgate Churchyard, EC2 (Liverpool St.), 020-7920 9207; fax 7920 9206 Ⓢ

www.pomodoro.co.uk

"By the end of the evening, all the tables join in singing and dancing" at this "funky" duo in Knightsbridge ("cramped", "with intimate caves") and the City ("down a quaint street"); whilst the "basic Italian", pizza-orientated menu "doesn't exactly tick the boxes for great food or service", the "live music acts each night [offer] both atmosphere and utter cheesiness in spades."

PJ's Bar & Grill ◐ 14 | 15 | 15 | £29

52 Fulham Rd., SW3 (South Kensington), 020-7581 0025; fax 7584 0820

30 Wellington St., WC2 (Covent Garden), 020-7240 7529; fax 7836 3426; www.pjsgrill.net

A "cracking atmosphere" that's "popular among the Chelsea Eurotrash" characterises this casual American-style brasserie whose "respectable", "large selection" of dishes is "pretty basic", but clocks in "at a pretty basic price" too; sliding Food and Decor scores support suggestions it's "on a declining streak", but it remains "useful" for weekend brunch and/or shopping breaks, whilst the Covent Garden affiliate is "perfect for something quick before the theatre."

Planet Hollywood ◐ 11 | 16 | 13 | £23

13 Coventry St., W1 (Leicester Sq./Piccadilly Circus), 020-7437 7639; fax 7734 0835; www.planethollywood.com

It's "always fun to see the memorabilia" of "movie props" and movie idols at this "loud" Piccadilly outpost of the planet-wide chain; but it's "all about the decor, as the food is mediocre at best", and whilst it's "worth hitting once" with "starstruck" kids, cynics suggest the "sign at the door should read: 'not for adults.'"

Plateau ☒ 19 | 21 | 18 | £46

Canada Pl., 4th fl., 8 Canada Sq., E14 (Canary Wharf), 020-7715 7100; www.conran.com

"Amidst the skyscrapers" of Canary Wharf – "an area that desperately needs a good restaurant" – the Conran Group's "welcome" glass-fronted rooftop eatery is split in two: the fine-dining section has a "perfectly decent", if "high-priced", New French menu with "an extensive wine list and knowledgeable sommelier", whilst the "noisy grill" and bar offers "less costly" Brasserie-style fare and a "hip atmosphere with enough reserve for a business dinner."

Poissonnerie de l'Avenue ● ☒ 22 | 20 | 21 | £49

82 Sloane Ave., SW3 (South Kensington), 020-7589 2457; fax 7581 3360; www.poissonnerie.co.uk

Likened to a "smooth sailing yacht", this "comfortable ol' friend" "has hardly changed for decades" and offers "exactly what one expects from a classy Chelsea" site: servers whose "golden warmth invites all to relax and enjoy" "Classic French fish that's fresh and not mucked about with"; if the scene's a bit "stodgy", that's apparently "what the well-heeled" "patrons want."

Pomegranates ● ☒ ▽ 17 | 9 | 13 | £54

94 Grosvenor Rd., SW1 (Pimlico), 020-7828 6560; fax 7828 2037

"Ultimate host" Patrick Gwynne Jones "prides himself" on the "truly Eclectic", mostly made-on-the-premises cuisine (from gravlax to brandy ice cream) they've been serving since the '70s at this Pimlico basement – "an amusing setting, if lacking in charm" fans find; but pessimists protest this "pricey" pomegranate has plenty of pips, from the "ever more decadent" decor to "waiters who don't know what they're doing."

Pomino ● – | – | – | M

35 Bellevue Rd., SW17 (Balham/Wandsworth Common B.R.), 020-8672 5888; fax 8672 8856; www.pomino.co.uk

Named after a hillside town in central Italy, this "vast' "new kid on the block" overlooking Wandsworth Common evokes a Tuscan eatery, with the "kitchen spilling out" into the tile-and-stone surrounds; the "rustic food" is "all very tasty" but the "service needs to improve, fast."

Pomodorino ☒ – | – | – | M

4/12 Lower Regent St., SW1 (Piccadilly Circus), 020-7321 2100; www.pomodorino.co.uk

Part of a seven-strong Rome-based chain, this stone-floored, low-ceilinged Piccadilly Circus yearling serves "*delicioso*", if "unimaginative" Southern Italian pastas and pizzas from a wood-fired oven, alongside a 450-label wine list; but whilst the "layout resembles a pizzeria, don't mistake it for one – or the bill will surprise you."

Poons 17 | 12 | 15 | £28

Whiteley's, 151 Queensway, W2 (Bayswater/Queensway), 020-7792 2884; fax 8458 0968
4 Leicester St., WC2 (Leicester Sq.), 020-7437 1528; fax 7437 2903 ◐
Royal National Hotel, 50 Woburn Pl., WC1 (Euston/Russell Sq.), 020-7580 1188; fax 8458 0968 ◐

"Downmarket decor and rushed service are more than compensated for by tasty" "classics" at this Cantonese chain converts claim; but critics cavil the "cost has gone up" – "bring your ivory chopsticks" – whilst the cuisine tastes "consistently bland" ("Chinese for people who don't really like Chinese food").

Porters ◐ 18 | 15 | 18 | £23

17 Henrietta St., WC2 (Covent Garden), 020-7836 6466; fax 7379 4296; www.porters.uk.com

For over 25 years, Lord Bradford's "pub getaway" in the heart of Covent Garden has been "a standby" for "generous portions" of "old-fashioned" Traditional British "comfort food" ("oooh, those pies!") "served with an unexpected smile"; true, it's "undeniably touristy" and "feels sort of chain-ish" (though it isn't), but it's "just the thing" "for families", "quick, pre-theatre dining" or somewhere to "take your out-of-town mates."

Portrait ▽ 16 | 23 | 16 | £30

The National Portrait Gallery, 3rd fl., 2 St. Martin's Pl., WC2 (Charing Cross/Leicester Sq.), 020-7312 2490; fax 7925 0244; www.searcys.co.uk

The "understated elegance" of its location "looking out over the rooftops of London" garners "top marks" for the National Portrait Gallery's Modern British dining room; the fare from Searcy's caterers is "entirely satisfactory", if "not much else" – "but with that view, they could serve an old Wellington boot and it wouldn't matter."

Potemkin ☒ ▽ 18 | 12 | 15 | £28

144 Clerkenwell Rd., EC1 (Farringdon), 020-7278 6661; fax 7278 5551; www.potemkin.co.uk

"Much better than you'd expect from the rather industrial feel to the building", this Clerkenwell corner named after Catherine the Great's renowned lover offers an "interesting" array of "real Russian" "staples uncommon in London", presented by "nonintrusive service"; there's also an "impressive selection of vodkas" that is "impossible to choose among."

Prince Bonaparte ▽ 17 | 16 | 14 | £18

80 Chepstow Rd., W2 (Bayswater/Notting Hill Gate), 020-7313 9491; fax 7792 0911

"Couches, easy chairs" and "a roaring fire" help make this "noisy" Notting Hill gastro-pub "a great place to hang out with friends" and "a few pints"; the "decent" Modern British grub will do "while you booze", but isn't "suitable for a 'proper' dinner"; N.B. no reservations.

Princess Garden ◐ 22 | 20 | 23 | £44

8-10 N. Audley St., W1 (Bond St.), 020-7493 3223; fax 7629 3130; www.princessgardenofmayfair.com

Adorned with "unique" Asian art, this "stylish" venue caters to a "high-end" clientele with "high-class Chinese food" served by highly "courteous" staff; it's on the "expensive" side, yes, but what do you expect in "posh" Mayfair? P.S. "try the private room for a party."

Prism ☒ 19 | 20 | 19 | £46

147 Leadenhall St., EC3 (Bank/Monument), 020-7256 3888; fax 7256 3883; www.harveynichols.com

"Serves its purpose as a business lunch" site say City suits of this Harvey Nichols–owned "converted bank", with "pricey" – some snap "overpriced" – "but very good" Modern British cooking, "tables far enough apart so [diners] are not squished" and "great buzz"; it's a shame the "soaring roof" makes "the room too loud" at times, and that the "professional" service slackens in the evenings when the space becomes a loungey bar.

Providores, The/Tapa Room 22 | 16 | 18 | £39

109 Marylebone High St., W1 (Baker St./Bond St.), 020-7935 6175; fax 7935 6877; www.theprovidores.co.uk

"Bring someone adventurous" to this Marylebone marvel, consisting of the "sparse", "all-white" upstairs Providores, whose "exciting", "enticing" Eclectic fare uses "ingredients you've never heard of mixed with other ingredients you've never heard of", and the ground-floor Tapa Room that's "cramped" but has a "great vibe" from "a cool crowd" and "lots of little dishes for sharing"; it's "pretty pricey" and "service depends on who you get", but some "ambrosial Kiwi wines" will help you mellow out.

Pug ▽ 18 | 18 | 16 | £30

66-68 Chiswick High Rd., W4 (Stamford Brook/Turnham Green), 020-8987 9988; fax 8987 9911

"Tucked at the quieter end of the Chiswick High Road", this "trendy bar" ("like having dinner in a pub") offers a "surprisingly good" Modern British menu, full of "innovative twists on classic dishes", alongside an "interesting wine list"; P.S. "in summer, make a reservation to snag one of their outdoor tables."

Quadrato 23 | 22 | 23 | £47

Four Seasons Hotel Canary Wharf, 46 Westferry Circus, E14 (Canary Wharf), 020-7510 1999; fax 7510 1998; www.fourseasons.com

There's "little to complain about" this "fine" Canary Wharf establishment, characterised by "great, hearty Northern

Italian cuisine, "modern, fabbo decor" and "Four Seasons–quality service"; given its popularity "for casual business meetings", the ambience can seem "slightly soulless"; so try "the outside areas – perfect for summer days."

Quaglino's ◐ 18 | 20 | 17 | £49

16 Bury St., SW1 (Green Park), 020-7930 6767; fax 7839 2866; www.quaglinos.co.uk

"For a trendy restaurant, it's survived a long time" (13 years) say surveyors of this "cavernous" St. James's basement; since the French Brasserie "dependables" are at best "decent" and the staff "is pretentious for no good reason", "the draw is the decor" and the "fantastic party ambience" – "from the movie-star staircase to the cool jazz strains"; whether this sort of "noisy", "splashy" "theme-park" scene is "still a kick" or "losing its caché" is your call.

Quality Chop House ◐ 20 | 17 | 17 | £34

92-94 Farringdon Rd., EC1 (Farringdon), 020-7837 5093; fax 7833 8748

"You feel thrown back into the 19th century" at this listed Victorian building, which offers its "old-school clientele" "reassuringly comforting" (if "not challenging") Traditional British cuisine; some "don't get it" – especially the "wildly uncomfortable", "narrow church pew seating that makes for swift dining" – but an overall ratings rise reinforces those who find this Farringdon "favourite" "worth going to."

Quilon ⊠ 24 | 22 | 21 | £41

Crowne Plaza London St. James, 41 Buckingham Gate, SW1 (St. James's Park/Victoria), 020-7821 1899; fax 7828 5802; www.thequilonrestaurant.com

"Never a disappointment" proclaim fans of this "quiet", "dressy" Bombay Brasserie brother near Buckingham Palace, where an "innovative", "distinct" menu of "Southern Indian delights" is "correctly spiced" and comes in "small" portions that "leave you feeling not stuffed"; service is "attentive but not suffocating."

Quirinale ⊠ 24 | 20 | 23 | £44

1 Great Peter St., SW1 (Westminster), 020-7222 7080; fax 7233 3080

"A slick, dependable modern Italian in a sea of Westminster mediocrity", this "intimate" eatery (named for Rome's presidential palace) "caters to politicos" with "impeccably attentive service" and "simple, but amazing food" at "reasonable prices given the quality"; regulars appreciate the fact "owner Nadine Gourgey is always on hand to chat."

Quod ◐⊠ 13 | 14 | 14 | £28

57 Haymarket, SW1 (Piccadilly Circus), 020-7925 1234; fax 7839 4545; www.quod.co.uk

"Big, friendly and with great art adorning the walls", this "contemporary" St James's "standby" offers "reliable", if "unspectacular", Anglo-Italian fare that's "ok for groups", especially "after work"; but unfortunately the "noise kills" it "for an intimate dinner", and the "hurried service is not terribly efficient."

Quo Vadis ☒ 20 | 21 | 18 | £46

26-29 Dean St., W1 (Leicester Sq./Tottenham Court Rd.), 020-7437 9585; fax 7736 7593; www.whitestarline.org.uk

With "more than a little history" to its "chic" Soho location ("Karl Marx laboured on *Das Kapital* upstairs"), Marco Pierre White's "comfortably quiet" "remodelling of an old favourite" draws a "well-heeled clientele" with "elegantly presented", "interesting" Italian cooking, "polished staff" and "modern art" on display; but antagonists ask "where are we going" with this "tired", "pompous" place – at this point, "you're paying for the memories."

RACINE 23 | 19 | 22 | £42

239 Brompton Rd., SW3 (South Kensington), 020-7584 4477; fax 7584 4900

"Served with grace and good humour", the "virtuoso French Bistro food" and "keenly priced, judiciously chosen wine list" offer "a taste of Parisian atmosphere" at this "civilised" yet "casual" Knightsbridge locale; some warn that "prices seem to be edging up", but most agree this "buzzy" "gem" manages to satisfy "a demanding clientele."

Rainforest Cafe 11 | 20 | 13 | £23

20-24 Shaftesbury Ave., W1 (Piccadilly Circus), 020-7434 3111; fax 7434 3222; www.rainforestcafe.com

Full of "scary" "screeching monkeys, cockatoos" and "plastic jungle plants", this "cheesy, friendly" Piccadilly eatery is more "like a ride at Disneyland" than a restaurant; but its "average, basic" menu of Yankee "staples", though "not cheap", works "for the young, or young at heart"; so let killjoys cry "the worst of America has crossed the pond" – haven't you always wanted to "share a cocktail with a life-sized baboon"?

Randall & Aubin 21 | 15 | 17 | £33

14-16 Brewer St., W1 (Piccadilly Circus), 020-7287 4447; fax 7287 4488

329-331 Fulham Rd., SW10 (Fulham Broadway/South Kensington), 020-7823 3515; fax 7823 3991 ◐

"Big queues" build up for this Soho citizen, an old converted butcher's shop "serving up an array of seafood" that's "simply prepared, very fresh" and "well priced"; but since this "noisy" "no-frills establishment saves effort on decor", with "a small space and hard stools that are not very comfortable", "avoid unless you're a fan of our water-loving friends"; the menu at the younger Chelsea sibling extends to Modern British brasserie-style "treats", making it a "top place to kick a night off."

Ransome's Dock 20 | 18 | 20 | £39

35-37 Park Gate Rd., SW11 (Sloane Sq./ South Kensington), 020-7223 1611; fax 7924 2614; www.ransomesdock.co.uk

Chef-owner "Martin Lam's ingredients are impeccable", and he uses them well in his "simple", but "well-executed" Modern British–Eclectic cuisine, backed by an "interesting and competitive wine list" and "attractively presented" by "fine service"; his dockside "setting on the Thames" at Battersea is "special", if somewhat "out-of-the-way."

Raoul's 20 | 15 | 14 | £22

13 Clifton Rd., W9 (Warwick Ave.), 020-7289 7313; fax 7266 4752

"A home away from home" for loyalists, this "small cafe" (with a "great deli" across the road) in Maida Vale is something of "a local institution" for a "perfect weekend brunch", with an "appetising, affordable" Med menu; but beware, it "can be hard to get a table" as they only take reservations at dinner, and service can be "the slowest in London"; N.B. in late summer, a sibling was set to open at 105-107 Talbot Road, W11.

Rasa 24 | 15 | 19 | £29

6 Dering St., W1 (Bond St./Oxford Circus), 020-7629 1346; fax 7637 0224 ☒

5 Charlotte St., W1 (Tottenham Court Rd.), 020-7637 0222; fax 7637 0224

55 Stoke Newington Church St., N16 (Stoke Newington B.R.), 020-7249 0344; fax 7637 0224

56 Stoke Newington Church St., N16 (Stoke Newington B.R.), 020-7249 1340; fax 7637 0224

www.rasarestaurants.com

There's "always a queue" at this "cosy", "kitschy" quartet, since the "scrumptious", "ambrosial" victuals offer an "excellent introduction in Keralan cooking" (aka Southern India); the signature veggie dishes leave even "the most devoted carnivore admitting vegetables are a beautiful thing"; P.S. "you may spend less" at one branch than another, "but that's real estate for you."

RASOI VINEET BHATIA ☒ 27 | 23 | 26 | £64

10 Lincoln St., SW3 (Sloane Sq.), 020-7225 1881; fax 7581 0220; www.vineetbhatia.com

With "transcendental", "innovative cuisine designed to challenge and delight", Vineet Bhatia's "cosy" Chelsea eatery offers a "sophisticated" "combo of modern elegance and fun foodie surprises"; a handful question whether "the service is over-attentive to a fault" ("constantly asking something"), but few deny this "stand-out" Indian from a revered chef "offers a special treat – even down to the remarkably delicious pappadams"; P.S. "the tasting menu is pricey, but worth every pence."

Ravi Shankar — | — | — | I

133-135 Drummond St., NW1 (Euston), 020-7388 6458; fax 7388 2494

In "a side street near Euston Station", this basic-looking spot has been "consistent for many years" as a "cheap, cheerful" place to "go when you get the craving" for "wonderful vegetarian Indian" food; "warm service makes you feel like a regular even on your first visit."

Real Greek, The ⊠ 20 | 17 | 15 | £33

15 Hoxton Mkt., N1 (Old St.), 020-7739 8212; fax 7739 4910
140-142 St. John St., EC1 (Farringdon), 020-7253 7234; fax 7253 7235
www.therealgreek.co.uk

"A great place to go on a winter's night for a quick fix of sunshine and happy days", this "lively" Hoxton hangout (with an adjacent mezze/wine bar named Mezedopolio) "takes Greek food to a new level", with an "imaginative", "innovative" menu and "interesting" Hellenic wines; its younger Clerkenwell cousin offers a "convivial canteen/bar-style [experience] where you rub shoulders with your fellow diners."

Red Fort 23 | 21 | 20 | £38

77 Dean St., W1 (Oxford Circus/Tottenham Court Rd.), 020-7437 2525; fax 7434 0721; www.redfort.co.uk

"If you are up for a posh dinner and feel like a great curry, look no further" than this "smart", "funky" Indian whose Soho site is "perfect for post-curry clubbing" and "theatregoers"; the "creative", "hearty" cuisine suits "all palates from smashingly savoury to fiery and fulsome"; a few fret it's "trying to be too fancy" (at least the prices are), but fans with more fort-titude feel that it "somehow all seems to work."

Redmonds ▽ 23 | 15 | 18 | £42

170 Upper Richmond Rd. W., SW14 (Mortlake B.R.), 020-8878 1922; fax 8878 1133; www.redmonds.org.uk

"Places like this are the reason people can't be bothered to go into town" opine the locals "lucky to live nearby" chef-owner Redmond Haywood's East Sheen "oasis"; the "imaginative", "tantalising" Modern British cooking comes "with a twist" and the "attentive service" "with a smile" (it's overseen by Redmond's wife, Pippa).

RED PEPPER 21 | 11 | 16 | £25

8 Formosa St., W9 (Warwick Ave.), 020-7266 2708; fax 7266 5522

Though "cramped" and "crowded" ("once you sit, you cannot move"), this "thriving" Maida Vale "neighbourhood Italian" packs 'em in for pastas and pizzas that are "brilliant for the price"; the "couldn't-care-less waiters" "take the shine off it" somewhat, but still the "homemade" eats are "not to be missed."

Refettorio ☒ 22 | 18 | 17 | £42

Crowne Plaza, 19 New Bridge St., EC4 (Blackfriars), 020-7438 8052; www.london-city.crowneplaza.com

"An amazing selection of ham, cheese and salami" on display greets guests at this Blackfriars Italian, "well hidden in the Crowne Plaza hotel"; constructed by consultant chef (and "genius") Giorgio Locatelli, its varied menu of "hearty, yet light regional" dishes brightens up the somewhat "clinical setting" that, with its "enormous banquettes" and communal table, seems especially "good for large groups."

Reubens 14 | 9 | 10 | £24

79 Baker St., W1 (Baker St.), 020-7486 0035; fax 7486 7079; www.reubensrestaurant.com

"Jewish carnivores" kvell at this "Kosher delicatessen" with downstairs dining room in Marylebone; but the less devout declare the food's "pricey considering the quality" – and they don't even "do a Reuben sandwich" yet; P.S. to add insult to injury, "the service is a little rude unless you're a local (then it's like talking to your mum")."

RHODES TWENTY FOUR ☒ 24 | 21 | 22 | £53

Tower 42, 24th fl., 25 Old Broad St., EC2 (Bank St./Liverpool St.), 020-7877 7703; fax 7877 7788; www.rhodes24.co.uk

"Getting through the security check on the ground floor is a drag", but once up on the 24th floor of the City's tallest skyscraper, "fantastic views across London" provide a backdrop for "master" chef Gary Rhodes' "Traditional British cuisine with a Modern touch", a "wonderful combination of creativity in idea and excellence in execution"; service is quite "helpful", and if the "decor resembles an airline lounge, it's definitely first class"; P.S. "don't forget to go up to Vertigo 42", a separate bar on the top floor.

RIB ROOM & OYSTER BAR 23 | 21 | 23 | £51

Carlton Tower, 2 Cadogan Pl., SW1 (Knightsbridge/Sloane Sq.), 020-7858 7053; fax 7823 1708; www.carltontower.com

Within the Carlton Tower hotel, this "comfortable, wood-lined" dining room "continues to meet modern tastes without losing any of its classic values" as a "traditional chophouse" with "beef, beef and more beef" – plus a "good selection of seafood and oysters"; "a bit on the expensive side", perhaps, but it's "something of a luxury" to have "tables well spaced to enable a discreet conversation" and "attentive service."

Riccardo's ◐ 18 | 12 | 18 | £32

126 Fulham Rd., SW3 (Gloucester Rd./South Kensington), 020-7370 6656; fax 7373 0604

"Fab for children" and "perfect on summer days" when the covered front patio is opened up, this "lively" Chelsea trattoria in decidedly "unpretentious" premises is "a place to head when you want to feel at home"; the "wholesome", "un-Anglicised Italian" menu features "small dishes that give a different perspective from standard" fare.

RICHARD CORRIGAN AT LINDSAY HOUSE ☒ 27 | 23 | 23 | £63

21 Romilly St., W1 (Leicester Sq./Piccadilly Circus), 020-7439 0450; fax 7437 7349; www.lindsayhouse.co.uk

"In the middle of Soho", a "rather residential setting"– a "cosy" "converted townhouse" complete with "creaky stairs", fireplaces and "bare interior" – provides the characterful canvas for chef-owner Richard Corrigan's "exquisite" Modern British–Irish menu (no, "it's not all about the potato", but rather "incredible combinations, artfully presented"), an "expansive, if expensive, wine list" and "considerate, subtle service"; a rise in the Food score confirms the cuisine "is worth the time spent."

Richoux 15 | 14 | 14 | £23

172 Piccadilly, W1 (Green Park/Piccadilly Circus), 020-7493 2204; fax 7495 6658

41A S. Audley St., W1 (Bond St.), 020-7629 5228; fax 7491 0825

86 Brompton Rd., SW3 (Knightsbridge), 020-7584 8300; fax 7589 8547

3 Circus Rd., NW8 (St. John's Wood), 020-7483 4001; fax 7483 3810

www.richoux.co.uk

"Not the place for weight-watchers", this "reliable chain" of "touristy" tearooms tenders "all the classics" all day long, from a "full English breakfast" to the "perfect cream tea" to a "late-night Welsh rarebit"; it "never changes" – which trendoids translate as "dated" and "dreary" – but "sometimes, that's exactly what you want."

RITZ, THE 24 | 28 | 26 | £60

Ritz Hotel, 150 Piccadilly, W1 (Green Park), 020-7300 2370; fax 7907 2681; www.theritzlondon.com

"Get dressed up" for "a trip to 18th-century Versailles" at this "luxuriant, regal" dining room in the Ritz Hotel – yet again the *Survey*'s No. 1 for Decor; from the "exemplary service" (always "solicitous", if a bit "smug") to the "excellent" cuisine ("a mixture of Classic French and English dishes"), it's a "sheer, extravagant heaven" that "one never wants to leave"; P.S. whilst the weekend "dinner dances are something special", "nothing tops afternoon tea" at the adjacent Palm Court: "take granny and you'll stay in the will."

Riva 22 | 16 | 19 | £48

169 Church Rd., SW13 (Hammersmith), 020-8748 0434; fax 8748 0434

"Top-class food in an unlikely place" report regulars "raving about" Andrea Riva's quirky Barnes eatery, which attracts a "sharp crowd" with "stunningly fresh, seasonal Northern Italian cuisine" and "naughty puddings"; on the flip side, the "drab interior could do with a makeover" and the "service can be erratic" (there's a sense "they favour the locals" and "celebs").

RIVER CAFÉ 26 | 21 | 23 | £57

Thames Wharf, Rainville Rd., W6 (Hammersmith), 020-7386 4200; fax 7386 4201; www.rivercafe.co.uk

"Have yet to have a bad meal here, after all these years" affirm admirers of this Hammersmith institution that's "hard to find but worth it"; "a busy open kitchen" produces "robust", "rustic" Italian dishes that are "big on fresh herbs" and delivered by "invisibly attentive" staff; those who find the "austere blue-and-silver" interior too "noisy to relax and savour" "can dine amidst the trees" on the "pretty" riverside patio; N.B. residential restrictions mean tables have to be vacated by 11 PM.

Rivington Grill Bar Deli ▽ 15 | 13 | 14 | £33

28-30 Rivington St., EC2 (Old St.), 020-7729 7053; fax 7729 7086; www.rivingtongrill.co.uk

"Seems to know what it's doing" say those who know this converted Shoreditch warehouse where the "cold, white interior somehow suits" the "warm", "if unadventurous", Traditional British menu; however, it's "probably not worth making the journey if you're out of the neighbourhood"; N.B. try takeaway from the titular deli next door.

Rocket 18 | 18 | 15 | £28

4 Lancashire Ct., W1 (Bond St.), 020-7629 2889; fax 7629 2881 Ⓢ

Putney Wharf, Brewhouse St., SW15 (East Putney), 020-8789 7875; fax 8789 7876

www.rocketrestaurants.co.uk

"Charge your rockets" at this "popular" pair "perfectly positioned in Putney" and in a "charming" Mayfair mews; there's "always a good vibe" from an "after-work crowd" chowing down on the "reasonably priced" Italian-Med meals that include "huge pizzas and interesting salads"; "shame the service can be patchy", though.

Rodizio Rico ▽ 18 | 11 | 14 | £27

111 Westbourne Grove, W2 (Bayswater), 020-7792 4035; fax 7243 1401

77-78 Upper St., N1 (Angel), 020-7354 1076; fax 7359 8052 Ⓢ

"If you're a carnivore, this is your new home" profess fans of this Brazilian churrascaria in Westbourne Grove, whose "all-you-can-eat fest" of grilled meats is "good value for the money" (unless "you just want a light meal"); however, the less-enthused find the "endless, endless" parade of flesh "all so dull"; N.B. the Islington branch opened post-*Survey*.

Roka ◐ 24 | 21 | 18 | £46

37 Charlotte St., W1 (Goodge St./Tottenham Court Rd.), 020-7580 6464; fax 7153 4502; www.rokarestaurant.com

"Much more casual than its sister, Zuma", this "fashionable" Japanese yearling with "floor-to-ceiling windows" fronting

Charlotte Street is dominated by a "great grill" producing "mouth-watering" robata dishes, plus tempura and sushi selections that "hit the spot" too; however, some slam the "plain decor" and staff that "make you feel you ought to show gratitude"; P.S. "beneath the restaurant", the "amazing Shochu lounge" is "an option if you can't get a table" upstairs.

Rosmarino 23 | 19 | 21 | £39

1 Blenheim Terrace, NW8 (St. John's Wood), 020-7328 5014; fax 7625 2639

"Best on a summer's night when the front of the restaurant opens onto the patio", this "little authentic Italian tucked away in St. John's Wood" is an "understated", yet "classy joint" with "lots of touch and warmth"; both the "pleasing food" and the "guaranteed smooth service" have risen in the ratings since an ownership change in 2004.

ROUSSILLON ⊠ 25 | 21 | 24 | £66

16 St. Barnabas St., SW1 (Sloane Sq./Victoria), 020-7730 5550; fax 7824 8617; www.roussillon.co.uk

It's "surprisingly unknown" – perhaps because it's "in a hidden Pimlico block" – but those familiar with this "pretty" New French "love it dearly" for its "exquisite food" that's long on "quality" vegetarian dishes, "staff that have a sense of humour" and "a sommelier who is a master at finding something delicious for a good price"; "prices are climbing", true, but this "charming little restaurant is perfect for a romantic night out."

Rowley's ◐ 20 | 17 | 20 | £39

113 Jermyn St., SW1 (Piccadilly Circus), 020-7930 2707; fax 7839 4240

23 Conduit St., W1 (Oxford Circus), 020-7493 7050

www.rowleys.co.uk

Accompanied by "unlimited chips", the "steak comes recommended" at this "grown-up" St. James's stalwart in a 1790s butcher shop; the "simple" Traditional British menu has "the odd touch of something new" (e.g. Modern European faves), but some still knock it for being "a one-note affair"; N.B. the new Mayfair locale opened on the old Deca site post-*Survey*.

ROYAL CHINA 23 | 15 | 15 | £29

13 Queensway, W2 (Queensway), 020-7221 2535; fax 7792 5752

24-26 Baker St., W1 (Baker St.), 020-7487 4688; fax 7935 7893

68 Queen's Grove, NW8 (St. John's Wood), 020-7586 4280; fax 7722 4750

30 Westferry Circus, E14 (Canary Wharf), 020-7719 0888; fax 7719 0889

"Hit the dim-sum craving square on the head" at this "top-notch" Chinese quartet where the "piping hot", "well-prepared" reliables are only "bettered by Hong Kong"; but beware, it's usually "impossible to get a table" on weekends, and the "poker face" staff show "no concern for customers waiting in queues"; P.S. the decor's a trifle "tacky" at all but the "stunning, panelled" Canary Wharf outpost, which has "outdoor seating on the river."

Royal Exchange Grand Café & Bar ⊠ ▽ 15 | 24 | 16 | £29

The Royal Exchange, The Courtyard, EC3 (Bank), 020-7618 2480; fax 7618 2490; www.conran.com

"The unique, impressive setting in the middle of the Royal Exchange" makes a "welcome island of quiet" to enjoy an "interesting" menu of "fresh, light" Modern European cold dishes (like "great seafood") at the Conran Group's all-day, upscale cafe; the "downside is, it gets very busy" and some prefer just to "come here for cocktails" to avoid the staff's "annoying power selling" of side dishes, etc.

R.S.J. ⊠ 21 | 15 | 20 | £37

33 Coin St., SE1 (Waterloo), 020-7928 4554; fax 7401 2455; www.rsj.uk.com

"Overlook the crowded tables" and "tatty decor" command "those in-the-know" who call this "accommodating" address "one of London's best-kept secrets", with a "fine wine list" that's is an "education in Loire" labels and a "creative Modern British menu"; it's "a perfect spot pre-theatre", as it's "right near the National" and offers a "great-value" early-bird prix fixe.

RULES ◐ 22 | 24 | 22 | £48

35 Maiden Ln., WC2 (Covent Garden), 020-7836 5314; fax 7497 1081; www.rules.co.uk

"As olde world as it comes", this 208-year-old Covent Garden "institution" – allegedly a "former haunt of kings and their mistresses" – is "a must for out-of-towners looking for a taste of history" in an Edwardian "gentleman's club" scene; the "hearty", "quintessential" Traditional British menu ("prime rib in its prime!") "maintains a consistent high standard", and even though some find the place "too fuddy-duddy" or "touristy" for their tastes, most concede "London's oldest restaurant" still rules.

Saigon ◐⊠ 22 | 13 | 17 | £31

45 Frith St., W1 (Leicester Sq./Piccadilly Circus), 020-7437 7109; fax 7734 1668

"If you love Vietnamese" this site "in the middle of Soho" "is a terrific choice" thanks to "consistently excellent" dishes made with "proper spices"; the "unassuming surroundings" are "in serious need of refurbishment", though.

Sakura 19 | 9 | 11 | £26

9 Hanover St., W1 (Oxford Circus), 020-7629 2961

The "'70s decor adds to the homely atmosphere" at this "casual", "no-frills" Japanese "joint" near Oxford Street with "lots of people and things to amuse" you, from "nice" sushi to cooked dishes "at a decent price"; that said, the lack of "ventilation" and "legendary rude service" cast a "depressive" air antagonists argue.

Sale e Pepe ◐ ⊠ 22 | 15 | 21 | £38

9-15 Pavilion Rd., SW1 (Knightsbridge), 020-7235 0098; fax 7225 1210

"Singing and arguing", the "raucous waiters" create an "atmosphere just short of crazy" at this "hectic" 32-year-old trattoria where the "old-style", "consistently good" Italian menu is "reasonably priced" (for Knightsbridge, at least); "beware if you feel claustrophobic at tightly spaced tables", but if you crave the corny, "this is the place for you."

Salloos ◐ ⊠ 22 | 16 | 20 | £41

62-64 Kinnerton St., SW1 (Hyde Park Corner/Knightsbridge), 020-7235 4444

"Tucked out of the way" in "a charming Belgravia side street", this "old standby" from the '70s sustains with "heavy" Indo-Pakistani fare that's still "solidly good", even "unrivalled when the chef is on form"; but a slide in the Food score suggests it's being "left behind by the newer Indians", and naysayers note wryly that whilst the cuisine "quality is variable, the prices are consistently high."

Salt Yard ⊠ – | – | – | M

54 Goodge St., W1 (Goodge Street), 020-7637 0657; fax 7580 7435; www.saltyard.co.uk

Three restaurant debutantes with a passion for tapas-style dining have created this casual Fitzrovia newcomer, whose Modern European menu also includes moderately priced charcuterie boards and cheeses; a prominent old-fashioned meat slicer dominates the decadent ground-floor bar, whilst the minimalist dining room downstairs is all chalky-coloured walls, mirrors and wooden tables.

Salusbury Pub & Dining Room ▽ 19 | 18 | 16 | £34

50-52 Salusbury Rd., NW6 (Queen's Park), 020-7328 3286

A "lively crowd" congregates at this boisterous Queen's Park gastro-pub where "big wooden tables" and a cosy fireplace create "nice atmosphere"; and whilst most appreciate the "above-average" Italian menu, antagonists argue it's "too ambitious by half" – and "taking a couple of quid off the mains" wouldn't hurt either.

San Lorenzo ◐ ⊠ ⊭ 20 | 18 | 18 | £52

22 Beauchamp Pl., SW3 (Knightsbridge), 020-7584 1074; fax 7584 1142; www.sanlorenzo.com

San Lorenzo Fuoriporta

38 Wimbledon Hill Rd., SW19 (Wimbledon), 020-8946 8463; fax 8947 9810

With some of the "best people-watching in London" ("*Hello!* magazine come to life"), "delightful" Italian food and "quick service", this Knightsbridge "landmark" is "always a winner", especially – some say "only" – "if you are a friend" of legendary owners Mara and Lorenzo Berni; but critics cavil it's "coasting" on past glories ("more celebs than substance") and "too expensive not to take credit cards"; N.B. the family-run Wimbledon sibling is a magnet for players during the tennis championships.

Santa Fe ▽ 17 | 14 | 13 | £26

75 Upper St., N1 (Angel), 020-7288 2288; fax 7288 2287; www.santafe.co.uk

Quite a "loud contingent patronises this Wild West outpost", partly for the "tempting margaritas" and partly for the Southwestern American fare that provides "an interesting diversion for Islington" – even if it's "mediocre", as some muchachos mutter; the "basic surroundings" are "looking a bit tired now."

Santa Lucia ◐ 19 | 13 | 11 | £28

2 Hollywood Rd., SW10 (South Kensington), 020-7352 8484; fax 7351 2390

"For a relaxed night out with tasty, simple food", this "buzzing" bi-level Chelsea trattoria ("same [ownership] as Made in Italy") has *paisanos* who praise the "really good, very Italian" victuals, notably "the definitive pizza"; but the service is often "sloppy", and "never changing the menu makes life boring for the regulars."

Santini 23 | 19 | 21 | £50

29 Ebury St., SW1 (Victoria), 020-7730 4094; fax 7730 0544; www.santini-restaurant.com

If you want "delicious" "Northern Italian fare that can't be beat", this "pleasant", sometimes "hectic" venue near Victoria Station is "a real find"; there's "kind service" and a "smart", "heterogeneous crowd"; but as with many "fashionable" places, the menu can be "a bit overpriced."

Sardo ⊠ 22 | 14 | 21 | £37

45 Grafton Way, W1 (Warren St.), 020-7387 2521; fax 7387 2559; www.sardo-restaurant.com

"It's not cheap, but given the quality, it's very good value" proclaim lovers of this "lively" Fitzrovian where "many ad executives and young couples" enjoy "home-cooked", "authentic Sardinian" dishes with "original touches", along with wines from a "brilliant list"; the servers' "warm charm" compensates for the "small" surroundings.

Sardo Canale ⊠ 21 | 20 | 18 | £38

42 Gloucester Ave., NW1 (Chalk Farm), 020-7722 2800

This "welcome" "addition to the Primrose Hill dining scene" is "perfect for the area", offering "delicious Sardinian" fare in a "fantastic canal-side location" that creates an "atmosphere better than its sister Sardo's"; but "not everyone loves it", citing "hit-and-miss" fare and service.

Sarkhel's 24 | 15 | 21 | £30

197-199 Replingham Rd., SW18 (Southfields), 020-8870 1483; fax 8871 0808
199 Upper Richmond Rd. W., SW14 (Mortlake B.R.), 020-8876 6220
www.sarkhels.com

"Full of people having fun", this "good quality curry house" has "been well received in Southfields" – and now Sheen too – thanks to "a regularly changing" menu of "marvellous" Indian "dishes with an unexpected twist" from revered chef Udit Sarkhel; although some quibble the "quality varies", most agree it's "well worth the trip."

Sartoria ⊠ 19 | 20 | 19 | £52

20 Savile Row, W1 (Oxford Circus/Piccadilly Circus), 020-7534 7000; fax 7534 7070; www.conran.com

"Decorated with items from the clothing industry" – "very fitting as it's on Savile Row" – this "calm" Conran Group venue offers "perfectly good" Modern Italian cuisine allied with "attentive staff"; some come unravelled at the "pricey" bill and find the "cool decor" "verging on cold", but the 27 different grappas available make it a "most relaxing spot after a hectic day."

Satsuma 18 | 12 | 15 | £21

56 Wardour St., W1 (Leicester Sq./Piccadilly Circus), 020-7437 8338; fax 7437 3389

"Just don't wear anything that clashes with orange" at this "bright", "funky" Soho site where "huge queues at busy times" are testimony to the "inventive", "affordable" Japanese "staples"; the "backache-inducing benches" and "communal tables can be a bit of a drag", but that does not deter a "hip crowd" from having their sushi and noodle "cravings satisfied."

SAVOY GRILL 24 | 24 | 24 | £59

Savoy Hotel, The Strand, WC2 (Covent Garden/Embankment), 020-7592 1600; fax 7592 1601; www.gordonramsay.com

With "smooth-as-silk" service, this "subtly elegant" act on The Strand is enjoying the fruits of its "modernised room and menu" under chef Marcus Wareing, whose "sublime" Modern British–European cooking is "pricey, but worth it"; although some are "still not convinced by the makeover" (a "bit stuffy", "unadventurous"), most claim this "divine art deco" destination – "you can almost sense David Niven lurking in the room" – remains a "London treasure and special treat."

Scalini ◐ 24 | 16 | 20 | £46

1-3 Walton St., SW3 (Knightsbridge/South Kensington), 020-7225 2301; fax 7225 3953

"Always crowded with beautiful people" "next to families with kids", this "noisy" Chelsea Italian "never fails to come up with the goods" – specifically, an "excellent array" of dishes (including "some not on the menu they prepare for you"); whilst generally the waiters are "warm" and "genial", some jest that "it would help if they remembered who ordered what"; P.S. "ask for the front room."

Seashell ☒ 20 | 10 | 16 | £18

49-51 Lisson Grove, NW1 (Marylebone), 020-7224 9000; fax 7724 9071; www.seashellrestaurant.co.uk

"You don't come here for atmosphere, but they do have some of the tastiest fish in town" (available "fried, "broiled or baked") at this "basic"-looking, "mildly famous" Marylebone veteran; cynics snap it's a shell of its former self – certainly "they're all at sea" in the dining room – but at least the "takeaway is reliable and good value."

Shanghai Blues ◐ – | – | – | E

193-197 High Holborn, WC1 (Holborn), 020-7404 1668; www.shanghaiblues.co.uk

Situated in a "chic" converted public library in Holborn ("an area becoming trendy"), this "great newcomer" has two high-ceilinged, lantern-hung dining rooms and a cosy mezzanine level with a piano bar and regular live bands; the "interesting" menu features "innovative dim sum" and "high-end" Shanghai fare, courtesy of a former chef to the Chinese government.

Shepherd's ☒ 17 | 17 | 17 | £34

Marsham Ct., Marsham St., SW1 (Pimlico/St. James's Park), 020-7834 9552; fax 7233 6047; www.langansrestaurants.co.uk

"Bustling with MPs who all rush out at 9:45 PM in time for the Division Bell", this "discreet" Westminster venue (it's "hard to overhear other tables' conversations") is "utterly reliable" for "unfussy" Traditional British "comfort food"; but a disgruntled minority maintain culinary "things have moved on" from the "formulaic approach" of this "old hat."

Shikara ◐ – | – | – | M

87 Sloane Ave., SW3 (South Kensington), 020-7581 6555; fax 7581 8988; www.shikara.co.uk

Once Jimmy'z Bar, this space within the Chelsea Cloisters building at Brompton Cross has become a white-walled, family-run Indian; the menu offers full-bodied, wholesome dishes from the north (also listing the healthy properties of herbs and spices), served by staff wearing natty traditional black attire; N.B. the takeaway menu is mainly tandoori fare.

Shogun ▽ 19 | 18 | 18 | £51

Millennium Hotel Mayfair, Adam's Row, W1 (Bond St.), 020-7493 1255; fax 7493 1255

"In the cave of the Millennium Hotel", this "dark, hidden" retreat – "seductive" to some, "threatening" to others – is "packed with a Japanese clientele" sampling "wonderfully fresh sushi" and other "innovative" Asian fare; a few snipers find the "less-than-impressive" offerings "overpriced."

Signor Sassi ◐ Ⓢ 22 | 16 | 21 | £37

14 Knightsbridge Green, SW1 (Knightsbridge), 020-7584 2277; fax 7225 3953

"Everyone is warmly welcomed when they enter" this Knightsbridge trattoria, a "popular haunt" for "excellent, if not exceptional Italian food" with, "of course, large pepper grinders" wielded by "singing staff"; it's "noisy, but it's probably supposed to be" – part of the "congenial" "charm."

Signor Zilli ◐ Ⓢ 20 | 12 | 17 | £37

41 Dean St., W1 (Leicester Sq./Tottenham Court Rd.), 020-7734 3924; fax 7734 8156; www.zillialdo.com

This eponymous "celebrity chef's flagship" in Soho "never disappoints" disciples who praise its "delightful" Italian cucina ("best described as hearty") and "sweet staff", "who do everything to fit you in, no matter how full" it is; but dissenters declare the "cheesy decor" and "mediocre" meals fit "only for tourists and day-trippers."

Silk Ⓢ – | – | – | VE

Courthouse Hotel Kempinski, 19-21 Great Marlborough St., W1 (Oxford Circus), 020-7297 5555; www.courthouse-hotel.com

The ancient silk trade route through Italy, the Middle East and Asia inspires the name – as well as the cuisines covered by the dinner-only Eclectic menu – of this grand oak-panelled and jury-style, wood-chaired dining room (a former courthouse) in a smart new Soho hotel; prices are almost as high as the glass-vaulted ceilings, but budget-watchers can benefit from the all-day brasserie, The Carnaby, on the premises.

Silks & Spice ▽ 17 | 12 | 15 | £29

95 Chiswick High Rd., W4 (Turnham Green), 020-8995 7991; fax 8994 7773

Temple Ct., 11 Queen Victoria St., EC4 (Bank/Mansion House), 020-7248 7878; fax 7248 9595 Ⓢ

www.silksandspice.net

"Cheap and cheerful", this chain in Chiswick and "the heart of the City" rustles up "trusty", "tasty" Thai-Malaysian dishes, presented by "petite, stunning" servers; they're perpetually "popular", even if the "noisy" ambience is "not so nice."

Simply Nico Ⓢ 20 | 15 | 18 | £43

12 Sloane Sq., SW1 (Sloane Sq.), 020-7896 9909; fax 7896 9908

48A Rochester Row, SW1 (St. James's Park/Victoria), 020-7630 8061; fax 7828 8541

"Fine for a longggg lunch" or "intimate dinner" declare devotees of these "delightful neighbourhood bistros" in Sloane Square and Rochester Row, with their "reliable", decent" French fare; however, they're "simply expensive" to sceptics who say they "need someone to liven things up" – starting with the "aloof staff."

Simpson's-in-The-Strand 19 | 22 | 22 | £46

100 The Strand, WC2 (Charing Cross), 020-7836 9112; fax 7836 1381; www.fairmont.com/savoy

For those "tired of chasing after the chichi places", try "a trip back in time" at this 178-year-old Savoy-owned Strand "institution" ("Sherlock would feel right at Holmes") that "oozes history", right down to the "old-fashioned British" "meaty classics" "carved from the [silver domed] trolley" ("remember to tip the carver") and "waiters who know it all, not unlike one's own Jeeves"; even "though it's touristy and somewhat worn", this "classic is still shipshape."

Singapore Garden 20 | 12 | 16 | £25

83/83A Fairfax Rd., NW6 (Swiss Cottage), 020-7328 5314; fax 7624 0656

Supporters sing the praises of the "tasty, homestyle" Chinese–Southeast Asian eats (especially the "exceptional Singaporean specialities") at this "lively", "local favourite" in Swiss Cottage; despite some "reasonably priced" prix fixes (from £10 at dinner), however, several say it's "pricey" "for what you get."

Singapura ⊠ ▽ 16 | 14 | 14 | £32

1-2 Limeburner Ln., EC4 (Blackfriars/St. Paul's), 020-7329 1133; fax 7236 1805

78-79 Leadenhall St., EC3 (Aldgate/Tower Hill), 020-7929 0089; fax 7621 0366

31 Broadgate Circle, EC2 (Liverpool St.), 020-7256 5045

www.singapuras.co.uk

"One of the best-kept secrets around" for a "business lunch or dinner", this City trio offers "solid" Southeast Asian cuisine; however, even those who "love the food" find the "service variable"; P.S. the Broadgate Circle's new deli "is worth the detour."

Sir Charles Napier ▽ 21 | 24 | 19 | £41

Spriggs Alley, Chinnor, Oxfordshire, 01494 483011; fax 01494 485311; www.sircharlesnapier.co.uk

A "wonderful location", surrounded by beechwoods and fields in the Chiltern Hills, makes this "esoteric" 18th-century coaching inn "lovely for a winter's supper" or an "amazing summer afternoon", when you can "enjoy a table outside"; there's a "great" (albeit "a bit expensive") Modern British menu and "good wine list", as well.

Six-13 ⊠ ▽ 16 | 17 | 18 | £46

19 Wigmore St., W1 (Bond St./Oxford Circus), 020-7629 6133; fax 7629 6135; www.six13.com

"An upmarket kosher restaurant", this "reserved" art deco–styled Marylebone Modern European "always hits the mark" with its strictly observed menu (no dairy), the devout declare; opponents opine it's "ok, but does it need to be satisfied with being just, well, ok?"; N.B. closed weekends.

Sketch – The Gallery ☒ 16 | 24 | 15 | £60

9 Conduit St., W1 (Oxford Circus), 0870-777 4488; fax 7629 1698; www.sketch.uk.com

"The paparazzi outside the door will make you feel like a star" at this "totally hip", "very showy" dinner-only Mayfair venue/club (it's a video art gallery during the day) with "tons of room between the tables" and a liberal sprinkling of "shiny fashionistas", models, etc.; although it's "creative", Pierre Gagnaire's New French cuisine strikes sceptics as "all style and no substance", and that, plus "lacklustre service", means many prefer to "go just for the drinks" at the "funky" bar; P.S. "the toilets are to die for."

Sketch – The Lecture Room & Library ☒ 22 | 23 | 20 | £101

9 Conduit St., W1 (Oxford Circus), 0870-777 4488; fax 7629 1684; www.sketch.uk.com

"Impressive", "eccentric" and "witheringly expensive" epitomises the experience at chef Pierre Gagnaire's "theatrical" restaurant off Regent Street; all award his New French fare "an A for bravery", but what strikes supporters as "a stunning gastronomic experience", "surprising the taste buds at every turn", sceptics see as "over-the-top" and "contrived"; "service is great, though", and "you do feel like you're in the most fabulous place in town" – just "wait for the trust fund to kick in" before you go.

Smiths of Smithfield – Dining Room ☒ 18 | 17 | 16 | £34

67-77 Charterhouse St., 2nd fl., EC1 (Barbican/Farringdon), 020-7251 7950; fax 7236 0488; www.smithsofsmithfield.co.uk

"If you want a restaurant/bar combo", this "buzzy" bi-level bistro beside Smithfield Market is "a reliable choice", with "decent-value" Modern British fare that supporters say is "straightforward", "if lacking personality"; the ground-floor bar "with huge comfy sofas" gets "full of raucous City boys" after work, so you'll excuse if "service can be a bit dodgy at times."

SMITHS OF SMITHFIELD – TOP FLOOR 22 | 21 | 19 | £53

67-77 Charterhouse St., EC1 (Barbican/Farringdon), 020-7251 7950; fax 7236 0488; www.smithsofsmithfield.co.uk

"Hard on the arteries and wallet" it may be, but praise goes out to the "wonderful cuts of meat from your favourite cow or pig" at this "airy, spacious top-floor" Traditional British chophouse with "top-flight views" overlooking Smithfield Market; if a few finicky souls feel it "never quite hits" the heights – certainly the often "indifferent service" is a drag – most claim it's "hard to beat" for "meat lovers", both "young and old."

Smollensky's American Bar & Grill 13 | 15 | 14 | £28

Bradmore House, Queen Caroline St., W6 (Hammersmith), 020-8741 8124; fax 8741 5695 ⊠
105 The Strand, WC2 (Charing Cross/Covent Garden), 020-7497 2101; fax 7836 3270
1 Nash Ct., E14 (Canary Wharf), 020-7719 0101; fax 7719 0060 ⊠
Hermitage Wharf, 22 Wapping High St., E1 (Tower Bridge/ Wapping High St.), 020-7680 1818; fax 7680 1787
62 Carter Ln., EC4 (St. Paul's), 020-7248 4220; fax 7248 4221 ⊠
www.smollenskys.co.uk

"Delivering what it promises without frills", this "cheery", "relaxed" quintet is "good for taking the kids out" ("with magicians and performers" at some branches) and "after-work drinking"; but the "run-of-the-mill" American fare's Food score has dropped, and regulars recommend "order the burgers, as that's the best thing they do."

Snows on the Green ⊠ ▽ 22 | 16 | 17 | £33

166 Shepherd's Bush Rd., W6 (Hammersmith), 020-7603 2142; fax 7602 7553; www.snowsonthegreen.co.uk

A "hidden gem" agree admirers of chef-owner Sebastian Snow's Brook Green (get the name now?) Modern British menu – which includes "good country" fare and game – served in his casual but "delightful" eatery; but some say the kitchen "can surprise one night, but disappoint" the next.

Sofra 18 | 13 | 17 | £25

18 Shepherd St., W1 (Green Park), 020-7493 3320; fax 7499 8282 ◐
1 St. Christopher's Pl., W1 (Bond St.), 020-7224 4080; fax 7224 0022 ◐
36 Tavistock St., WC2 (Covent Garden), 020-7240 3773; fax 7836 6633
11 Circus Rd., NW8 (St. John's Wood), 020-7586 9889; fax 7586 8778
19-21 Exmouth Mkt., EC1 (Angel), 020-7833 1111
www.sofra.co.uk

"Well-loved by students, but with food good enough for connoisseurs", this "bustling" chain around town provides "succulent Turkish delights" in "large portions" at "an amazing price"; although the "unremarkable", "cramped" environment and "erratic service" ruffle some feathers, this "treasure" is "popular at all hours of the day and night."

Soho House ◐ 17 | 20 | 18 | £42

Private club; inquiries: 020-7734 5188

"No wonder it's a legend" proclaim those enamoured by "genius Nick Jones'" "sophisticated" private club in a "comfy" Soho townhouse, attracting "famous members" and an "elite" crowd with a "great vibe", "dependable" Modern British "comfort food" and "well-meaning service"; those who find it "difficult to eat and pose at the same time" may prefer the "great bar and roof garden."

Soho Spice ◐ 18 | 15 | 15 | £26

124-126 Wardour St., W1 (Tottenham Court Rd.), 020-7434 0808; fax 7434 0799; www.sohospice.co.uk

The "new look and menus" introduced by new owner Kuldeep Singh (also with Mela and Chowki under his wing) have definitely "spiced it up" at this "clean, crisp" Soho spot; the "delicious, contemporary Indian" cuisine offers a "good price/quality ratio", which along with a "lively" atmosphere, leaves people "feeling fulfilled" – if also sometimes "with a headache from the noise" emanating from the downstairs bar and dance floor.

Solly's 20 | 12 | 13 | £29

148A Golders Green Rd., NW11 (Golders Green), 020-8455 2121

"For authentic schwarma" and "plenty of variety" on the Middle Eastern menu, this basic, bi-level Golders Green venue is just about "as good as it gets" if you're going kosher; the "decor's a bit old now", but service is "quick", even if it isn't always "friendly"; N.B. opening and closing times on weekends vary in accordance with sundown.

Song Que Café ▽ 23 | 6 | 11 | £13

134 Kingsland Rd., E2 (Old St.), 020-7613 3222

"Don't be deceived by its divey looks" ("how else can they keep the prices so low?") – this "always busy" Vietnamese-Chinese in Shoreditch has "delightfully fresh, delicately flavoured food", including the "most authentic pho in London"; even if the "service leaves a little to be desired", all agree the place is "perfect for filling up on the way home, or on the way out"; P.S. "going to the loo is still an experience in itself."

Sonny's ▽ 20 | 15 | 18 | £39

94 Church Rd., SW13 (Barnes Bridge B.R.), 020-8748 0393; fax 8748 2698

This "terrifically reliable local favourite" (celebrating its 20th anniversary) in Barnes is a "comfortable, fairly casual" spot for "not-too-complicated" Modern British fare that hits "right in the middle of the taste buds"; "slow service", however, has the peripatetic preferring to "check out their adjoining deli for cheaper options."

SOPHIE'S STEAKHOUSE & BAR ◐ 21 | 16 | 17 | £31

311-313 Fulham Rd., SW10 (South Kensington), 020-7352 0088; fax 7349 9776; www.sophiessteakhouse.com

"Expect to spend some time at the bar to get a coveted seat" at this "constantly crowded" Chelsea chophouse that "doesn't accept reservations"; however, it does offer a "sociable", "vibrant" setting for a "diverse", "hearty" American menu starring "very reliable steaks"; even after sitting you "must have patience" with the "easy-going service", but the fact that a "young, chic crowd keeps coming back" suggests the place has the "right mix."

Souk ◐ 16 | 22 | 17 | £25

27 Litchfield St., WC2 (Leicester Sq.), 020-7240 1796; fax 7240 3382; www.soukrestaurant.net

"You'll think you're in Morocco" – "on a good night, the staff grab instruments off the wall and begin playing music" – at this site "tucked away" near Leicester Square; and if the "interesting" North African fare "is not haute cuisine", the "fabulous atmosphere more than compensates."

Spago ◐⊭ 21 | 16 | 17 | £28

6 Glendower Pl., SW7 (South Kensington), 020-7225 2407

The service is "a little rough around the edges", but this "casual", "unheard-of pizza place in South Kensington" is still "a worthy destination" for "simple, straightforward Italian" staples at a "good, cheap" price; P.S. "downstairs is a great venue to watch football, especially if Italy is playing."

Spiga 18 | 12 | 17 | £27

84-86 Wardour St., W1 (Leicester Sq./Piccadilly Circus), 020-7734 3444; fax 7734 3332

"A regular, safe bet" for "real Italian-style pasta and pizza", plus "decent wines" say surveyors of this "brightly lit" Soho "standby"; and if the "decor is nothing to write home about", at least there's "no need to break the bank" to dine here.

Spighetta ▽ 19 | 12 | 16 | £27

43 Blandford St., W1 (Baker St.), 020-7486 7340; fax 7486 7340; www.spighetta.co.uk

Wood oven–baked, "correctly done pizzas are the best bet" at this easy-going Marylebone "basement venue"; "it's a pity" about "the less-than-romantic decor" and slightly "complacent" service, but surveyors are "satisfied with everything" else, from the "interesting Sardinian"-accented menu to the "prices and ambience."

Spoon at Sanderson ◐ 20 | 24 | 19 | £54

(fka Spoon+)

Sanderson Hotel, 50 Berners St., W1 (Goodge St./Oxford Circus), 020-7300 1444; fax 7300 5540; www.chinagrillmgt.com/spoon

The "mixing and matching [of meat, sauces and veggies] allows for creative meals" at this "ultramodern, ultrachic" Eclectic eatery in the Sanderson Hotel; although a few find chef Alain Ducasse's "jigsaw puzzle" too "complicated" – especially "after a few of the fabulous mojitos" – and choke at the "heart-attack prices", most consider it "interesting all-round", especially when the "really cool bar" and "fantastic summer terrace" are factored in.

SQUARE, THE 27 | 23 | 26 | £77

6-10 Bruton St., W1 (Bond St./Green Park), 020-7495 7100; fax 7495 7150; www.squarerestaurant.com

"It's hip to be Square" proclaim mavens of Mayfair's "tastefully appointed" "temple to gastronomy" where chef-owner Philip Howard's "stupendous" New French cooking costs "a lot of moola" but still is "superb on all counts"; traditionalists may find the "modernistic" "atmosphere a little sterile", but the combination of "discreet, conscientious service", "imposing wine list" and "amazing cheese platter" ensures this "top-notch" wonder "has the wow factor every time."

Sri Nam ⊠ 16 | 15 | 13 | £26

10 Cabot Sq., E14 (Canary Wharf), 020-7715 9515; www.orientalrestaurantgroup.co.uk

"Convenient for those working in Canary Wharf", this colourful citizen spread over two floors offers "nicely spiced Thai" cuisine; although some slam the "sloooooow service" and recommend a "refocus on food", it remains a "lively lunchtime spot", whilst the "happy-hour bar in the evenings" is a big draw.

Sri Siam City ⊠ 19 | 16 | 17 | £29

85 London Wall, EC2 (Liverpool St.), 020-7628 5772; fax 7628 3395; www.orientalrestaurantgroup.co.uk

"For Thai at a convenient City location, you won't go wrong" with this basement-dweller; "always nicely fragranced", the fare (which refreshingly "doesn't revolve around meat") is "good without being expensive" and the "staff efficient" – a "perfect" business-meal formula, though "the lack of mobile phone coverage can be a blessing or a curse."

Sri Thai Soho ▽ 21 | 17 | 19 | £28

16 Old Compton St., W1 (Leicester Sq.), 020-7434 3544; fax 7287 1311; www.orientalrestaurantgroup.co.uk

"Ideally located" in the centre of Soho, this "relaxed" Thai "looks tantalising" with its deep red walls and "flavourful", "fresh" food; overall it offers "a good change of pace", even if the "friendly" staff can be "slightly ditzy" at busy times.

Star of India ◐ 23 | 16 | 18 | £33

154 Old Brompton Rd., SW5 (Gloucester Rd./South Kensington), 020-7373 2901; fax 7373 5664

In its 50-odd years, this "fabulous old staple" in South Kensington has "consistently pleased" with Indian cooking from a "changing menu" that "varies by province", along with "waiters who welcome you like family"; "whilst it's a step up in price from your local curry" joint, and the "decor's tired", most salute this star's power – "my taste buds wake up at the very mention" of its name.

Sticky Fingers 13 | 16 | 15 | £27

1A Phillimore Gardens, W8 (High St. Kensington), 020-7938 5338; fax 7937 0145; www.stickyfingers.co.uk

Jammed with Rolling Stones "memorabilia" (and boasting Bill Wyman as one of the owners), this "loud", music-themed Kensington American is "about as good as it gets for a burger fix" and a "saviour" if one's "with kids"; but nonrockers rant the "fast-food–quality fare" is strictly "for the tourists" and declare the digs "could use a good scrubbing", citing "sticky fingers, sticky floors, sticky tables."

ST. JOHN ☒ | 26 | 17 | 21 | £46

26 St. John St., EC1 (Farringdon), 020-7251 0848; fax 7251 4090; www.stjohnrestaurant.com

"Be open-minded and you will discover great new tastes" at this "unique" Smithfield site where "terrific chef Fergus Henderson" turns "parts of an animal you wouldn't think to eat", "from snout to tail", into "amazingly simple" Modern British dishes that "catch the eye and charm the taste buds"; the staff are "reliable and articulate", and if a few find the "butcher-shop-chic" decor "somewhat sterile", none deny this "offally good place" is "something that London can be proud of."

St. John Bread & Wine | 23 | 16 | 18 | £31

94-96 Commercial St., E1 (Liverpool St.), 020-7247 8724; fax 7247 8924; www.stjohnbreadandwine.com

"The place to go when you have a hankering for pig spleen salad", this "stark-walled" Spitalfields sibling of St. John is open all day from 9 AM, with a "short", "challenging" Modern British menu – "a meat-eater's delight" – that's "more about tastes than a big" meal, hence "great for a quick bite"; a "buzzy atmosphere, full of rising Brit-art celebs and trendy locals" enlivens the "simple, canteenlike" digs; N.B. take it away at the on-site bakery and wine shop.

Strada | 18 | 15 | 16 | £21

15-16 New Burlington St., W1 (Oxford Circus), 020-7287 5967; fax 7287 6074
9-10 Market Pl., W1 (Oxford Circus), 020-7580 4644; fax 7580 7877
6 Great Queen St., WC2 (Holborn), 020-7405 6293; fax 7405 6284
91 Wimbledon High St., SW19 (Wimbledon), 020-8946 4363
11-13 Battersea Rise, SW11 (Clapham Junction), 020-7801 0794; fax 7801 0754
175 New King's Rd., SW6 (Parsons Green), 020-7731 6404; fax 7731 1431
237 Earl's Court Rd., SW5 (Earl's Court), 020-7835 1180; fax 7835 2093
102-104 Clapham High St., SW4 (Clapham North), 020-7627 4847; fax 7720 2153
105-106 Upper St., N1 (Angel), 020-7226 9742; fax 7226 9187
8-10 Exmouth Mkt., EC1 (Farringdon), 020-7278 0800; fax 7278 6901
www.strada.co.uk
Additional locations throughout London

"Buzzy, lively, but never too noisy to converse" in, this "casual yet smart" chain has a "decent" Italian menu majoring on "huge pizzas with imaginative toppings", plus "very drinkable house wine"; and if foes find it too "formulaic" ("can't remember what you've eaten five minutes after" departure), supporters hail this "refreshing" presence on *la strada* of London; P.S. "complimentary spring water is a nice touch."

Stratford's ▽ 26 | 21 | 25 | £44

7 Stratford Rd., W8 (High St. Kensington), 020-7937 6388; fax 7938 3435; www.stratfords-restaurant.com

"Bright, with tasteful decor", this small seafooder in a "quiet Kensington" street serves "delicious fish", "immaculately done" in "orthodox" Classic French style; "charming service" and "reasonable set menus" add to its appeal.

Sugar Hut ◐ ▽ 20 | 25 | 16 | £40

374 North End Rd., SW6 (Fulham Broadway), 020-7386 8950; fax 7386 8428; www.sugarhutfulham.com

Diners "feel in a different world" at this "über-cool" Fulham Thai with "amazing" Asian/Moroccan decor, including bed-style seating to "lie back on and relax", "succulent cuisine at soothing prices" and "even better cocktails"; however, sceptics are soured on the "smoky" scene ("a nightclub, not a restaurant"), suggesting the "front-of-house team needs to study the art of humility."

Sugar Reef ◐ ⊠ 13 | 16 | 12 | £35

41-44 Great Windmill St., W1 (Piccadilly Circus), 020-7851 0800; fax 7851 0807; www.sugarreef.net

"Noisy and cavernous", this oh-so-"cool" space for "chavs" and "footballers' wives" on a "prime piece of" Piccadilly "isn't sure if it's a nightclub or a restaurant" – the "hoodlumlike doormen do not bode well for fine dining" and the Modern European fare "could be more inspiring"; but sweet-hearted surveyors shrug "this place is all about the music afterwards", anyway.

Sumosan ◐ 23 | 20 | 18 | £54

26 Albemarle St., W1 (Green Park), 020-7495 5999; fax 7355 1247; www.sumosan.com

This "minimalist" Mayfair Japanese (part of a Moscow-based chain) "may not be full of celebs like Nobu", but it still attracts "beautiful people" with an "innovative" menu – "have anything, it's all good"; that said, "nonchalant", "Keystone Cops-esque service" and "expensive prices" cause aggravation, leaving many to prefer the "fantastic cocktails" and DJ (Thursday–Saturday) in the J Bar below.

Suze ⊠ – | – | – | M

41 N. Audley St., W1 (Bond St.), 020-7491 3237; fax 7495 3806; www.suzewinebar.com

Something of a "rallying point for homesick Kiwis", this easy-going brasserie/wine bar has a "great" vino list that's "strong on New Zealand" labels; but it also serves "surprisingly excellent Pacific Rim cuisine" (the "green shell mussels are a must") at "reasonable prices given its location" in Mayfair; "attentive, helpful staff" also make it a "favourite."

SWEETINGS ☒ 23 | 16 | 21 | £34

39 Queen Victoria St., EC4 (Mansion House), 020-7248 3062

"You don't get more British" than this "informal" "City institution", one of "a dying breed", where an "old-school"-tie bunch bring "a good sense of neighbourliness and humour to enjoy" "superb quality seafood" and service over a "multiple-bottle-of-wine lunch"; expect "large crowds, so get there early" as there's an "egalitarian no-booking policy"; P.S. "save room for puds like nanny used to make."

Taman gang ◐☒ 19 | 24 | 18 | £58

141 Park Ln., W1 (Marble Arch), 020-7518 3160; fax 7518 3161; www.tamangang.co.uk

"Be prepared to blow lots of money" at Mayfair's "super-trendy" "beautiful" Balinese-style site filled "with a sexy crowd" consuming "wonderfully tasty" Southeast Asian fare and "cocktails that hit their mark"; cynical wags wonder "does London need another design-led, show-off place" – especially since "service is, well, a bit variable"; but gleeful gang-members "recommend it" for a "romantic evening."

TAMARIND ◐ 25 | 21 | 22 | £47

20 Queen St., W1 (Green Park), 020-7629 3561; fax 7499 5034; www.tamarindrestaurant.com

Proves "the terms gourmet and Indian food go together" gush groupies of this "sophisticated" Mayfair basement, a site of "outstanding" cuisine with an "avant-garde" approach, "elegantly and effectively served" amidst a setting of "quiet, modern elegance"; a few lament it's "lost the subtlety that made it unique", and baulk at "such inflated prices", but they are outvoted by those who rave it's "worth every rupee."

Tampopo ▽ 14 | 15 | 15 | £22

140 Fulham Rd., SW10 (South Kensington), 020-7370 5355; www.tampopo.co.uk

"Comforting soups" and "healthfully tasty", "spicy dishes" are found at this "speedy" Asian with "big windows to watch the world go by"; although "being crammed into communal tables is a minus", most agree it's "great after a movie" (there's a "cinema right across the road") even if it can "get very crowded."

Tas ◐ 20 | 16 | 18 | £23

20 New Globe Walk, SE1 (London Bridge), 020-7928 3300; fax 7261 1166
33 The Cut, SE1 (Southwark), 020-7928 1444; fax 7633 9686
72 Borough High St., SE1 (London Bridge), 020-7403 7200; fax 7403 7022
www.tasrestaurant.com

"Tangy, tasty, terrific" "Turkish eats" make these "nice little secrets" "reliable" venues "to try something different" at "reasonable prices", with the added perks of a "crooning guitarist" and a "not-too-shabby wine list"; sure, the normally "cheerful service" "suffers on busy evenings", but most "give a thumbs up" to this trio.

Tate Gallery Restaurant 18 | 20 | 17 | £27

Tate Britain, Millbank, SW1 (Pimlico), 020-7887 8825; fax 7887 8902; www.tate.org.uk

"An excellent place to unwind after the rigours of all that art", this "beautiful", yet "minimalist" daytime cafe (dominated by "a great Rex Whistler mural") in the Tate Britain is "a treasure for the hungry museum fan" looking for "delightful" Modern British dishes with a "wine list that continues to impress", thanks to "the number of half bottles available."

Tate Modern 17 | 19 | 12 | £28

(fka Restaurant 7)

Tate Modern, Bankside, SE1 (Blackfriars/London Bridge), 020-7401 5020; www.tate.org.uk/modern

The "panoramic Thames view" is "stunning" from this "cafeterialike setting" in the Tate Modern; the Eclectic menu is "perfectly fine", if typically "overpriced", "but never worth the trip on its own"; "complacent service" comes in for criticism, too.

Tatsuso ⊠ ▽ 23 | 13 | 18 | £59

32 Broadgate Circle, EC2 (Liverpool St.), 020-7638 5863; fax 7638 5864

"Japanese to the smallest detail", this minimalist bi-level Broadgate venue offers "some of the nicest dishes you'll [ever] eat", including "unbelievably good sashimi"; "but you will have to take out a mortgage to pay" the "astronomical prices" – especially "in the evening when following the chef's choice"; "service without a smile" saddens some.

TECA ⊠ 20 | 19 | 17 | £51

54 Brooks Mews, W1 (Bond St.), 020-7495 4774; fax 7491 3545

"Should be more popular" attest admirers of this "quite decent find" down a Mayfair mews; in "bright, clean-lined" premises, it features a "solid" Italian menu offering "interesting variations and an excellent wine list"; yet foes feel "something about it doesn't excite" – perhaps it's the "indifferent service" or the feeling you pay "too much for too little."

TENTAZIONI ⊠ 25 | 16 | 22 | £44

Lloyd's Wharf, 2 Mill St., SE1 (London Bridge/Tower Hill), 020-7237 1100; fax 7237 1100; www.tentazioni.co.uk

"Out of the way, but worth the trek" to Shad Thames say the "regulars who are treated like royalty" as they indulge in a "small", but "ever-changing menu" of "inventive", "sophisticated modern Italian" eats "cooked to perfection", supported by a "keenly priced wine list almost completely" from The Boot.

Terminus 15 | 14 | 14 | £28

Great Eastern Hotel, 40 Liverpool St., EC2 (Liverpool St.), 020-7618 7400; fax 7618 7401; www.great-eastern-hotel.co.uk

"It's a bit noisy, so you can meet and not worry about being overheard" at this all-day, "buzzing" brasserie/bar – "part train station waiting room, part pickup joint" – by Liverpool Street Station; those in a rush regard it as "reliable" "for a quick business lunch", "breakfast or snack"; but foes are ready to terminate visits to this "mediocre" Modern British.

Terrace ⊠ 19 | 20 | 19 | £43

Le Meridien Piccadilly, 2nd fl., 21 Piccadilly, W1 (Green Park/ Piccadilly Circus), 020-7851 3085; fax 7851 3090

"A safe place to take your in-laws", this glassy dining room on Le Meridien's "mezzanine overlooking Piccadilly" has a "consistently good", if rather "ordinary" French menu, with service that's "friendly, if a little slow"; best bets are the "tremendous breakfasts" and "Sunday jazz brunch buffet."

Texas Embassy Cantina 13 | 17 | 16 | £23

1 Cockspur St., SW1 (Charing Cross/Piccadilly Circus), 020-7925 0077; fax 7925 0444; www.texasembassy.com

"To get a rib or taco fix, American expats go" to this Trafalgar Square Tex-Mex that, with its "über-cheesy decor" and "all sorts of fellow adventurers", "generally succeeds" in providing a "rip-snortin' time"; however, hostile hombres recommend partaking of the "brilliant margaritas" and "good variety of cold beer", all the better "to forget" the "pedestrian" "approximation of Southwestern food" here.

T.G.I. Friday's ◐ 11 | 12 | 14 | £21

96-98 Bishop's Bridge Rd., W2 (Bayswater/Queensway), 020-7229 8600; fax 7727 4150

25-29 Coventry St., W1 (Piccadilly Circus), 020-7839 6262; fax 7839 6296

6 Bedford St., WC2 (Charing Cross/Covent Garden), 020-7379 0585; fax 7240 3239

www.tgifridays.com

"Americana kitsch at its finest" reigns at this West End chain trio, "the same as every other location in the world": "hyperactive waiters", "loud music" and a "basic", "big" burger-dominated menu of "predictable food"; caustic cognoscenti confide "this is a place you try to avoid, but sometimes it's just convenient", especially when "with large groups", "children or those with childish palates."

Thai Pavilion ▽ 17 | 18 | 17 | £26

42 Rupert St., W1 (Leicester Sq./Piccadilly Circus), 020-7287 6333; fax 7587 0484; www.thaipavilion.com ◐

82 Kennington Rd., SE11 (Lambeth North), 020-7587 0455; fax 7587 0484; www.pavilioneast.com

"Whether for business or pleasure", this "beautiful space" – complete with waterfall – "in the heart" of Soho (with a

Kennington sibling) has fans claiming they "will definitely be going back" for "tasty" Thai cooking at "reasonable prices" – like lunch for a "bargain £5"; the staff's a bit "slow in arriving", though.

Thai Square 18 | 17 | 15 | £26

27-28 St. Anne's Ct., W1 (Tottenham Court Rd.), 020-7287 2000 ◐ Ⓢ
5 Princes St., W1 (Oxford Circus), 020-7499 3333 Ⓢ
148 The Strand, WC2 (Covent Garden), 020-7497 0904 ◐ Ⓢ
2-4 Lower Richmond Rd., SW15 (Putney/Putney Bridge), 020-8780 1811; fax 8780 1211 ◐
19 Exhibition Rd., SW7 (South Kensington), 020-7584 8359
21-24 Cockspur St., SW1 (Charing Cross/Piccadilly Circus), 020-7839 4000; fax 7839 0839
347-349 Upper St., N1 (Angel), 020-7704 2000; fax 7704 2277
1 Great St. Thomas Apostle, EC4 (Mansion House), 020-7329 0001 Ⓢ
136-138 Minories, EC3 (Tower Hill), 020-7680 1111; fax 7680 1112 Ⓢ
www.thaisq.com

Even if it "never surprises", the "uniformity of this chain" of Thais mushrooming around town ensures a "decent dining experience", with a "wide choice of spicy" dishes and even "a certain romance" in the artefact-heavy (Buddhas, etc.) setting; but sceptical savants shrug it's "average food at an above-average price", bemoaning "hit-and-miss service."

Thierry's Ⓢ ▽ 18 | 14 | 18 | £34

342 King's Rd., SW3 (Sloane Sq./South Kensington), 020-7352 3365; fax 7352 3365

"Extremely popular with locals" "for a cosy dinner", this "sweet little place" in King's Road serves "the Classic food of a true, local French Bistro" that's "just the right side of inventive"; whilst the "service is endearingly disorganised", everyone is "treated as a regular customer."

Tiger Lil's 13 | 11 | 11 | £21

16A Southside Clapham Common, SW4 (Clapham Common), 020-7720 5433; fax 7622 5995
270 Upper St., N1 (Highbury & Islington), 020-7226 1118; fax 7288 1108
www.tigerlils.com

This "Mongolian BBQ" pair in Clapham and Islington offers a "make-your-own stir-fry" format where "you can go up as many times as you like" with your chosen ingredients and enlist the help of "entertaining wok men" to prepare "fresh" Asian-Eclectic dishes; still, a few wonder "why it all tastes the same", and warn the "pick-and-mix" principle works well "so long as you don't have to queue."

Timo 22 | 19 | 21 | £46

343 Kensington High St., W8 (High St. Kensington), 020-7603 3888; fax 7603 8111

An "appealing" menu of "simple preparations with fantastic ingredients" is the formula that fans applaud at this "serene" Kensington Italian with "caring staff" and a "neighbourhood feel"; "if a little predictable, it's very reliable" – just "don't sit downstairs" regulars recommend.

Tokyo Diner ◐ 19 | 10 | 17 | £17

2 Newport Pl., WC2 (Leicester Sq.), 020-7287 8777; fax 7434 1415; www.tokyodiner.com

Little beyond "blond woods and bright lights" sets the scene for "beautiful bento boxes full of mouth-watering delights" and other "fresh, simple" Japanese fare at this "tiny, two-story" Chinatown "diner"; "service is quick" – and, more importantly, "takes no tips"; hence, a "good budget place."

TOM AIKENS ⊠ 26 | 22 | 24 | £81

43 Elystan St., SW3 (South Kensington), 020-7584 2003; fax 7584 2001; www.tomaikens.co.uk

At his "blow-out place for gourmands", "gifted" chef-owner Tom Aikens offers "inventiveness, intensity" and "beautifully presented" "paintings on a plate" at his "austere" but "elegant" Chelsea New French; some say it's "all too over-the-top", from the "frothy" cuisine to the "warm service" ("you feel as if you're always being watched"); still, most agree this "memorable experience" is "worth every penny", as well as "all the hassle of getting a reservation."

Tom's Delicatessen 20 | 15 | 14 | £18

226 Westbourne Grove, W11 (Notting Hill Gate), 020-7221 8818; fax 7221 7717

"Seating is at a premium" – indeed, "one feels rushed to vacate one's table for the next hungry person" – at Tom Conran's "tiny deli/sandwich shop" with a popular "little back garden" and sprinkling of celebs in Notting Hill; and if there are "irritating queues" (especially Saturday and Sunday mornings), "don't be put off" as the "consistently good, healthy" Eclectic fare "is well worth it."

Tootsies 14 | 12 | 15 | £20

120 Holland Park Ave., W11 (Holland Park), 020-7229 8567
35 Haven Green, W5 (Ealing Broadway), 020-8566 8200; fax 8991 1491
148 Chiswick High Rd., W4 (Turnham Green), 020-8747 1869; fax 8987 0686
35 James St., W1 (Bond St.), 020-7486 1611; fax 7935 4957
48 High St., SW19 (Wimbledon), 020-8946 4135
1 Battersea Rise, SW11 (Clapham Junction), 020-7924 4935
107 Old Brompton Rd., SW7 (South Kensington), 020-7581 8942; fax 7590 0979
177 New King's Rd., SW6 (Parsons Green), 020-7736 4023

(continued)
Tootsies
36-38 Abbeville Rd, SW4 (Clapham South), 020-8772 6646; fax 8772 0672
196-198 Haverstock Hill, NW3 (Belsize Park), 020-7431 3812; fax 7794 8478
www.tootsiesrestaurants.co.uk
Additional locations throughout London
"Great if you want to take the sprogs out", this chain of "firm favourites" is "an easy place to please all tastes", with "basic" American diner grub (including "no-nonsense burgers with all the trimmings"); even if the "service is not the best" and the "decor could use some modernising", "you know what you're going to get whichever branch you go to"; P.S. "when hungover, nothing beats their all-day breakfast dish."

Toto's 23 | 21 | 21 | £48
Walton House, Walton St. at Lennox Garden Mews, SW3 (Knightsbridge), 020-7589 2062; fax 7581 9668
"Rich cooking matches the rich clientele" at this "romantic", "chichi" Chelsea Italian, with "a grown-up" experience that's "like dining in a grand house", from the "quality" cuisine to the "professional" service (however, it helps "to know them to get good treatment"); it's a "favourite" "for a long, languid Sunday lunch" or "special occasion" – just be sure to give "your credit card some warning."

Troubadour, The ◐ 13 | 20 | 15 | £19
265 Old Brompton Rd., SW5 (Earl's Court), 020-7370 1434; fax 7341 6329; www.troubadour.co.uk
"Still going after 50 years", this "funky", all-day Earl's Court coffeehouse "oozes decades of cultural history" – having been "a '60s hangout for musicians" and now a nightly source of "great live music downstairs"; the Eclectic fare is "nothing haute", but then "it's not really about the food", it's about the "unbeatable" "bohemian" ambience, complete with "extremely atmospheric courtyard at the back."

Truc Vert 21 | 16 | 15 | £29
42 N. Audley St., W1 (Bond St.), 020-7491 9988; fax 7491 7717
"Forget hectic London life" at this "quaint" French Bistro bringing "a bit of Gallic sunshine" to those "grabbing a bite in Mayfair"; you "can pop in anytime" for "delicious, homemade" fare, consumed at "small wooden tables"; however, "service is apologetic and slow", so some prefer takeaway from the "exquisite deli."

Tsunami ⊠ 25 | 18 | 17 | £39
5-7 Voltaire Rd., SW4 (Clapham North), 020-7978 1610; fax 7978 1591; www.tsunamijapaneserestaurant.co.uk
"Despite its now-unfortunate name, this is a wonderful Japanese" say surveyors high on this "hip, cool" corner of

Clapham, where much "innovative flair" goes into the "fresh" Asian fare; the "reasonable" price/value ratio leads some to compare this to "a poor man's Nobu" (and indeed, the chef worked there); only wet spot is the "somewhat aloof service."

Tugga — | — | — | E

312-314 King's Rd., SW3 (Sloane Square), 020-7351 0101; www.tugga.com

Four Tuggas – the nickname for Portuguese nationals – have clubbed together to open this smart, cosy eatery in King's Road showcasing respected Porto-based chef Miguel Castro e Silva's modern morsels, including tapas-size dishes called *petiscos* (prices, however, are far from pint-sized); the kitchen swings from noon until 11 PM, and, in addition to a sunken private dining room, there's a contemporary bar.

Tuttons Brasserie ◐ 16 | 16 | 16 | £27

11-12 Russell St., WC2 (Covent Garden), 020-7836 4141; fax 7379 9979

"When you don't want fancy schmancy", just "solid" sustenance, this "lively" Modern British "somehow suits all" options, whether "with partner, friends or family"; whilst it's "fun to watch the Covent Gardeners go by", "especially after the theatre", it tends to be "full of tourists in summer – so, a better bet in the off-season."

Two Brothers Fish ⊠ 21 | 11 | 17 | £20

297-303 Regent's Park Rd., N3 (Finchley Central), 020-8346 0469; fax 8343 1978

. . . and they get a very good catch, judging by the acclaim for the "generous portions" of "beautifully fresh fish" (and "top chips") that make it "well worth the schlep" to this "tired"-looking seafooder; "be prepared to queue, though" (they take no reservations at night), unless you want to "use the takeaway counter."

202 18 | 21 | 16 | £24

Nicole Farhi, 202 Westbourne Grove, W11 (Notting Hill Gate), 020-7727 2722; fax 7792 9217

"Populated by yummy mummies and models" and the "occasional celebrity", Nicole Farhi's "lively" "clothing-store-cum-restaurant" located in "chic" Westbourne Grove premises is "great for weekend brunch"; the Modern European menu offers "solid", "fresh" fare, but the "best part is sitting outside" and "gazing at the glamorous people waltzing by."

UBON ⊠ 25 | 22 | 20 | £54

34 Westferry Circus, E14 (Canary Wharf), 020-7719 7800; fax 7719 7801; www.noburestaurants.com

For "miso cod without the crowds", converts congregate at Nobu's Canary Wharf cousin – "not as fashionable, but easier to get a table"; it's also "easy to rack up a sizeable bill" from the "fabulous", "innovative" Japanese–South American menu, served by staff that are "smooth" (though possessing "an unmerited superior attitude"); "spectacular views" make it "better-looking" than its sire, and whilst the "chefs' skill isn't quite as good", "if you love the food, who cares?"; N.B. the name is Nobu spelt backwards.

Uli ☒ ∇ 25 | 15 | 26 | £31

16 All Saints Rd., W11 (Ladbroke Grove), 020-7727 7511

Near Portobello Road (admittedly "an area better known for trendiness than taste"), this "intimate", "aspirational Asian" has patrons pleading "don't let the word out" about its "creative" cuisine and "incredibly nice staff"; "prices are slightly higher" than some like, but this is "a diamond in the rough."

Umu ☒ ∇ 16 | 24 | 18 | £78

14-16 Bruton Pl., W1 (Bond St.), 020-7499 8881

Located behind a hidden, "James Bond–like entrance" in a discreet Mayfair mews, this "stylish", "showy" site offers a "grandiose menu", reputedly the first in London to focus on Kyoto cuisine, preferably served kaiseki (small, set courses) style; whilst there are many "little gems" on the plate and an "impressive selection of sakes" on display, "disappointed" dissidents feel "let down" given the "*Goldfinger* prices" – it's "for people with more money than taste."

Union Cafe ☒ 20 | 15 | 19 | £31

96 Marylebone Ln., W1 (Bond St.), 020-7486 4860; fax 7486 4860; www.brinkleys.com

"Never crowded and never loud", this "trusted" brother to Brinkley's in Marylebone embodies a "delightful" union of "comforting", "consistently good" Modern British–Med fare and a "well-chosen wine list with minimal markup"; a "lively crowd" attests it's "nice for lunch" or "midweek dinner."

Vale, The – | – | – | M

99 Chippenham Rd., W9 (Maida Vale), 020-7266 0990; fax 7286 7224

"Still undiscovered" after seven years – perhaps it's the location in a "slightly insalubrious" part of Maida Vale – this Modern British makes a "good local choice" for "consistent" dishes from a "daily-changing menu" with some competitive "set deals"; "charming" "staff who genuinely seem to care" get a pat on the back.

Vama ◐ 24 | 18 | 19 | £39

438 King's Rd., SW10 (Sloane Sq.), 020-7565 8500; fax 7565 8501; www.vama.co.uk

Be "blown away by" a "perfectly balanced", "wonderfully innovative Indian" "menu that will challenge your taste buds" at this "atmospheric, classy" King's Road eatery that offers "friendly staff" and some "celeb-spotting" to boot ("we saw Jude Law"); some caution "the cost can skyrocket if you're not careful."

Vasco & Piero's Pavilion ⊠ ▽ 23 13 22 £35

15 Poland St., W1 (Oxford Circus), 020-7437 8774; fax 7437 0467; www.vascosfood.com

Granted, this "tiny" pavilion "needs a fresh lick of paint", but the few Soho stalwarts who know it don't mind a bit, since it "does everything right", from the "interesting", "homestyle" Italian cucina at "decent prices" to the "personal service"; plus, the "adventurous wine list is speckled with gems."

Veeraswamy ◐ 22 19 19 £38

Victory House, 99-101 Regent St., W1 (Piccadilly Circus), 020-7734 1401; fax 7439 8434; www.realindianfood.com

"Perched above the Regent Street bustle", this "venerable Indian" "institution" – it celebrates its 80th birthday this year – "keeps on ticking", preparing "mouth-watering", "upscale" dishes (e.g. lobster curry); but if it's "still a place to impress", that's for the "food more than the decor" – the "rich colours in an ultracontemporary setting" seem "somewhat jarring" – or the staff, which range in attitude from "friendly" to "rather grudging"; N.B. a scheduled refurb may soon redeem the digs.

Verbanella ◐ 20 17 23 £38

30 Beauchamp Pl., SW3 (Knightsbridge), 020-7584 1107; fax 7589 9662

It "never lets you down" say staunch supporters of this "cute little Italian" in Knightsbridge, where "the staff treat you as an old friend" and the "solid-value", "dependable" (if "not unusual") menu fits the bill "for a leisurely lunch or a less-expensive dinner."

Viet Hoa ◐ 21 5 17 £17

70-72 Kingsland Rd., E2 (Old St.), 020-7729 8293; fax 7729 8293

"Still worth a trip" to Shoreditch say surveyors of this "good-value Vietnamese", offering "divine" dishes from an "extremely cheap" menu; there's "no atmosphere", but the "very quick service" means you don't have to linger amidst "laundry room–like" decor.

Villandry 18 16 14 £33

170 Great Portland St., W1 (Great Portland St.), 020-7631 3131; fax 7631 3030; www.villandry.com

"You get hungry just walking in the door" of this "relaxed" "gourmet food shop" "with restaurant attached"; "freshness rules" on the "wholesome" "rather Eclectic menu" that's "adventurous and traditional at the same time"; but sceptics say it's "spoilt by staff" who "seem too cool to bother serving" and suggest the "expensive prices" mean the Marylebone "rent must be pretty high."

Vine, The ▽ 21 | 19 | 15 | £33

86 Highgate Rd., NW5 (Kentish Town B.R.), 020-7209 0038; fax 7209 9001

Ratings may not reflect the relaunch by new management of this "cool pub tucked away from the hassles of life" in Kentish Town; the hardy few who are familiar with it say that it remains "a fun place to meet and mingle", with a "pleasant garden out back" and a "good cross-section" of dishes on its "reliable" Modern European menu; however, hostiles huff that "service is haphazard."

Vineyard at Stockcross ▽ 22 | 25 | 24 | £61

Vineyard at Stockcross, Stockcross, Newbury, Berkshire, 01635 528770; fax 01635 528398; www.the-vineyard.co.uk

Take "a trip to Napa Valley, just outside Newbury" when you visit this "beautiful", white and wrought-iron "wine-lovers' paradise" within the Berkshire hotel of the same name, whose main claim to fame is a huge, "remarkable wine list – American-orientated, but with plenty of fine European bottles"; accompanying it is an "imaginative" Modern British–Classic French menu; "expensive, but worth it" surveyors summarise.

Vingt-Quatre ◐ 13 | 12 | 14 | £24

325 Fulham Rd., SW10 (South Kensington), 020-7376 7224; fax 7352 2643

"As the name says, it serves food around the clock" (*vingt-quatre* means 24 *en français*), "getting maddeningly busy after midnight when it's the only decent place open" in Chelsea; its coterie of "clubbers" and "celebrity-spotters" confide the Eclectic brasserie-style menu is "nothing spectacular", even sometimes "below par, but in the wee hours does it matter?"

Vivat Bacchus ⊠ – | – | – | E

47 Farringdon St., EC4 (Chancery Ln./Farringdon), 020-7353 2648; www.vivatbacchus.co.uk

Bacchus himself might smile at this bright Holborn basement where, amidst bottles, one dines on Modern European cooking with some "inventive twists"; it features three "walk-in wine cellars" with an "excellent South African" selection, and a "great cheese room" with 80 varieties; add in "caring staff", and you've got one "great find."

Vrisaki ◐⊠ ▽ 22 | 7 | 17 | £25

73 Myddelton Rd., N22 (Bounds Green/Wood Green), 020-8889 8760; fax 8889 0103

"From the front it looks just like a kebab shop, but once inside, [all] is beautiful" at this Wood Green Greek – thanks to the "fabulous choice" of food that "just keeps on coming and coming" (so "do not eat for several days" beforehand); one of "North London's best-kept secrets", it's "unparalleled value for money" too.

WAGAMAMA 19 | 14 | 17 | £16

26A Kensington High St., W8 (High St. Kensington), 020-7376 1717
101A Wigmore St., W1 (Bond St./Oxford Circus), 020-7409 0111
10A Lexington St., W1 (Oxford Circus/Piccadilly Circus), 020-7292 0990
1 Tavistock St., WC2 (Covent Garden), 020-7836 3330; fax 7240 8846
4A Streatham St., WC1 (Holborn/Tottenham Court Rd.), 020-7323 9223; fax 7436 7834
Harvey Nichols, 109-125 Knightsbridge, SW1 (Knightsbridge), 020-7201 8000; fax 7201 8080
40 Parkfield St., N1 (Angel), 020-7226 2664
11 Jamestown Rd., NW1 (Camden Town), 020-7428 0800; fax 7482 4887
109 Fleet St., EC4 (Blackfriars/St. Paul's), 020-7583 7889 ⊠
1A Ropemaker St., EC2 (Moorgate), 020-7588 2688 ⊠
www.wagamama.com
Additional locations throughout London

Using a "match of yin and yang – a cool environment and warm, comforting" Japanese fare – this "high-tech noodle shop conquers London" and our surveyors, who've voted it the *Survey*'s Most Popular; "running the risk of giving chains a good name", all branches "maintain the same standard", with "long bench-seating and tables" to entice "diners to commune with each other"; but it's the "fast, furious" servers with the handheld computers that make it so "appealing"– plus it's"perfect when on a budget" to boot.

Wapping Food 17 | 23 | 16 | £36

Wapping Hydraulic Power Station, Wapping Wall, E1 (Wapping), 020-7680 2080

"The setting in an old electricity station" adds "oodles of character" to this Wapping eatery "with an attached gallery for exhibits"; the "well-prepared, interesting" Eclectic–Modern European fare comes at "decent prices", and even if the "amateur service" causes some dismay, most feel it's "worth a hike" to this "quite remote" spot.

Waterloo Fire Station 12 | 13 | 13 | £24

150 Waterloo Rd., SE1 (Waterloo), 020-7620 2226; fax 7633 9161

It's "not often you get to eat in a fire station", so many "want to try" this "lively" renovated Waterloo venue for the "interesting decor" alone; alas, the "basic" Modern European menu is not so hot, whilst the "scarce service" and siren-level sound has many "calling 999"; it's best "for a quick pint" to wet your whistle whilst waiting for a train or curtain at the Old or New Vic nearby.

WATERSIDE INN ⊠ 28 | 25 | 26 | £90

Waterside Inn, Ferry Rd., Bray-on-Thames, Berkshire, 01628 620691; fax 01628 784710; www.waterside-inn.co.uk

"Situated on the Thames, in a setting out of a picture book", the Roux brothers' Berkshire destination "provides a massage of all the senses and a reminder of what life is all about"; the "French haute cuisine" is "a perpetual delight", and all's "presided over with care" by "service without equal" in a "pleasant", "old-fashioned" room; it's "extraordinarily expensive", but it's "perfect to swoon your lover", so go on, have a "big splurge" – and make use of the "overnight accommodation" as well.

Wells, The 20 | 19 | 15 | £37

30 Well Walk, NW3 (Hampstead), 020-7794 3785; www.thewellshampstead.co.uk

"Filling the gastro vacuum in Hampstead", this "rambling" 18th-century pub contents a "well-mannered clientele" with "interesting" Modern European cooking and "real beer, perfectly served"; cynics, however, cite serious "staff lapses" – "food's good, if and when it arrives"; still, it's "cosy in winter, a treat on the terrace in summer", so all's well that ends at The Wells.

Westbourne, The 18 | 16 | 13 | £21

101 Westbourne Park Villas, W2 (Royal Oak/Westbourne Park), 020-7221 1332; fax 7243 8081

"In clique-y Notting Hill", this "casual" "hangout" "will never go out of fashion"; and whilst many prefer to "go for the scene first, fare second", the Eclectic–Modern European eats offer "among the best food-for-money deals" around; outside tables on "that amazing terrace" make it "a bit of a scrum in the summer."

Wheeler's, St. James's ☒ 19 | 18 | 19 | £47

12A Duke of York St., SW1 (Piccadilly Circus), 020-7930 2460; fax 8839 2394

Recently acquired by chef Matthew Brown (ex Belvedere), St. James's "landmark" last "link in an old-time London chain" is still a source for "Classic" French–British fish and pretty "professional service"; malcontents may mutter "the food has slipped, whilst prices have gone in the other direction", but regulars confide "dress like a banker" and "don't do anything beyond sole, and you'll dine royally."

White Swan Pub & Dining Room ☒ – | – | – | M

108 Fetter Ln., EC4 (Chancery Ln./Farringdon), 020-7242 9696; www.thewhiteswanlondon.com

"Don't let the publike exterior deceive you": this Holborn "unexpected little gem" (formally a journalists' boozer, the Mucky Duck) offers a "homey" first-floor dining room with a "lovely" Modern British menu, all overseen by "sociable, welcoming owners"; N.B. the £15 Express lunch guarantees two courses in an hour.

Whit's ☒ – | – | – | M

21 Abingdon Rd., W8 (High St. Kensington), 020-7938 1122

"Keep up the good work" urge the few familiar with this eatery "tucked away on a Kensington side street"; chef/

co-owner Steve Whitney cooks "consistent", "very English food" with Gallic accents that, whilst "delicious", strikes some as "too fancy" for a "friendly neighbourhood" place.

Wilton's ⊠ 23 | 21 | 23 | £56

55 Jermyn St., SW1 (Green Park/Piccadilly Circus), 020-7629 9955; fax 7495 6233; www.wiltons.co.uk

A "dignified, clublike atmosphere" (gentlemen, jackets please) reigns in this "quintessentially British" veteran in St. James's, where diners can "rub shoulders with the political elite"; chef Jerome Ponchelle "strikes a great balance" between the Classic and Modern, offering "the epitome of English cooking", "with an emphasis on fresh seafood" "superbly served"; even advocates admit it's pretty "pricey" and pretty "predictable – and may it stay that way."

Windows on the World 20 | 24 | 20 | £56

Hilton Park Lane, 22 Park Ln., W1 (Hyde Park Corner), 020-7208 4021; fax 7208 4144

"It's all about the view" "overlooking the city, including the back garden of Buckingham Palace" at this "gentrified" aerie atop the Hilton Park Lane; nevertheless, there's also "smart" staff serving "surprisingly good" Classic French cuisine, although the worldly wail it's "way too hotel-ish" ("which means poor value" for the price); however, you can "get a drink and snack without breaking the bank in the nice lounge area", often populated by "lots of older men with their 'nieces.'"

Wizzy ◐ – | – | – | M

616 Fulham Rd., SW6 (Parsons Green), 020-7736 9171

Hwi 'Wizzy' Shim was most recently working front of house at Hakkasan until she dug deep into her own pockets to make her restaurant debut as a chef at this small, pocket-size Parsons Green venue; the concise, well-priced menu features modern interpretations of classic Korean dishes and BBQ, making good use of native ingredients shipped in.

Wòdka ◐ 20 | 15 | 20 | £37

12 St. Albans Grove, W8 (High St. Kensington), 020-7937 6513; fax 7937 8621; www.wodka.co.uk

With an "awesome" variety of "unusual, flavoured vodkas" (the "homemade cherry – wow!"), "stunning waitresses" and an "interesting Polish" menu – a "great twist on classic Eastern European fare" – this "cosy" Kensington haunt offers "something different"; the "contemporary" "decor's nothing much", but "who can remember after you taste all sorts of specialty" spirits?

WOLSELEY, THE ◐ 20 | 25 | 20 | £45

160 Piccadilly, W1 (Green Park), 020-7499 6996; fax 7499 6888; www.thewolseley.com

"The celebrities keep coming" and "the dramatic, elegant interior makes anyone feel important" at this "buzzy"

Piccadilly establishment where the "sophisticated" Modern European menu "suits all tastes" and is "served all day"; a few are frustrated at the "rigid" time sittings and "indifferent service", but most applaud this "alive, exciting" venue as "a gem for breakfast" and "spot-on for afternoon tea."

Wong Kei ◐⊭ 16 | 6 | 6 | £14

41-43 Wardour St., W1 (Leicester Sq./Piccadilly Circus), 020-7437 8408

The "surly service" may be "crass, but that's the fun part" of this "unique" Chinatown institution, which remains "as popular as ever", despite the "manky" decor and communal "tables for sharing"; the "simple" Cantonese menu is "brilliant value" – indeed, some suggest "there's no other reason to go" than for a "bargain" meal.

W'Sens ◐ – | – | – | M

12 Waterloo Pl., SW1 (Piccadilly Circus), 020-7484 1355; fax 7484 1366; www.wsens.co.uk

A "newcomer to the scene" in St. James's, this "funky", flashy outpost of restaurant group La Compagnie des Comptoirs has admirers who appreciate the "tempting", "but not mind-blowing" Med-inspired Eclectic menu ("some superb dishes, others average"), whilst others bemoan "patchy service"; P.S. "the bar is a great place to meet after work."

YAUATCHA 24 | 22 | 17 | £36

15 Broadwick St., W1 (Oxford Circus), 020-7494 8888; fax 7494 8889

"Divine dim sum" and a "varied, inventive Chinese menu" are the culinary draws at owner Alan Yau's "hectic, vibrant" yearling in the basement of the Ingeni building in Soho; there's an "ethos of 90-minute tables" that the "helpful servers" strictly enforce, prompting some to suggest "it needs to be less rushed"; P.S. the "fantastic patisserie and teahouse" on the ground floor is also "worth the trip."

Ye Olde Cheshire Cheese 16 | 23 | 18 | £20

145 Fleet St., EC4 (Blackfriars), 020-7353 6170; fax 7353 0845; www.yeoldecheshirecheese.com

"Atmospheric is an understatement" for this "timeworn" 340-year-old landmark tavern on Fleet Street that apparently was "a favourite hangout of Charles Dickens"; even though it's inevitably "a tourist hot spot", the "good ales keep it popular" with a "lively" local crowd, whilst the "comforting", "consistent" Traditional British "pub grub" is "better than you might expect."

Yoshino ☒ 23 | 16 | 20 | £31

3 Piccadilly Pl., W1 (Piccadilly Circus), 020-7287 6622; fax 7287 1733; www.yoshino.net

"No frills, just some of the finest sushi", along with other "decent", "authentic" Japanese dishes "at reasonable prices", are the hallmarks of this "great little gem" "smack bang in Piccadilly", with "charmingly demure" service and a "diverse crowd, comprised mainly of Asian bohemians"; P.S. "go for the bento box set and you will be full at the end of it."

YO! SUSHI 16 | 14 | 15 | £23

Whiteley's, Unit 218, 151 Queensway, W2 (Bayswater), 020-7727 9392; fax 7727 9390
Unit R07, Paddington Station, W2 (Paddington), 020-7706 9550
Selfridges, 400 Oxford St., W1 (Bond St.), 020-7318 3944; fax 7318 3885
52 Poland St., W1 (Oxford Circus), 020-7287 0443; fax 7439 3660
11-13 Bayley St., WC1 (Tottenham Court Rd.), 020-7636 0076; fax 7439 3663
Fulham Broadway Ctr., 1st fl., Fulham Rd., SW6 (Fulham Broadway), 020-7385 6077; fax 7385 9584
Harvey Nichols, 5th fl., Knightsbridge, SW1 (Knightsbridge), 020-7235 5000; fax 7318 3885
County Hall, Unit 3B, Belvedere Rd., SE1 (Westminster), 020-7928 8871; fax 7928 5619
Unit 2, N1 Ctr., 39 Parkfield St., N1 (Angel), 020-7359 3502
95 Farringdon Rd., EC1 (Farringdon), 020-7841 0785; fax 7841 0798
www.yosushi.com
Additional locations throughout London

"If you've got a craving for quick Japanese food", this "futuristic eating experience" around town offers "conveyor belt sushi" with "non-daring", "reliable" fare on "colour-coded dishes so prices are easy to understand", plus a "drinks service robot"; but some say "the novelty's worn off" from this "gimmicky" venture, and conclude there's "better for less elsewhere."

ZAFFERANO 25 | 19 | 22 | £56

15 Lowndes St., SW1 (Knightsbridge), 020-7235 5800; fax 7235 1971

"Relaxed and classy", this "*splendido*" Italian in "low-key" Belgravia "knows how to make both celebrities and locals feel at home" and remains "a must for foodies", thanks to Andrew Needham's "first-class" menu of "excellent rustic" dishes and the "comprehensive wine list"; a handful hiss it's "lost some of its sparkle", especially as the bill's gotten stiffer, but even those who pout it's "pricey" concede the "set lunch is extremely good value"; N.B. in September, a small expansion was due to be unveiled.

Zaika 24 | 22 | 20 | £49

1 Kensington High St., W8 (High St. Kensington), 020-7795 6533; fax 7937 8854; www.zaika-restaurant.co.uk

With an "inspired, upscale" menu and an "excellent wine list", this "contemporary", "comfortable" Kensington venue is a "textbook example of how to turn Indian flavours into haute cuisine"; a few find it "pricey" and claim the departure of chef Vineet Bhatia "is making a difference";

nevertheless, this "sensual dining experience" remains "a great date place."

Zamoyski ▽ 22 | 17 | 21 | £29

85 Fleet Rd., NW3 (Belsize Park), 020-7794 4792

This "small, friendly Polish" place with bare brick walls in Belsize Park has a "great", hearty menu and a "wide range of vodkas" for "scrumptious shots to finish off your meal with"; there's also "entertaining live music" on Saturday nights.

Zen Central ◐ 21 | 17 | 19 | £37

20 Queen St., W1 (Green Park), 020-7629 8089; fax 7493 6181; www.zencentralrestaurant.com

There's an "emphasis on vegetarian dishes" and "lovely Peking duck" on the "upscale" Mandarin menu at this "elegant", modern Mayfair eatery, and whilst some feel there's a surfeit of "Westernised dishes", most are not surprised it "continues to keep going" after almost 20 years.

ZeNW3 ◐ 21 | 16 | 16 | £39

83-84 Hampstead High St., NW3 (Hampstead), 020-7794 7863; fax 7794 6956; www.zenw3.com

"You can't top the variety and combinations" on the "reliable" Chinese-Japanese menu at this 20-year-old Hampstead venue, and even though many now feel the "tired decor needs a face-lift" and the "hurried service" ruffles a few feathers, the steadfast insist it remains a "solid" standby; P.S. "try the Sunday buffet: it's good value and you can stay all day."

Zetter Restaurant & Rooms 20 | 18 | 18 | £34

The Zetter, 86-88 Clerkenwell Rd., EC1 (Farringdon), 020-7324 4455; fax 7324 4445; www.thezetter.com

Set in the former warehouse base of Zetter Football Pools, this "trendy restaurant in a hip hotel" in Clerkenwell offers a "relaxed bar to chill out at" and an "understated" dining area with an "inventive", "carefully conceived" modern Italian menu delivered by "attentive" servers; still, a few feel the place "could do with a bit more atmosphere."

Ziani ◐ 23 | 18 | 21 | £39

45 Radnor Walk, SW3 (Sloane Sq.), 020-7351 5297; fax 7244 8387

"Boisterous, busy" and "upbeat", this "tiny" Chelsea site where "everyone is jammed in" is "a find" for "excellent, basic Italian cooking"; but be warned, the "noise levels can defeat conversation", and the staff "need to slow down" – though they still ensure everyone is "treated like family."

Zilli Fish ☒ 21 | 16 | 19 | £36

36-40 Brewer St., W1 (Piccadilly Circus), 020-7734 8649; www.zillialdo.com

Celebrity chef Aldo Zilli – a "food hero" to some – is the man to "cook up a storm" at this "bubbly seafooder" in "casual" Soho premises where "the prices are fairly high, but the quality is superb"; "at rush times" expect it to be "noisy" and the "service to get a little spotty."

Zimzun ▽ 14 | 20 | 16 | £24

Retail Ctr., Fulham Rd., SW6 (Fulham Broadway), 020-7385 4555; fax 7386 8555; www.zimzun.co.uk

It's "not in the school canteen style", exactly, but "be prepared to share" one of the "big square tables" for communal dining at this stylish eatery that features a "good" Thai menu of green curry and the like; being located in the shopping centre above Fulham Broadway tube station, "so close to the cinema, makes for a great night out", especially "for big groups."

Zinc Bar & Grill 15 | 17 | 16 | £32

11 Jerdan Pl., SW6 (Fulham Broadway), 020-7386 2250; fax 7386 2260

21 Heddon St., W1 (Oxford Circus/Piccadilly Circus), 020-7255 8899; fax 7255 8888 ⊠

www.conran.com

A "younger crowd" seeking a "meeting point for adventures in Mayfair" populates this establishment in "light, airy" premises off Regent Street that's a "reliable place for a not-too-expensive" Modern British–European meal; however, few critics feel it "could do better", claiming that "there's just something missing"; the lesser-known, younger Fulham sibling has an outside terrace that's "good in the sun."

Zizzi 16 | 15 | 14 | £21

231 Chiswick High Rd., W4 (Chiswick), 020-874 7940 ◐
110-116 Wigmore St., W1 (Bond St.), 020-7935 2336 ◐
35-38 Paddington St., W1 (Baker St.), 020-7224 1450 ◐
33-41 Charlotte St., W1 (Goodge St.), 020-7436 9440 ◐
73-75 The Strand, WC2 (Charing Cross), 020-7240 1717; fax 7379 9753 ◐
20 Bow St., WC2 (Holborn), 020-7836 6101
35-37 Battersea Rise, SW11 (Clapham South), 020-7924 7311 ◐
194-196 Earl's Court Rd., SW5 (Earl's Court), 020-7370 1999 ◐
87 Allitsen Rd., NW8 (St. John's Wood), 020-7722 7296
1-3 Hampstead Ln., N6 (Highgate), 020-8347 0090 ◐
www.zizzi.co.uk
Additional locations throughout London

This "casual", "comforting" and "cheap" ("by London standards") Italian chain offers "unpretentious pastas and delicious wood oven–baked pizza"; even if it can be "noisy and non-romantic" at times, most agree it's an easy option "after a long day at the office" and a "popular place to take children", whereas the less convinced suggest "the name is the zippiest thing about the place."

Zucca 18 | 17 | 17 | £29

188 Westbourne Grove, W11 (Notting Hill Gate), 020-7727 0060; fax 7727 0069

"It certainly benefits from a great location" in Notting Hill, but the "simple pleasures" of "fresh", "decent" Italian fare from a "varied, authentic menu" also get a thumbs up at this "relaxed", minimalist trattoria; there's also a "cosy bar downstairs, popular with the locals."

ZUMA 25 | 24 | 20 | £56

5 Raphael St., SW7 (Knightsbridge), 020-7584 1010; fax 7584 5005; www.zumarestaurant.com

"Book in advance" for this "emperor of the sushi scene", a "fashionable" Knightsbridge venue that "thrills all the senses" thanks to a "flashy crowd" "alive with famous faces", "hopping bar" and "sublime" Japanese menu that also boasts "terrific" dishes from the robata grill; sure, there are some who baulk at the "wallet-damaging" prices and "snobby waiters" that result from the "ridiculous hype"; but most maintain it "wholly deserves its reputation" as one of the "trendiest" spots around.

Indexes

CUISINES
LOCATIONS
SPECIAL FEATURES

CUISINES

American
Arkansas Cafe (E1)
Banquette (WC2)
Battersea Grill/Chel. (multi. loc.)
Big Easy (SW3)
Bodeans (multi. loc.)
Christopher's (WC2)
Ed's Easy Diner (multi. loc.)
Hard Rock Cafe (W1)
Harlem (multi. loc.)
Joe Allen (WC2)
Lucky 7 (W2)
PJ's B&G (multi. loc.)
Planet Hollywood (W1)
Rainforest Cafe (W1)
Reubens (W1)
Santa Fe (N1)
Smollensky's (multi. loc.)
Sophie's Steak (SW10)
Sticky Fingers (W8)
T.G.I. Friday's (multi. loc.)
Tootsies (multi. loc.)

Argentinean
El Gaucho (multi. loc.)
Gaucho Grill (multi. loc.)

Asian
Asia de Cuba (WC2)
Blakes (SW7)
Cicada (EC1)
Cocoon (W1)
e&o (W11)
Eight Over Eight (SW3)
Fifty (SW1)
Great Eastern (EC2)
L'Etranger (SW7)
Maze (W1)
Pacific Oriental (EC2)
Pengelley's (SW1)
Singapura (EC3)
Tampopo (SW10)
Tiger Lil's (multi. loc.)
Uli (W11)

Bangladeshi
Ginger (W2)

Belgian
Abbaye (EC1)
Belgo (multi. loc.)
Bierodrome (multi. loc.)

Brazilian
Rodizio Rico (W2)

British (Modern)
Abbey (NW1)
Admiral Codrington (SW3)
Admiralty (WC2)
Alastair Little (W1)
Anchor & Hope (SE1)
Anglesea Arms (W6)
Annie's (multi. loc.)
Atlantic B&G (W1)
Aurora (EC2)
Axis (WC2)
Balans (multi. loc.)
Balham Kitchen (SW12)
Bankside (multi. loc.)
Barnsbury (N1)
Belvedere (W8)
Bistrot 190 (SW7)
Boxwood Café (SW1)
Bradley's (NW3)
Brinkley's (SW10)
Cafe at Sotheby's (W1)
Chez Bruce (SW17)
Clarke's (W8)
Cow Din. Rm. (W2)
Duke of Cambridge (N1)
Duke of Clarence (SW5)
1802 (E14)
Engineer (NW1)
Farm (SW6)
ffiona's (W8)
Fifth Floor (SW1)
Fifth Floor Cafe (SW1)
First Floor (W11)
Fishmarket (EC2)
Fish Shop on St. John (EC1)
Frederick's (N1)
Frontline (W2)

Glasshouse (Richmond)
Globe (NW3)
Gravetye Manor (W. Sus)
Groucho Club (W1)
Gun (E14)
Havelock Tavern (W14)
Homage (WC2)
Home House (W1)
Hush (W1)
Ifield (SW10)
Island Rest. (W2)
Ivy, The (WC2)
Joe's (SW3)
Joe's Rest./Bar (SW1)
Julie's (W11)
Just St. James's (SW1)
Kensington Pl. (W8)
Launceston Place (W8)
Le Caprice (SW1)
Lilly's (E1)
Livebait (multi. loc.)
Medcalf (EC1)
Odette's (NW1)
Palmerston (SE22)
Paternoster Chop (EC4)
Petersham (Richmond)
Portrait (WC2)
Prince Bonaparte (W2)
Prism (EC3)
Pug (W4)
Randall & Aubin (multi. loc.)
Ransome's Dock (SW11)
Redmonds (SW14)
Rhodes 24 (EC2)
Richard Corrigan (W1)
R.S.J. (SE1)
Savoy Grill (WC2)
Sir Charles Napier (Oxon)
Smiths/Dining Rm. (EC1)
Snows on Green (W6)
Soho House (W1)
Sonny's (SW13)
St. John (EC1)
St. John Bread/Wine (E1)
Tate Gallery (SW1)
Terminus (EC2)
Troubadour (SW5)
Truc Vert (W1)
Tuttons Brasserie (WC2)
Union Cafe (W1)
Vale (W9)
Vineyard/Stockcross (Berks)
Wheeler's (SW1)
White Swan (EC4)
Wilton's (SW1)
Zinc B&G (multi. loc.)

British (Traditional)

Abbeville (SW4)
Annabel's (W1)
Battersea Grill/Chel. (multi. loc.)
Bentley's (W1)
Boisdale (multi. loc.)
Brian Turner (W1)
Browns (multi. loc.)
Builders Arms (SW3)
Butlers Wharf (SE1)
Cafe Fish (W1)
Coach & Horses (EC1)
fish! (SE1)
Fortnum's Fountain (W1)
Goring Din. Rm. (SW1)
Green's (SW1)
Grenadier (SW1)
Grill Room (W1)
Grumbles (SW1)
Guinea Grill (W1)
Inn The Park (SW1)
Kew Grill (Richmond)
Langan's Bistro (W1)
Langan's Brasserie (W1)
Maggie Jones's (W8)
Mark's Club (W1)
Medcalf (EC1)
Montagu (W1)
North Sea (WC1)
Notting Grill (W11)
Odin's (W1)
Paternoster Chop (EC4)
Porters (WC2)
Quality Chop Hse. (EC1)
Quod (SW1)
Rhodes 24 (EC2)
Richoux (multi. loc.)

Ritz (W1)
Rivington Grill (EC2)
Rowley's (multi. loc.)
Rules (WC2)
Shepherd's (SW1)
Simpson's (WC2)
Smiths/Top Floor (EC1)
Whit's (W8)
Wilton's (SW1)
Ye Olde Cheshire (EC4)

Burmese

Mandalay (W2)

Chinese

(* dim sum specialist)
Chinese Exp. (W1)
Chino Latino (SE1)
Chuen Cheng Ku (W1)*
dim t (N6)*
ECapital (W1)
Four Seasons (W2)
Fung Shing (WC2)
Golden Dragon (W1)*
Good Earth (multi. loc.)
Gung-Ho (NW6)
Hakkasan (W1)
Harbour City (W1)*
Hunan (SW1)
Imperial China (WC2)*
Imperial City (EC3)
Jade Garden (W1)*
Jenny Lo's Tea Hse. (SW1)
Joy King Lau (WC2)*
Kai Mayfair (W1)
Lee Ho Fook (W1)*
Mandarin Kitchen (W2)
Mao Tai (multi. loc.)
Memories/China (multi. loc.)
Mr. Chow (SW1)
Mr. Kong (WC2)
New Culture Rev. (multi. loc.)
New World (W1)*
Nyonya (W11)
Phoenix Palace (NW1)*
Ping Pong (W1)*
Poons (multi. loc.)
Princess Garden (W1)*
Royal China (multi. loc.)*
Shanghai Blues (WC1)*
Singapore Garden (NW6)
Song Que Café (E2)
Wong Kei (W1)
Yauatcha (W1)*
Zen Central (W1)
ZeNW3 (NW3)

Chophouse

Black & Blue (multi. loc.)
Butlers Wharf (SE1)
Christopher's (WC2)
El Gaucho (multi. loc.)
Gaucho Grill (multi. loc.)
Kew Grill (Richmond)
Notting Grill (W11)
Paternoster Chop (EC4)
Quality Chop Hse. (EC1)
Rib Room (SW1)
Rules (WC2)
Smiths/Top Floor (EC1)
Smollensky's (multi. loc.)
Sophie's Steak (SW10)

Cuban

Asia de Cuba (WC2)
Floridita (W1)

Danish

Lundum's (SW7)

Eclectic

Archipelago (W1)
Axis (WC2)
Bibendum Oyster (SW3)
Blakes (SW7)
Books for Cooks (W11)
Boxwood Café (SW1)
Brinkley's (SW10)
Brunello (SW7)
Cafe Med (multi. loc.)
Cantina Vinopolis (SE1)
Canyon (Richmond)
Chino Latino (SE1)
Collection (SW3)
Ebury Wine Bar (SW1)
Electric Brasserie (W11)
Enterprise (SW3)
Fifty (SW1)

Giraffe (multi. loc.)
Graze (W9)
Hoxton Apprentice (N1)
Ifield (SW10)
Kettners (W1)
Lanes (W1)
Lanesborough (SW1)
Lansdowne (NW1)
Light House (SW19)
Lonsdale (W11)
Michael Moore (W1)
Mosimann's (SW1)
Motcombs (SW1)
MVH (SW13)
Naked Turtle (SW14)
Oxo Tower (SE1)
Pomegranates (SW1)
Providores/Tapa (W1)
Ransome's Dock (SW11)
Silk (W1)
Spoon (W1)
Tate Modern (SE1)
Tiger Lil's (multi. loc.)
Tom's Deli (W11)
Troubadour (SW5)
Villandry (W1)
Vingt-Quatre (SW10)
Wapping Food (E1)
Westbourne (W2)
W'Sens (SW1)

European (Modern)

Abbeville (SW4)
Abbey (NW1)
Abingdon (W8)
Admiral Codrington (SW3)
Albannach (WC2)
Allium (SW1)
Andrew Edmunds (W1)
Angela Hartnett's (W1)
Avenue (SW1)
Babylon (W8)
Bank Aldwych (WC2)
Bank Westminster (SW1)
Banquette (WC2)
Bingham (Richmond)
Blandford St. (W1)
Bluebird Club (SW3)
Blue Print Café (SE1)
Brackenbury (W6)
Bush B&G (W12)
Chalcot (NW1)
Chancery (EC4)
Circus (W1)
Clerkenwell (EC1)
Criterion Grill (W1)
Don (EC4)
Draper's Arms (N1)
Drones (SW1)
Ebury Din. Rm. (SW1)
1880 (SW7)
Embassy (W1)
Fat Duck (Berks)
Foliage (SW1)
43 South Molton (W1)
Frederick's (N1)
Gate (W6)
George (W1)
Greyhound (SW11)
Homage (WC2)
Home House (W1)
Indigo (WC2)
Ivy, The (WC2)
Ladbroke Arms (W11)
Lansdowne (NW1)
Le Café du Jardin (WC2)
Le Caprice (SW1)
Le Deuxième (WC2)
Little Bay (multi. loc.)
Lola's (N1)
Mash (W1)
Montagu (W1)
Nicole's (W1)
noble rot. (W1)
Notting Hill Brass. (W11)
1 Lombard Brass. (EC3)
Oriel (SW1)
Rowley's (multi. loc.)
Royal Exchange (EC3)
Salt Yard (W1)
Savoy Grill (WC2)
Six-13 (W1)
Sugar Reef (W1)
Troubadour (SW5)

202 (W11)
Union Cafe (W1)
Vine (NW5)
Vivat Bacchus (EC4)
Wapping Food (E1)
Waterloo Fire (SE1)
Wells (NW3)
Westbourne (W2)
Wolseley (W1)
Zinc B&G (multi. loc.)

Fish 'n' Chips
fish! (SE1)
Fish Shop on St. John (EC1)
Geales Fish (W8)
Livebait (multi. loc.)
Nautilus Fish (NW6)
North Sea (WC1)
Seashell (NW1)
Sweetings (EC4)
Two Bros. Fish (N3)

French (Bistro)
Aubaine (SW3)
Bibendum Oyster (SW3)
Bistrotheque (E2)
Bistrot 190 (SW7)
Café Boheme (W1)
Café Rouge (multi. loc.)
Elena's l'Etoile (W1)
French House (W1)
Grumbles (SW1)
La Bouchée (SW7)
La Poule au Pot (SW1)
Le Café du Marché (EC1)
Le Colombier (SW3)
Le Petit Max (SW11)
L'Escargot (W1)
Mon Plaisir (WC2)
Pat. Valerie (multi. loc.)
Racine (SW3)
Simply Nico (SW1)
Thierry's (SW3)

French (Brasserie)
Bellamy's (W1)
Brasserie Roux (SW1)
Brass. St. Quentin (SW3)
Café des Amis (WC2)
Cheyne Walk (SW3)
Chez Gérard (multi. loc.)
Incognico (WC2)
La Brasserie (SW3)
Langan's Brasserie (W1)
La Trouvaille (N1)
Le Palais du Jardin (WC2)
Malmaison Hotel (EC1)
Oriel (SW1)
Quaglino's (SW1)

French (Classic)
Almeida (N1)
Annabel's (W1)
Aurora (EC2)
Belgo (multi. loc.)
Bradley's (NW3)
Brass. St. Quentin (SW3)
Chez Gérard (multi. loc.)
Chez Kristof (W6)
Foliage (SW1)
French Horn (Berks)
Hush (W1)
La Bouchée (SW7)
La Brasserie (SW3)
La Fromagerie (W1)
Langan's Bistro (W1)
Langan's Brasserie (W1)
La Poule au Pot (SW1)
La Trouvaille (multi. loc.)
L'Aventure (NW8)
Le Boudin Blanc (W1)
Le Café du Marché (EC1)
Le Colombier (SW3)
Le Gavroche (W1)
Le Palais du Jardin (WC2)
Le Petit Max (SW11)
Le Pont de la Tour (SE1)
L'Estaminet (WC2)
Les Trois Garçons (E1)
Le Suquet (SW3)
Le Vacherin (W4)
Lobster Pot (SE11)
L'Oranger (SW1)
Lou Pescadou (SW5)
Mirabelle (W1)
Mon Plaisir (WC2)
Novelli/Auberge du Lac (Herts)

Odin's (W1)
Oslo Court (NW8)
Poissonnerie/l'Ave. (SW3)
Racine (SW3)
Ritz (W1)
Stratford's (W8)
Terrace (W1)
Thierry's (SW3)
Vineyard/Stockcross (Berks)
Waterside Inn (Berks)
Wheeler's (SW1)
Whit's (W8)
Windows on World (W1)

French (New)
Aubergine (SW10)
Belvedere (W8)
Berkeley Square (W1)
Bibendum (SW3)
Bingham (Richmond)
Bleeding Heart (EC1)
Café des Amis (WC2)
Capital (SW3)
Cellar Gascon (EC1)
Club Gascon (EC1)
Coq d'Argent (EC2)
Criterion Grill (W1)
1880 (SW7)
Gordon Ramsay/Claridge's (W1)
Gordon Ramsay/68 Royal (SW3)
Graze (W9)
Greenhouse (W1)
Incognico (WC2)
La Trompette (W4)
La Trouvaille (W1)
Le Cercle (SW1)
Ledbury (W11)
Le Manoir/Quat (Oxon)
Le Mercury (N1)
L'Escargot (W1)
Le Soufflé (W1)
L'Etranger (SW7)
LMNT (E8)
Maggiores (WC2)
Maze (W1)
Morgan M (N7)
Morton's (W1)
Nathalie (SW3)
Odette's (NW1)
1 Lombard St. (EC3)
One-O-One (SW1)
Orrery (W1)
Patterson's (W1)
Pearl (WC1)
Pétrus (SW1)
Pied à Terre (W1)
Pig's Ear (SW3)
Plateau (E14)
Roussillon (SW1)
Sketch/Gallery (W1)
Sketch/Lecture Rm. (W1)
Square (W1)
Terrace (W1)
Tom Aikens (SW3)
Waterside Inn (Berks)

Greek
Costas Grill (W8)
Daphne (NW1)
Halepi (multi. loc.)
Lemonia (NW1)
Real Greek (multi. loc.)
Vrisaki (N22)

Hamburgers
Arkansas Cafe (E1)
Ed's Easy Diner (multi. loc.)
Gourmet Burger (multi. loc.)
Hard Rock Cafe (W1)
Joe Allen (WC2)
Kettners (W1)
Lucky 7 (W2)
Planet Hollywood (W1)
Smollensky's (multi. loc.)
Sophie's Steak (SW10)
Sticky Fingers (W8)
T.G.I. Friday's (multi. loc.)
Tootsies (multi. loc.)
Vingt-Quatre (SW10)

Hungarian
Gay Hussar (W1)

Indian
Amaya (SW1)
Benares (W1)
Bengal Clipper (SE1)

Bombay Bicycle (multi. loc.)
Bombay Brasserie (SW7)
Cafe Lazeez (multi. loc.)
Café Spice Namasté (E1)
Chor Bizarre (W1)
Chowki Bar (W1)
Chutney Mary (SW10)
Chutney's (NW1)
Cinnamon Club (SW1)
Deya (W1)
Gopal's (W1)
Kastoori (SW17)
Khan's (W2)
Khan's/Kensington (SW7)
La Porte des Indes (W1)
Ma Goa (SW15)
Malabar (W8)
Malabar Junction (WC1)
Masala Zone (multi. loc.)
Mela (WC2)
Mint Leaf (SW1)
Noor Jahan (multi. loc.)
Painted Heron (multi. loc.)
Parsee (N19)
Quilon (SW1)
Rasa (multi. loc.)
Rasoi Vineet Bhatia (SW3)
Ravi Shankar (NW1)
Red Fort (W1)
Salloos (SW1)
Sarkhel's (multi. loc.)
Shikara (SW3)
Soho Spice (W1)
Star of India (SW5)
Tamarind (W1)
Vama (SW10)
Veeraswamy (W1)
Zaika (W8)

Irish

Richard Corrigan (W1)

Italian

Abbey Rd. Pub (NW8)
Al Duca (SW1)
Alloro (W1)
Aperitivo (W1)
Arancia (SE16)
Ark (W8)
Artigiano (NW3)
Ask Pizza (multi. loc.)
Assaggi (W2)
Bertorelli (multi. loc.)
Brunello (SW7)
Buona Sera (multi. loc.)
Caldesi (W1)
Camerino (W1)
Cantina del Ponte (SE1)
Caraffini (SW1)
Caravaggio (EC3)
Carluccio's (multi. loc.)
Carpaccio (SW3)
Casale Franco (N1)
Cecconi's (W1)
Cipriani (W1)
Como Lario (SW1)
Daphne's (SW3)
De Cecco (SW6)
Del Buongustaio (SW15)
Diverso (W1)
Drones (W1)
Eco (multi. loc.)
Edera (W11)
Elena's l'Etoile (W1)
Elistano (SW3)
Emporio Armani (SW3)
Enoteca Turi (SW15)
Essenza (W11)
Fiore (SW1)
Frankie's Italian (SW3)
Friends (SW10)
Getti (multi. loc.)
Giovanni's (WC2)
Green Olive (W9)
Harry's Bar (W1)
Il Bordello (E1)
Il Convivio (SW1)
Il Falconiere (SW7)
Il Portico (W8)
Iniga (SW3)
La Famiglia (SW10)
La Fontana (SW1)
La Fromagerie (W1)
La Genova (W1)
La Porchetta (multi. loc.)
Latium (W1)
L'Incontro (SW1)
Little Italy (W1)
Locanda Locatelli (W1)

Locanda Ottoemezzo (W8)
Lucio (SW3)
Luigi's Covent Gdn. (WC2)
Made in Italy (SW3)
Maggiores (WC2)
Manicomio (SW3)
Mediterraneo (W11)
Metrogusto (N1)
Mimmo d'Ischia (SW1)
Montpeliano (SW7)
Monza (SW3)
Neal Street (WC2)
Oak (W2)
Oliveto (SW1)
Olivo (SW1)
Orso (WC2)
Osteria Antica (SW11)
Osteria Basilico (W11)
Osteria dell'Arancio (SW10)
Passione (W1)
Pellicano (SW3)
Pizza Express (multi. loc.)
Pizza Metro (SW11)
Pizza Pomodoro (multi. loc.)
Pomino (SW17)
Pomodorino (SW1)
Quadrato (E14)
Quirinale (SW1)
Quod (SW1)
Quo Vadis (W1)
Red Pepper (W9)
Refettorio (EC4)
Riccardo's (SW3)
Riva (SW13)
River Café (W6)
Rosmarino (NW8)
Sale e Pepe (SW1)
Salusbury Pub (NW6)
San Lorenzo (multi. loc.)
Santa Lucia (SW10)
Santini (SW1)
Sardo (W1)
Sartoria (W1)
Scalini (SW3)
Signor Sassi (SW1)
Signor Zilli (W1)
Spago (SW7)
Spiga (W1)
Spighetta (W1)
Strada (multi. loc.)
TECA (W1)
Tentazioni (SE1)
Timo (W8)
Toto's (SW3)
Vasco & Piero's (W1)
Verbanella (SW3)
Zafferano (SW1)
Zetter (EC1)
Ziani (SW3)
Zilli Fish (W1)
Zizzi (multi. loc.)
Zucca (W11)

Japanese

(* sushi specialist)
Abeno (WC1)
Benihana (multi. loc.)
Café Japan (NW11)
Chino Latino (SE1)*
City Miyama (EC4)*
Defune (W1)*
Hi Sushi (multi. loc.)*
Ikeda (W1)*
Ikkyu (W1)
itsu (multi. loc.)*
Jin Kichi (NW3)*
Kiku (W1)*
Koi (W8)*
Kulu Kulu Sushi (multi. loc.)*
Matsuri (multi. loc.)
Michiaki (W1)*
Mitsukoshi (SW1)*
Miyama (W1)
Moshi Moshi (multi. loc.)
Nobu (W1)*
Noto (multi. loc.)*
Roka (W1)*
Sakura (W1)*
Satsuma (W1)
Shogun (W1)*
Sumosan (W1)
Tatsuso (EC2)*
Tokyo Diner (WC2)
Tsunami (SW4)
Ubon (E14)*
Umu (W1)
Wagamama (multi. loc.)

Yoshino (W1)*
Yo! Sushi (multi. loc.)*
ZeNW3 (NW3)
Zuma (SW7)*

Korean
(* Barbecue specialist)
Wizzy (SW6)*

Kosher
Bloom's (NW11)
Reubens (W1)
Six-13 (W1)
Solly's (NW11)

Lebanese
Al Bustan (SW7)
Al Hamra (W1)
Al Sultan (W1)
Al Waha (W2)
Beiteddine (SW1)
Dish Dash (SW12)
Fairuz (multi. loc.)
Fakhreldine (W1)
Ishbilia (SW1)
Levant (W1)
Levantine (W2)
Maroush (multi. loc.)
Noura (multi. loc.)

Malaysian
Champor (SE1)
Nyonya (W11)
Silks & Spice (multi. loc.)

Mediterranean
Atlantic B&G (W1)
Baker & Spice (multi. loc.)
Cafe Med (multi. loc.)
Camden Brasserie (NW1)
Cantaloupe (EC2)
Cantina Vinopolis (SE1)
Canyon (Richmond)
Chalcot (NW1)
Chino Latino (SE1)
Citrus (W1)
Coach & Horses (EC1)
Cru (N1)
Eagle (EC1)
Fifteen (N1)
Fifth Floor Cafe (SW1)
Food Room (SW8)
Frontline (W2)
Levant (W1)
Little Bay (multi. loc.)
L'Oranger (SW1)
Moro (EC1)
Nicole's (W1)
Ottolenghi (multi. loc.)
Oxo Tower Brass. (SE1)
Pescatori (W1)
Raoul's (W9)
Rocket (multi. loc.)
Union Cafe (W1)
W'Sens (SW1)

Mexican
Cafe Pacifico (WC2)
Crazy Homies (W2)

Middle Eastern
Aziz (SW6)
Gallipoli (N1)
Ottolenghi (multi. loc.)
Solly's (NW11)

Moroccan
Aziz (SW6)
OCCO (W14)
Pasha (SW7)

North African
Momo (W1)
Moro (EC1)
Original Tagine (W1)
Souk (WC2)

Pacific Rim
Grocer on Warwick (W1)
I-Thai (W2)
Mju (SW1)
Oxo Tower Brass. (SE1)
Pacific Oriental (EC2)
Suze (W1)

Pakistani
Original Lah. Kebab (multi. loc.)
Salloos (SW1)

Persian/Iranian
Alounak (multi. loc.)
Dish Dash (SW12)
Kandoo (W2)

Peruvian
Fina Estampa (SE1)

Pizza
Ask Pizza (multi. loc.)
Buona Sera (multi. loc.)
Cantina del Ponte (SE1)
Casale Franco (N1)
Eco (multi. loc.)
Friends (SW10)
Il Bordello (E1)
Kettners (W1)
La Porchetta (multi. loc.)
Made in Italy (SW3)
Oak (W2)
Oliveto (SW1)
Orso (WC2)
Osteria Basilico (W11)
Pizza Express (multi. loc.)
Pizza Metro (SW11)
Pizza on Park (SW1)
Pizza Pomodoro (multi. loc.)
Red Pepper (W9)
Rocket (multi. loc.)
Spago (SW7)
Spiga (W1)
Spighetta (W1)
Strada (multi. loc.)
Zizzi (multi. loc.)
Zucca (W11)

Polish
Baltic (SE1)
Daquise (SW7)
Wòdka (W8)
Zamoyski (NW3)

Portuguese
Tugga (SW3)

Russian
Potemkin (EC1)

Scottish
Albannach (WC2)
Boisdale (multi. loc.)

Seafood
Belgo (multi. loc.)
Bentley's (W1)
Bertorelli (EC4)
Bibendum Oyster (SW3)
Big Easy (SW3)
Cafe Fish (W1)
Chamberlain's (EC3)
deep (SW6)
fish! (SE1)
Fish Hoek (W4)
Fishmarket (EC2)
Fish Shop on St. John (EC1)
FishWorks (multi. loc.)
Geales Fish (W8)
Green's (SW1)
J. Sheekey (WC2)
Le Pont de la Tour (SE1)
Le Suquet (SW3)
Livebait (multi. loc.)
Lobster Pot (SE11)
Lou Pescadou (SW5)
Manzi's (WC2)
North Sea (WC1)
One-O-One (SW1)
Pescatori (W1)
Poissonnerie/l'Ave. (SW3)
Randall & Aubin (multi. loc.)
Seashell (NW1)
Stratford's (W8)
Sweetings (EC4)
Two Bros. Fish (N3)
Wheeler's (SW1)
Wilton's (SW1)
Zilli Fish (W1)

Small Plates
Amaya (SW1)
Aperitivo (W1)
Cellar Gascon (EC1)
Club Gascon (EC1)
Fina Estampa (SE1)
Fino (W1)
Hunan (SW1)
Le Cercle (SW1)
Lonsdale (W11)
Maze (W1)

Moro (EC1)
Providores/Tapa (W1)

South African
Fish Hoek (W4)

South American
Armadillo (E8)
1492 (SW6)
La Piragua (N1)
Ubon (E14)

Southeast Asian
Grocer on Warwick (W1)
Jim Thompson's (multi. loc.)
Patara (multi. loc.)
Singapore Garden (NW6)
Singapura (multi. loc.)
Taman gang (W1)

Spanish
(* tapas specialist)
Cambio de Tercio (SW5)
Cigala (WC1)*
El Blason (SW3)*
El Pirata (W1)*
Eyre Brothers (EC2)
Fino (W1)*
Galicia (W10)*
La Rueda (multi. loc.)*
Meson Don Felipe (SE1)*
Meza (W1)*
Moro (EC1)
Salt Yard (W1)*

Swedish
Garbo's (W1)
Glas (SE1)
Lundum's (SW7)

Tex-Mex
Texas Embassy (SW1)

Thai
Ben's Thai (W9)
Blue Elephant (SW6)
Busaba Eathai (multi. loc.)
Busabong (SW10)
Chiang Mai (W1)
Churchill Arms (W8)
Crazy Bear (W1)
Esarn Kheaw (W12)
I-Thai (W2)
Mango Tree (SW1)
Nahm (SW1)
Pepper Tree (SW4)
Silks & Spice (multi. loc.)
Sri Nam (E14)
Sri Siam City (EC2)
Sri Thai Soho (W1)
Sugar Hut (SW6)
Thai Pavilion (multi. loc.)
Thai Square (multi. loc.)
Zimzun (SW6)

Turkish
Efes Kebab (W1)
Iznik (N5)
Ozer (W1)
Pasha (N1)
Sofra (multi. loc.)
Tas (SE1)

Vegetarian
Blah! Blah! Blah! (W12)
Chutney's (NW1)
Eat & Two Veg (W1)
Food for Thought (WC2)
Gate (W6)
Kastoori (SW17)
Mildreds (W1)
Morgan M (N7)
Rasa (multi. loc.)
Ravi Shankar (NW1)
Roussillon (SW1)

Vietnamese
Bam-Bou (W1)
Nam Long-Le Shaker (SW5)
Saigon (W1)
Song Que Café (E2)
Viet Hoa (E2)

LOCATIONS

CENTRAL LONDON

Belgravia
Amaya
Baker & Spice
Beiteddine
Boxwood Café
Drones
Ebury Wine Bar
Grenadier
Il Convivio
Ishbilia
Jenny Lo's Tea Hse.
Lanesborough
Memories/China
Mimmo d'Ischia
Mosimann's
Motcombs
Nahm
Oliveto
Pat. Valerie
Pétrus
Pizza on Park
Rib Room
Salloos
Santini
Zafferano

Bloomsbury/Fitzrovia
Abeno
Archipelago
Ask Pizza
Bam-Bou
Bertorelli
Busaba Eathai
Camerino
Carluccio's
Chez Gérard
Cigala
Crazy Bear
Efes Kebab
Elena's l'Etoile
Fino
Hakkasan
Ikkyu
Latium
Malabar Junction
Mash
North Sea
Passione
Pescatori
Pied à Terre
Poons
Rasa
Roka
Salt Yard
Sardo
Spoon
Villandry
Wagamama
Yo! Sushi
Zizzi

Chinatown
Chinese Exp.
Chuen Cheng Ku
ECapital
Fung Shing
Golden Dragon
Harbour City
Imperial China
Jade Garden
Joy King Lau
Lee Ho Fook
Manzi's
Mr. Kong
New World
Noto
Tokyo Diner
Wong Kei

Covent Garden/Holborn
Admiralty
Asia de Cuba
Axis
Bank Aldwych
Banquette
Belgo

Bertorelli
Bierodrome
Bleeding Heart
Browns
Café des Amis
Cafe Pacifico
Café Rouge
Chancery
Chez Gérard
Christopher's
Food for Thought
Gaucho Grill
Giovanni's
Homage
Indigo
Ivy, The
Joe Allen
J. Sheekey
Kulu Kulu Sushi
La Porchetta
Le Café du Jardin
Le Deuxième
Le Palais du Jardin
L'Estaminet
Livebait
Luigi's Covent Gdn.
Maggiores
Matsuri
Mon Plaisir
Neal Street
New Culture Rev.
Orso
Pat. Valerie
Pearl
Pizza Express
PJ's B&G
Poons
Porters
Rules
Savoy Grill
Shanghai Blues
Simpson's
Smollensky's
Sofra
Strada
T.G.I. Friday's
Thai Square
Tuttons Brasserie
Wagamama
White Swan
Zizzi

Knightsbridge

Brass. St. Quentin
Café Rouge
Capital
Emporio Armani
Fifth Floor
Fifth Floor Cafe
Foliage
Frankie's Italian
Good Earth
Ishbilia
Joe's Rest./Bar
Maroush
Mju
Montpeliano
Monza
Mr. Chow
Noto
One-O-One
Patara
Pat. Valerie
Pengelley's
Pizza Express
Pizza Pomodoro
Racine
Richoux
Sale e Pepe
San Lorenzo
Signor Sassi
Verbanella
Wagamama
Yo! Sushi
Zuma

Marylebone

Black & Blue
Blandford St.
Caldesi
Carluccio's
Chutney's
Defune
Deya
Eat & Two Veg

Fairuz
FishWorks
Garbo's
Getti
Giraffe
Home House
Kandoo
La Fromagerie
Langan's Bistro
La Porte des Indes
La Rueda
Levant
Locanda Locatelli
Mandalay
Maroush
Michael Moore
Michiaki
Momo
Montagu
OCCO
Odin's
Original Tagine
Orrery
Ozer
Pat. Valerie
Phoenix Palace
Providores/Tapa
Ravi Shankar
Reubens
Royal China
Seashell
Six-13
Sofra
Spighetta
Strada
Tootsies
Union Cafe
Wagamama
Yo! Sushi
Zizzi

Mayfair

Al Hamra
Alloro
Al Sultan
Angela Hartnett's
Annabel's
Ask Pizza
Bellamy's
Benares
Benihana
Berkeley Square
Brian Turner
Browns
Cafe at Sotheby's
Carluccio's
Cecconi's
Chez Gérard
Chor Bizarre
Cipriani
Drones
El Pirata
Embassy
43 South Molton
George
Gordon Ramsay/Claridge's
Greenhouse
Grill Room
Guinea Grill
Harry's Bar
Hush
Ikeda
itsu
Kai Mayfair
Kiku
La Genova
Lanes
Langan's Brasserie
Le Boudin Blanc
Le Gavroche
Le Soufflé
Mark's Club
Masala Zone
Maze
Mirabelle
Miyama
Morton's
Nicole's
noble rot.
Nobu
Noura
Patara
Patterson's
Pescatori

Princess Garden
Rasa
Richoux
Rocket
Rowley's
Sakura
Sartoria
Shogun
Sketch/Gallery
Sketch/Lecture Rm.
Sofra
Square
Strada
Sumosan
Suze
Taman gang
Tamarind
TECA
Thai Square
Truc Vert
Umu
Veeraswamy
Windows on World
Zen Central

Piccadilly

Atlantic B&G
Bentley's
Chowki Bar
Citrus
Cocoon
Criterion Grill
Diverso
Ed's Easy Diner
Fakhreldine
Gaucho Grill
Hard Rock Cafe
Mitsukoshi
Momo
Noura
Pat. Valerie
Planet Hollywood
Pomodorino
Rainforest Cafe
Richoux
Sugar Reef
Terrace
Wolseley
W'Sens
Yoshino
Zinc B&G

Soho

Alastair Little
Albannach
Andrew Edmunds
Aperitivo
Balans
Bertorelli
Bodeans
Busaba Eathai
Café Boheme
Cafe Fish
Cafe Lazeez
Café Rouge
Chiang Mai
Circus
Ed's Easy Diner
Floridita
French House
Gay Hussar
Gopal's
Grocer on Warwick
Groucho Club
Hi Sushi
Incognico
itsu
Kettners
Kulu Kulu Sushi
La Trouvaille
L'Escargot
Little Italy
Mela
Meza
Mildreds
Patara
Pat. Valerie
Ping Pong
Pizza Express
Portrait
Quo Vadis
Randall & Aubin
Red Fort
Richard Corrigan

Saigon
Satsuma
Signor Zilli
Silk
Soho House
Soho Spice
Souk
Spiga
Sri Thai Soho
Thai Pavilion
Thai Square
Vasco & Piero's
Wagamama
Yauatcha
Yo! Sushi
Zilli Fish
Zizzi

St. James's

Al Duca
Avenue
Brasserie Roux
Fifty
Fiore
Fortnum's Fountain
Getti
Green's
Inn The Park
Just St. James's
Le Caprice
L'Oranger
Matsuri
Mint Leaf
Noura
Quaglino's
Quilon
Quod
Ritz
Rowley's
Texas Embassy
Thai Square
Wheeler's
Wilton's

Victoria

Ask Pizza
Bank Westminster
Boisdale
Chez Gérard
Goring Din. Rm.
Mango Tree
Noura
Olivo
Simply Nico

Westminster

Cinnamon Club
Quirinale
Shepherd's
Tate Gallery
Yo! Sushi

EAST/SOUTH EAST LONDON

Blackfriars/City

Aurora
Bankside
Bertorelli
Boisdale
Browns
Café Spice Namasté
Caravaggio
Chamberlain's
Chez Gérard
City Miyama
Coq d'Argent
Don
Fishmarket
Gaucho Grill
Imperial City
Little Bay
Moshi Moshi
Noto
1 Lombard St.
1 Lombard Brass.
Pacific Oriental
Paternoster Chop
Pizza Express
Pizza Pomodoro
Prism
Refettorio
Rhodes 24

Royal Exchange
Silks & Spice
Singapura
Smollensky's
Sri Siam City
Sweetings
Tatsuso
Terminus
Thai Square
Vivat Bacchus
Wagamama
Ye Olde Cheshire

Bow/Mile End/Hackney/ Bethnal Green
Armadillo
Bistrotheque
LMNT

Canary Wharf/Docklands
Browns
Café Rouge
Carluccio's
1802
Gaucho Grill
Gun
itsu
Moshi Moshi
Plateau
Quadrato
Royal China
Smollensky's
Sri Nam
Ubon
Wapping Food

Clerkenwell/Smithfield/ Farringdon
Abbaye
Cafe Lazeez
Carluccio's
Cellar Gascon
Cicada
Clerkenwell
Club Gascon
Coach & Horses
Eagle
Fish Shop on St. John
La Porchetta
Le Café du Marché
Malmaison Hotel
Medcalf
Moro
Potemkin
Quality Chop Hse.
Real Greek
Smiths/Dining Rm.
Smiths/Top Floor
Sofra
St. John
Strada
Yo! Sushi
Zetter

Shoreditch/Spitalfields/ Hoxton/Whitechapel
Arkansas Cafe
Cantaloupe
Cru
Eyre Brothers
Fifteen
Great Eastern
Hoxton Apprentice
Les Trois Garçons
Real Greek
Rivington Grill
Song Que Café
St. John Bread/Wine
Viet Hoa

South Bank/Borough
Cantina Vinopolis
fish!
Glas
Oxo Tower
Oxo Tower Brass.
Tas
Tate Modern

Tower Bridge/Limehouse/ Wapping
Arancia
Bengal Clipper
Blue Print Café
Browns
Butlers Wharf
Cantina del Ponte

Champor
Fina Estampa
Il Bordello
Le Pont de la Tour
Lilly's
Original Lah. Kebab
Smollensky's
Tentazioni

Waterloo/Southwark/Kennington

Anchor & Hope
Baltic
Bankside
Chez Gérard
Chino Latino
Livebait
Lobster Pot
Meson Don Felipe
Painted Heron
R.S.J.
Tas
Thai Pavilion
Waterloo Fire

NORTH/NORTH WEST LONDON

Camden Town/Chalk Farm/Kentish Town/Primrose Hill

Abbey
Belgo
Camden Brasserie
Chalcot
Daphne
Engineer
Lansdowne
Lemonia
New Culture Rev.
Odette's
Sardo Canale
Vine
Wagamama

Golders Green/Finchley

Bloom's
Café Japan
Ed's Easy Diner
Jim Thompson's
Original Lah. Kebab
Solly's
Two Bros. Fish

Hampstead/Kilburn/Swiss Cottage

Artigiano
Ask Pizza
Baker & Spice
Black & Blue
Bombay Bicycle
Bradley's
Gaucho Grill
Giraffe
Globe
Gourmet Burger
Gung-Ho
Halepi
Hi Sushi
Jin Kichi
Little Bay
Nautilus Fish
Salusbury Pub
Singapore Garden
Tootsies
Wells
Zamoyski
ZeNW3

Highgate/Muswell Hill/Crouch End/Tufnell Park

dim t
Giraffe
La Porchetta
Parsee
Vrisaki
Zizzi

Islington

Almeida
Barnsbury
Bierodrome
Browns
Cafe Med

Carluccio's
Casale Franco
Draper's Arms
Duke of Cambridge
Frederick's
Gallipoli
Giraffe
Iznik
La Piragua
La Porchetta
La Trouvaille
Le Mercury
Lola's
Masala Zone
Metrogusto
Morgan M
New Culture Rev.
Ottolenghi
Pasha
Rodizio Rico
Santa Fe
Strada
Thai Square
Tiger Lil's
Wagamama
Yo! Sushi

St. John's Wood

Abbey Rd. Pub
Benihana
Ben's Thai
Cafe Med
Café Rouge
Graze
Green Olive
L'Aventure
Oslo Court
Raoul's
Red Pepper
Richoux
Rosmarino
Royal China
Sofra
Vale
Zizzi

Stoke Newington

La Porchetta
Rasa

SOUTH/SOUTH WEST LONDON

Barnes

Annie's
MVH
Riva
Sonny's

Battersea

Battersea Grill/Chel.
Buona Sera
Café Rouge
Food Room
Giraffe
Greyhound
Le Petit Max
Osteria Antica
Pizza Express
Pizza Metro
Ransome's Dock
Tootsies
Zizzi

Brixton/Clapham

Abbeville
Bierodrome
Bodeans
Bombay Bicycle
Café Rouge
Eco
Gourmet Burger
Harlem
La Rueda
Little Bay
Pepper Tree
Strada
Tiger Lil's
Tootsies
Tsunami

Chelsea

Admiral Codrington
Ask Pizza

Aubergine
Baker & Spice
Benihana
Big Easy
Bluebird Club
Brinkley's
Builders Arms
Buona Sera
Busabong
Caraffini
Carpaccio
Battersea Grill/Chel.
Cheyne Walk
Chutney Mary
Daphne's
Ed's Easy Diner
Eight Over Eight
El Blason
El Gaucho
Elistano
Enterprise
Friends
Gaucho Grill
Gordon Ramsay/68 Royal
itsu
La Famiglia
Le Cercle
Le Colombier
Le Suquet
Lucio
Made in Italy
Manicomio
Mao Tai
Nathalie
New Culture Rev.
Oriel
Osteria dell'Arancio
Painted Heron
Pat. Valerie
Pellicano
Pig's Ear
Pizza Express
PJ's B&G
Poissonnerie/l'Ave.
Randall & Aubin
Rasoi Vineet Bhatia
Riccardo's
Santa Lucia
Scalini
Simply Nico
Sophie's Steak
Tampopo
Thierry's
Tom Aikens
Toto's
Tugga
Vama
Vingt-Quatre
Ziani

Dulwich

Palmerston

Earl's Court

Balans
Ifield
Lou Pescadou
Masala Zone
Strada
Troubadour
Zizzi

Fulham

Aziz
Blue Elephant
Carluccio's
De Cecco
deep
Farm
1492
Gourmet Burger
Jim Thompson's
La Rueda
Mao Tai
Pizza Express
Strada
Sugar Hut
Tootsies
Wizzy
Yo! Sushi
Zimzun
Zinc B&G

Pimlico

Allium
Como Lario

Ebury Din. Rm.
Grumbles
Hunan
La Fontana
La Poule au Pot
L'Incontro
Pomegranates
Roussillon

Putney/Richmond
Ask Pizza
Bingham
Canyon
Carluccio's
Del Buongustaio
Enoteca Turi
Giraffe
Glasshouse
Gourmet Burger
Jim Thompson's
Kew Grill
Ma Goa
Naked Turtle
Petersham
Redmonds
Rocket
Sarkhel's
Thai Square

South Kensington
Al Bustan
Ask Pizza
Aubaine
Babylon
Bibendum
Bibendum Oyster
Bistrot 190
Black & Blue
Blakes
Bombay Brasserie
Cafe Lazeez
Cambio de Tercio
Collection
Daquise
Duke of Clarence
1880
El Gaucho
Il Falconiere
Iniga
Joe's
Khan's/Kensington
Kulu Kulu Sushi
La Bouchée
La Brasserie
L'Etranger
Lundum's
Nam Long-Le Shaker
Noor Jahan
Pasha
Patara
Shikara
Spago
Star of India
Thai Square
Tootsies

Wandsworth/Balham/ Wimbledon
Balham Kitchen
Chez Bruce
Dish Dash
Jim Thompson's
Kastoori
Light House
Pomino
San Lorenzo
Sarkhel's
Strada
Tootsies

WEST LONDON

Bayswater
Al Waha
Fairuz
Four Seasons
Ginger
Gourmet Burger
Halepi
Island Rest.
I-Thai
Khan's

Mandarin Kitchen
Poons
Rodizio Rico
Royal China
T.G.I. Friday's
Yo! Sushi

Chiswick
Annie's
Ask Pizza
Café Rouge
Fish Hoek
FishWorks
Giraffe
Gourmet Burger
La Trompette
Le Vacherin
Pug
Silks & Spice
Tootsies
Zizzi

Hammersmith
Brackenbury
Carluccio's
Chez Kristof
Gate
River Café
Smollensky's

Kensington
Abingdon
Ask Pizza
Balans
Black & Blue
Brunello
Clarke's
Edera
ffiona's
Giraffe
Il Portico
Kensington Pl.
Koi
Launceston Place
Locanda Ottoemezzo
Maggie Jones's
Memories/China
Pat. Valerie
Pizza Express
Sticky Fingers
Stratford's
Timo
Wagamama
Whit's
Wòdka
Zaika

Notting Hill/Holland Park/ Westbourne Grove
Alounak
Ark
Ask Pizza
Assaggi
Belvedere
Bombay Bicycle
Books for Cooks
Café Rouge
Churchill Arms
Costas Grill
Cow Din. Rm.
Crazy Homies
e&o
Electric Brasserie
Essenza
First Floor
Galicia
Geales Fish
Harlem
Julie's
Ladbroke Arms
Ledbury
Lonsdale
Lucky 7
Malabar
Mediterraneo
New Culture Rev.
Noor Jahan
Notting Grill
Notting Hill Brass.
Nyonya
Oak
Osteria Basilico
Ottolenghi
Pizza Express
Prince Bonaparte

Tom's Deli
Tootsies
202
Uli
Westbourne
Zucca

Olympia
Alounak
Havelock Tavern

Paddington
Frontline
Levantine

Shepherd's Bush
Anglesea Arms
Blah! Blah! Blah!
Bush B&G
Café Rouge
Esarn Kheaw
Snows on Green

IN THE COUNTRY

Fat Duck
French Horn
Gravetye Manor
Le Manoir/Quat
Novelli/Auberge du Lac
Sir Charles Napier
Vineyard/Stockcross
Waterside Inn

SPECIAL FEATURES

(Indexes list the best in each category. Multi-location restaurants' features may vary by branch.)

All-Day Dining

Annie's (SW13)
Aperitivo (W1)
Ask Pizza (multi. loc.)
Aubaine (SW3)
Baker & Spice (multi. loc.)
Balans (multi. loc.)
Balham Kitchen (SW12)
Banquette (WC2)
Belgo (WC2)
Bibendum Oyster (SW3)
Big Easy (SW3)
Black & Blue (multi. loc.)
Bloom's (NW11)
Browns (multi. loc.)
Busaba Eathai (multi. loc.)
Cafe at Sotheby's (W1)
Café Boheme (W1)
Café des Amis (WC2)
Cafe Lazeez (multi. loc.)
Café Rouge (multi. loc.)
Carluccio's (multi. loc.)
Chez Gérard (multi. loc.)
Chowki Bar (W1)
Chuen Cheng Ku (W1)
Cipriani (W1)
Dish Dash (SW12)
Eat & Two Veg (W1)
Ed's Easy Diner (multi. loc.)
Efes Kebab (W1)
El Pirata (W1)
Fifth Floor Cafe (SW1)
fish! (SE1)
Food for Thought (WC2)
Gaucho Grill (multi. loc.)
Giraffe (multi. loc.)
Gourmet Burger (multi. loc.)
Great Eastern (EC2)
Grenadier (SW1)
Halepi (W2)
Harbour City (W1)
Hard Rock Cafe (W1)
Harlem (W2)
Havelock Tavern (W14)
Hoxton Apprentice (N1)
Imperial City (EC3)
Indigo (WC2)
Inn The Park (SW1)
itsu (multi. loc.)
Jim Thompson's (SW19)
Joe Allen (WC2)
Joe's (SW3)
Joy King Lau (WC2)
La Brasserie (SW3)
La Fromagerie (W1)
La Rueda (W1)
Le Cercle (SW1)
Lee Ho Fook (W1)
Levant (W1)
Levantine (W2)
Lilly's (E1)
Livebait (multi. loc.)
Lucky 7 (W2)
New Culture Rev. (multi. loc.)
Noto (SW1)
Noura (multi. loc.)
1 Lombard Brass. (EC3)
Oriel (SW1)
Orso (WC2)
Ottolenghi (multi. loc.)
Ozer (W1)
Pat. Valerie (multi. loc.)
Ping Pong (W1)
Pizza Express (multi. loc.)
Pizza Metro (SW11)
Pizza on Park (SW1)
PJ's B&G (multi. loc.)
Planet Hollywood (W1)
Porters (WC2)
Portrait (WC2)
Quadrato (E14)
Rainforest Cafe (W1)
Randall & Aubin (multi. loc.)
Ransome's Dock (SW11)
Ravi Shankar (NW1)
Richoux (multi. loc.)

Royal China (multi. loc.)
Royal Exchange (EC3)
Rules (WC2)
Satsuma (W1)
Smollensky's (multi. loc.)
Sofra (multi. loc.)
Solly's (NW11)
Sophie's Steak (SW10)
Souk (WC2)
Sticky Fingers (W8)
St. John Bread/Wine (E1)
Suze (W1)
Tas (SE1)
Terrace (W1)
Texas Embassy (SW1)
T.G.I. Friday's (W1)
Thai Square (multi. loc.)
Tom's Deli (W11)
Tootsies (multi. loc.)
Troubadour (SW5)
Truc Vert (W1)
Tuttons Brasserie (WC2)
202 (W11)
Villandry (W1)
Vingt-Quatre (SW10)
Wagamama (multi. loc.)
Wolseley (W1)
W'Sens (SW1)
Ye Olde Cheshire (EC4)
Yo! Sushi (multi. loc.)
Zizzi (multi. loc.)

Breakfast

(See also Hotel Dining)
Annie's (multi. loc.)
Aubaine (SW3)
Baker & Spice (multi. loc.)
Balans (multi. loc.)
Balham Kitchen (SW12)
Bank Aldwych (WC2)
Books for Cooks (W11)
Cafe at Sotheby's (W1)
Café Boheme (W1)
Café Rouge (multi. loc.)
Carluccio's (multi. loc.)
Cinnamon Club (SW1)
Coq d'Argent (EC2)
Eat & Two Veg (W1)
Eco (multi. loc.)
Ed's Easy Diner (multi. loc.)
Electric Brasserie (W11)
Emporio Armani (SW3)
Engineer (NW1)
Fifth Floor Cafe (SW1)
Fortnum's Fountain (W1)
Giraffe (multi. loc.)
Grocer on Warwick (W1)
Harlem (multi. loc.)
Hush (W1)
Inn The Park (SW1)
Joe's (SW3)
Joe's Rest./Bar (SW1)
Julie's (W11)
La Brasserie (SW3)
La Fromagerie (W1)
Lucky 7 (W2)
Lundum's (SW7)
Nicole's (W1)
1 Lombard Brass. (EC3)
Oriel (SW1)
Ottolenghi (multi. loc.)
Pat. Valerie (multi. loc.)
Pizza on Park (SW1)
Portrait (WC2)
Providores/Tapa (W1)
Quality Chop Hse. (EC1)
Raoul's (W9)
Richoux (multi. loc.)
Royal Exchange (EC3)
Simpson's (WC2)
St. John Bread/Wine (E1)
Tate Gallery (SW1)
Tom's Deli (W11)
Tootsies (multi. loc.)
Troubadour (SW5)
Truc Vert (W1)
Tuttons Brasserie (WC2)
202 (W11)
Villandry (W1)
Vingt-Quatre (SW10)
Wolseley (W1)

Brunch

Abingdon (W8)
Admiral Codrington (SW3)
Annie's (multi. loc.)

Aubaine (SW3)
Avenue (SW1)
Aziz (SW6)
Balham Kitchen (SW12)
Bank Aldwych (WC2)
Big Easy (SW3)
Bistrot 190 (SW7)
Bluebird Club (SW3)
Blue Elephant (SW6)
Brasserie Roux (SW1)
Butlers Wharf (SE1)
Canyon (Richmond)
Cheyne Walk (SW3)
Christopher's (WC2)
Chutney Mary (SW10)
Clarke's (W8)
Coq d'Argent (EC2)
Cru (N1)
1802 (E14)
Fakhreldine (W1)
Fifth Floor Cafe (SW1)
Fish Shop on St. John (EC1)
1492 (SW6)
Garbo's (W1)
Giraffe (multi. loc.)
Harlem (multi. loc.)
Joe's Rest./Bar (SW1)
La Brasserie (SW3)
Lanesborough (SW1)
Le Caprice (SW1)
L'Etranger (SW7)
Lucky 7 (W2)
Lundum's (SW7)
Malmaison Hotel (EC1)
Motcombs (SW1)
Nicole's (W1)
PJ's B&G (multi. loc.)
Pomino (SW17)
Portrait (WC2)
Providores/Tapa (W1)
Pug (W4)
Quadrato (E14)
Ransome's Dock (SW11)
Salusbury Pub (NW6)
Sophie's Steak (SW10)
Tom's Deli (W11)
Troubadour (SW5)
Truc Vert (W1)
202 (W11)
Vale (W9)
Vama (SW10)
Villandry (W1)
Vine (NW5)
Vingt-Quatre (SW10)
Wapping Food (E1)
Zetter (EC1)

Business Dining

Al Duca (SW1)
Alloro (W1)
Almeida (N1)
Amaya (SW1)
Angela Hartnett's (W1)
Aubergine (SW10)
Aurora (EC2)
Avenue (SW1)
Axis (WC2)
Bank Aldwych (WC2)
Bank Westminster (SW1)
Bellamy's (W1)
Belvedere (W8)
Benares (W1)
Bentley's (W1)
Berkeley Square (W1)
Bibendum (SW3)
Blakes (SW7)
Bleeding Heart (EC1)
Bluebird Club (SW3)
Blue Print Café (SE1)
Bodeans (W1)
Boxwood Café (SW1)
Brian Turner (W1)
Brunello (SW7)
Capital (SW3)
Caravaggio (EC3)
Cecconi's (W1)
Chancery (EC4)
Chez Gérard (multi. loc.)
Christopher's (WC2)
Cinnamon Club (SW1)
Cipriani (W1)
Circus (W1)
Clarke's (W8)
Club Gascon (EC1)

Criterion Grill (W1)
Deya (W1)
Drones (SW1)
Edera (W11)
1880 (SW7)
Elena's l'Etoile (W1)
Embassy (W1)
Fakhreldine (W1)
Fifth Floor (SW1)
Fino (W1)
Fiore (SW1)
Foliage (SW1)
Glasshouse (Richmond)
Gordon Ramsay/Claridge's (W1)
Gordon Ramsay/68 Royal (SW3)
Goring Din. Rm. (SW1)
Gravetye Manor (W. Sus)
Greenhouse (W1)
Green's (SW1)
Grill Room (W1)
Il Convivio (SW1)
Imperial City (EC3)
Incognico (WC2)
Indigo (WC2)
I-Thai (W2)
Ivy, The (WC2)
J. Sheekey (WC2)
Just St. James's (SW1)
Kai Mayfair (W1)
La Genova (W1)
Lanes (W1)
Lanesborough (SW1)
Langan's Bistro (W1)
Langan's Brasserie (W1)
La Trompette (W4)
Launceston Place (W8)
Le Café du Marché (EC1)
Le Caprice (SW1)
Le Cercle (SW1)
Ledbury (W11)
Le Gavroche (W1)
Le Manoir/Quat (Oxon)
Le Pont de la Tour (SE1)
L'Escargot (W1)
Le Soufflé (W1)
L'Etranger (SW7)
L'Incontro (SW1)
Locanda Locatelli (W1)
L'Oranger (SW1)
Malmaison Hotel (EC1)
Manzi's (WC2)
Matsuri (multi. loc.)
Maze (W1)
Memories/China (multi. loc.)
Mirabelle (W1)
Mitsukoshi (SW1)
Miyama (W1)
Mju (SW1)
Montagu (W1)
Nahm (SW1)
Neal Street (WC2)
Nobu (W1)
Novelli/Auberge du Lac (Herts)
Odin's (W1)
One-O-One (SW1)
Orrery (W1)
Oxo Tower (SE1)
Paternoster Chop (EC4)
Pétrus (SW1)
Plateau (E14)
Poissonnerie/l'Ave. (SW3)
Princess Garden (W1)
Prism (EC3)
Providores/Tapa (W1)
Quadrato (E14)
Quaglino's (SW1)
Quirinale (SW1)
Quo Vadis (W1)
Rasa (multi. loc.)
Rasoi Vineet Bhatia (SW3)
Red Fort (W1)
Rhodes 24 (EC2)
Rib Room (SW1)
Richard Corrigan (W1)
Ritz (W1)
River Café (W6)
Roka (W1)
Rules (WC2)
Santini (SW1)
Savoy Grill (WC2)
Shanghai Blues (WC1)
Shepherd's (SW1)
Shogun (W1)
Silk (W1)

Sketch/Lecture Rm. (W1)
Smiths/Dining Rm. (EC1)
Smiths/Top Floor (EC1)
Spoon (W1)
Square (W1)
Tamarind (W1)
Tatsuso (EC2)
Terminus (EC2)
Tom Aikens (SW3)
Ubon (E14)
Umu (W1)
Vineyard/Stockcross (Berks)
Waterside Inn (Berks)
Wheeler's (SW1)
Wilton's (SW1)
Windows on World (W1)
W'Sens (SW1)
Zafferano (SW1)
Zaika (W8)
Zen Central (W1)
ZeNW3 (NW3)
Zuma (SW7)

Celebrity Chefs

Allium (SW1), *Anton Edelmann*
Angela Hartnett's (W1), *Angela Hartnett*
Banquette (WC2), *Marcus Wareing*
Belvedere (W8), *Marco Pierre White*
Benares (W1), *Atul Kochhar*
Boxwood Café (SW1), *Gordon Ramsay*
Brasserie Roux (SW1), *Albert Roux*
Brian Turner (W1), *Brian Turner*
Café Spice (E1), *Cyrus Todiwala*
Capital (SW3), *Eric Chavot*
Carluccio's (multi. loc.), *Antonio Carluccio*
Cellar Gascon (EC1), *Pascal Aussignac*
Chez Bruce (SW17), *Bruce Poole*
Cinnamon Club (SW1), *Vivek Singh*
Clarke's (W8), *Sally Clark*
Club Gascon (EC1), *Pascal Aussignac*
Criterion Grill (W1), *Marco Pierre White*
Drones (SW1), *Marco Pierre White*
Farm (SW6), *Paul Merrett*
Fat Duck (Berks), *Heston Blumenthal*
Fifteen (N1), *Jamie Oliver*
Frankie's Italian (SW3), *Marco Pierre White*
Gordon Ramsay/Claridge's (W1), *Gordon Ramsay*
Gordon Ramsay/68 Royal (SW3), *Gordon Ramsay*
Ifield (SW10), *Ed Baines*
Ivy, The (WC2), *Mark Hix*
J. Sheekey (WC2), *Mark Hix*
Kensington Pl. (W8), *Rowley Leigh*
Kew Grill (Richmond), *Antony Worrall Thompson*
Le Caprice (SW1), *Mark Hix*
Le Cercle (SW1), *Pascal Aussignac*
Le Gavroche (W1), *Michel Roux Jr.*
Le Manoir/Quat (Oxon), *Raymond Blanc*
Le Petit Max (SW11), *Max Renzland*
Locanda Locatelli (W1), *Giorgio Locatelli*
Maze (W1), *Gordon Ramsay*
Moro (EC1), *Sam & Sam Clark*
Nahm (SW1), *David Thompson*
Neal Street (WC2), *Antonio Carluccio*
Nobu (W1), *Nobu Matsuhisa & Mark Edwards*
Notting Grill (W11), *Antony Worrall Thompson*
Novelli/Auberge du Lac (Herts), *Jean-Christophe Novelli*
Pearl (WC1), *Jun Tanaka*

Pengelley's (SW1), *Ian Pengelley*
Pétrus (SW1), *Marcus Wareing*
Providores/Tapa (W1), *Peter Gordon*
Racine (SW3), *Henry Harris*
Randall & Aubin (multi. loc.), *Ed Baines*
Rasoi Vineet Bhatia (SW3), *Vineet Bhatia*
Real Greek (N1), *Theodore Kyriakou*
Refettorio (EC4), *Giorgio Locatelli*
Rhodes 24 (EC2), *Gary Rhodes*
Richard Corrigan (W1), *Richard Corrigan*
River Café (W6), *Rose Gray & Ruth Rodgers*
Roka (W1), *Rainer Becker*
Savoy Grill (WC2), *Marcus Wareing*
Sketch/Gallery (W1), *Pierre Gagnaire*
Sketch/Lecture Rm. (W1), *Pierre Gagnaire*
Smiths/Dining Rm. (EC1), *John Torode*
Smiths/Top Floor (EC1), *John Torode*
Spoon (W1), *Alain Ducasse*
Square (W1), *Philip Howard*
St. John (EC1), *Fergus Henderson*
St. John Bread/Wine (E1), *Fergus Henderson*
Tamarind (W1), *Cyrus Todiwala*
Tom Aikens (SW3), *Tom Aikens*
Waterside Inn (Berks), *Michel Roux*
Wolseley (W1), *Chris Galvin*
W'Sens (SW1), *Jacques & Laurent Pourcel*
Zilli Fish (W1), *Aldo Zilli*
Zuma (SW7), *Rainer Becker*

Cheese Boards

Almeida (N1)
Angela Hartnett's (W1)
Aubergine (SW10)
Aurora (EC2)
Bibendum (SW3)
Bistrotheque (E2)
Bleeding Heart (EC1)
Caravaggio (EC3)
Chez Bruce (SW17)
Christopher's (WC2)
Clarke's (W8)
Coq d'Argent (EC2)
Criterion Grill (W1)
Cru (N1)
1802 (E14)
Elena's l'Etoile (W1)
Fat Duck (Berks)
Fifteen (N1)
Foliage (SW1)
French Horn (Berks)
Glasshouse (Richmond)
Gordon Ramsay/Claridge's (W1)
Gordon Ramsay/68 Royal (SW3)
Goring Din. Rm. (SW1)
Gravetye Manor (W. Sus)
Greenhouse (W1)
Green's (SW1)
Grill Room (W1)
Julie's (W11)
La Fromagerie (W1)
Lanes (W1)
Lanesborough (SW1)
La Poule au Pot (SW1)
La Trompette (W4)
La Trouvaille (multi. loc.)
Le Cercle (SW1)
Le Gavroche (W1)
Le Manoir/Quat (Oxon)
Le Pont de la Tour (SE1)
L'Escargot (W1)
Le Soufflé (W1)
L'Estaminet (WC2)
Les Trois Garçons (E1)
L'Etranger (SW7)
L'Incontro (SW1)
Locanda Locatelli (W1)
L'Oranger (SW1)
Michael Moore (W1)
Mirabelle (W1)
Mju (SW1)

Montpeliano (SW7)
noble rot. (W1)
Novelli/Auberge du Lac (Herts)
One-O-One (SW1)
Orrery (W1)
Oslo Court (NW8)
Osteria dell'Arancio (SW10)
Paternoster Chop (EC4)
Pearl (WC1)
Pétrus (SW1)
Plateau (E14)
Refettorio (EC4)
Richard Corrigan (W1)
Ritz (W1)
River Café (W6)
Roussillon (SW1)
Royal Exchange (EC3)
Salt Yard (W1)
Sartoria (W1)
Savoy Grill (WC2)
Sir Charles Napier (Oxon)
Sketch/Lecture Rm. (W1)
Smiths/Top Floor (EC1)
Sonny's (SW13)
Square (W1)
St. John Bread/Wine (E1)
Tom Aikens (SW3)
Vale (W9)
Vineyard/Stockcross (Berks)
Vivat Bacchus (EC4)
Waterside Inn (Berks)
Wheeler's (SW1)
Windows on World (W1)
Zafferano (SW1)

Child-Friendly

(Besides the normal fast-food places; * children's menu available)
Abbeville (SW4)
Abingdon (W8)
Al Bustan (SW7)
Al Duca (SW1)
Almeida (N1)
Angela Hartnett's (W1)*
Aperitivo (W1)
Archipelago (W1)
Arkansas Cafe (E1)
Asia de Cuba (WC2)*
Ask Pizza (multi. loc.)
Assaggi (W2)
Aubaine (SW3)
Axis (WC2)*
Babylon (W8)*
Baker & Spice (multi. loc.)
Balham Kitchen (SW12)*
Baltic (SE1)*
Bank Aldwych (WC2)*
Banquette (WC2)
Belgo (multi. loc.)*
Benares (W1)
Benihana (multi. loc.)*
Berkeley Square (W1)*
Bibendum (SW3)
Bibendum Oyster (SW3)
Big Easy (SW3)*
Black & Blue (multi. loc.)
Blandford St. (W1)
Bloom's (NW11)*
Bluebird Club (SW3)
Blue Elephant (SW6)
Bodeans (multi. loc.)*
Books for Cooks (W11)
Boxwood Café (SW1)*
Brasserie Roux (SW1)*
Browns (multi. loc.)*
Buona Sera (multi. loc.)
Busaba Eathai (multi. loc.)
Cafe Fish (W1)*
Cafe Pacifico (WC2)*
Café Rouge (multi. loc.)*
Café Spice Namasté (E1)
Cantina del Ponte (SE1)
Canyon (Richmond)*
Caraffini (SW1)
Caravaggio (EC3)
Carluccio's (multi. loc.)*
Carpaccio (SW3)
Casale Franco (N1)
Cecconi's (W1)
Champor (SE1)
Cheyne Walk (SW3)
Chez Bruce (SW17)
Chez Gérard (multi. loc.)

Chez Kristof (W6)*
Christopher's (WC2)*
Chuen Cheng Ku (W1)
Churchill Arms (W8)
Cigala (WC1)
Cinnamon Club (SW1)
Cipriani (W1)
Circus (W1)
Citrus (W1)*
Coach & Horses (EC1)
Daphne's (SW3)
Del Buongustaio (SW15)
Drones (SW1)
Eagle (EC1)
e&o (W11)
Eat & Two Veg (W1)
Ebury Din. Rm. (SW1)
ECapital (W1)
Edera (W11)
Ed's Easy Diner (multi. loc.)*
Eight Over Eight (SW3)
Electric Brasserie (W11)
Elistano (SW3)
Emporio Armani (SW3)
Enoteca Turi (SW15)
Fakhreldine (W1)
Fifteen (N1)
Fifth Floor Cafe (SW1)
Fino (W1)
fish! (SE1)*
Fishmarket (EC2)
Fish Shop on St. John (EC1)
Fortnum's Fountain (W1)*
Frankie's Italian (SW3)*
Frederick's (N1)*
Friends (SW10)
Gaucho Grill (multi. loc.)
Gay Hussar (W1)
Giraffe (multi. loc.)*
Glasshouse (Richmond)*
Gourmet Burger (multi. loc.)*
Great Eastern (EC2)
Grenadier (SW1)
Grill Room (W1)*
Hakkasan (W1)
Hard Rock Cafe (W1)*
Harlem (multi. loc.)*
Indigo (WC2)*
Inn The Park (SW1)*
itsu (multi. loc.)
Jenny Lo's Tea Hse. (SW1)
Jim Thompson's (multi. loc.)*
Joe Allen (WC2)
Joe's Rest./Bar (SW1)
Julie's (W11)*
Just St. James's (SW1)*
Kensington Pl. (W8)*
Kettners (W1)
La Brasserie (SW3)
La Famiglia (SW10)
La Fromagerie (W1)
La Porchetta (multi. loc.)
La Trompette (W4)*
Le Caprice (SW1)
Le Manoir/Quat (Oxon)*
L'Etranger (SW7)
Livebait (multi. loc.)*
Locanda Locatelli (W1)
Locanda Ottoemezzo (W8)
Lola's (N1)
Lucio (SW3)
Lucky 7 (W2)*
Made in Italy (SW3)
Mango Tree (SW1)
Manicomio (SW3)
Maroush (multi. loc.)
Masala Zone (multi. loc.)*
Mediterraneo (W11)
Mela (WC2)
Mitsukoshi (SW1)*
Nathalie (SW3)
Nicole's (W1)
Nobu (W1)
Noura (multi. loc.)
Oak (W2)
Oliveto (SW1)
Oriel (SW1)
Orso (WC2)
Ottolenghi (multi. loc.)
Oxo Tower (SE1)
Oxo Tower Brass. (SE1)*
Patara (multi. loc.)
Pat. Valerie (multi. loc.)
Pellicano (SW3)

Petersham (Richmond)
Pizza Express (multi. loc.)
Pizza Metro (SW11)
Pizza on Park (SW1)
PJ's B&G (multi. loc.)*
Planet Hollywood (W1)*
Plateau (E14)
Pomino (SW17)*
Porters (WC2)*
Quadrato (E14)*
Quaglino's (SW1)*
Quality Chop Hse. (EC1)
Quilon (SW1)
Quirinale (SW1)
Quod (SW1)*
Rainforest Cafe (W1)*
Randall & Aubin (multi. loc.)
Ransome's Dock (SW11)
Raoul's (W9)
Rasa (multi. loc.)
Rasoi Vineet Bhatia (SW3)
Real Greek (multi. loc.)
Red Pepper (W9)
Reubens (W1)
Riccardo's (SW3)
Richoux (multi. loc.)*
Ritz (W1)*
Riva (SW13)
River Café (W6)
Rocket (multi. loc.)*
Rosmarino (NW8)
Royal China (multi. loc.)
Rules (WC2)
Sale e Pepe (SW1)
Salloos (SW1)
San Lorenzo (SW3)
Santa Fe (N1)*
Santini (SW1)
Sarkhel's (multi. loc.)*
Seashell (NW1)*
Shepherd's (SW1)
Shogun (W1)
Sir Charles Napier (Oxon)*
Six-13 (W1)
Smollensky's (multi. loc.)*
Sofra (multi. loc.)*
Solly's (NW11)*
Sonny's (SW13)*
Sophie's Steak (SW10)*
Spiga (W1)
Spighetta (W1)
Sticky Fingers (W8)*
Strada (multi. loc.)*
Tas (SE1)
Tentazioni (SE1)*
Texas Embassy (SW1)*
T.G.I. Friday's (multi. loc.)*
Thierry's (SW3)
Tiger Lil's (multi. loc.)*
Tom's Deli (W11)
Tootsies (multi. loc.)*
Truc Vert (W1)
Tsunami (SW4)
Tuttons Brasserie (WC2)*
Two Bros. Fish (N3)*
202 (W11)
Ubon (E14)
Uli (W11)
Vama (SW10)
Villandry (W1)
Vingt-Quatre (SW10)
Wagamama (multi. loc.)*
Waterside Inn (Berks)*
Wòdka (W8)
Wolseley (W1)
Yauatcha (W1)
Yoshino (W1)
Yo! Sushi (multi. loc.)*
Zafferano (SW1)
Zen Central (W1)
ZeNW3 (NW3)
Zetter (EC1)*
Zilli Fish (W1)*
Zizzi (multi. loc.)*
Zucca (W11)
Zuma (SW7)

Delivery/Takeaway

(D=delivery, T=takeaway)
Alounak (multi. loc.) (D,T)
Arkansas Cafe (E1) (T)
Baker & Spice (multi. loc.) (T)
Beiteddine (SW1) (D,T)
Big Easy (SW3) (T)

Bloom's (NW11) (D,T)
Blue Elephant (SW6) (D,T)
Cafe Lazeez (multi. loc.) (D,T)
Café Spice Namasté (E1) (D,T)
Cantina del Ponte (SE1) (T)
Carluccio's (multi. loc.) (T)
Chor Bizarre (W1) (T)
Chuen Cheng Ku (W1) (T)
Churchill Arms (W8) (T)
Chutney Mary (SW10) (T)
Cigala (WC1) (D,T)
Crazy Homies (W2) (T)
Defune (W1) (T)
Eat & Two Veg (W1) (T)
ECapital (W1) (T)
Ed's Easy Diner (multi. loc.) (T)
Esarn Kheaw (W12) (T)
Fairuz (multi. loc.) (D,T)
Fakhreldine (W1) (D,T)
Frankie's Italian (SW3) (T)
Friends (SW10) (T)
Garbo's (W1) (T)
Gaucho Grill (multi. loc.) (T)
Geales Fish (W8) (T)
Giraffe (multi. loc.) (T)
Golden Dragon (W1) (T)
Halepi (multi. loc.) (T)
Harbour City (W1) (T)
Harlem (multi. loc.) (T)
Havelock Tavern (W14) (T)
Ikeda (W1) (T)
Il Falconiere (SW7) (T)
Imperial City (EC3) (T)
Inn The Park (SW1) (T)
Ishbilia (SW1) (D,T)
itsu (multi. loc.) (D,T)
Jenny Lo's Tea Hse. (SW1) (D,T)
Jin Kichi (NW3) (T)
Khan's (W2) (T)
Khan's/Kensington (SW7) (D,T)
Kiku (W1) (T)
Koi (W8) (D,T)
Kulu Kulu Sushi (multi. loc.) (T)
La Fromagerie (W1) (D,T)
La Piragua (N1) (T)
La Porchetta (multi. loc.) (T)
La Porte des Indes (W1) (T)
Levant (W1) (T)
Levantine (W2) (T)
Lucky 7 (W2) (T)
Ma Goa (SW15) (T)
Mandalay (W2) (T)
Mango Tree (SW1) (T)
Mao Tai (multi. loc.) (D,T)
Masala Zone (multi. loc.) (T)
Matsuri (multi. loc.) (T)
Mela (WC2) (T)
Memories/China (multi. loc.) (T)
Moshi Moshi (multi. loc.) (D,T)
Mr. Chow (SW1) (T)
North Sea (WC1) (T)
Noura (multi. loc.) (D,T)
Nyonya (W11) (T)
Oliveto (SW1) (T)
Orig. Lah. Kebab (multi. loc.) (T)
Ottolenghi (multi. loc.) (T)
Ozer (W1) (T)
Painted Heron (multi. loc.) (T)
Patara (multi. loc.) (T)
Pizza Express (multi. loc.) (T)
Pizza Metro (SW11) (T)
Rasa (multi. loc.) (T)
Red Pepper (W9) (T)
Reubens (W1) (D,T)
Riccardo's (SW3) (D,T)
Richoux (multi. loc.) (T)
Royal China (multi. loc.) (T)
Salloos (SW1) (D,T)
Santa Lucia (SW10) (T)
Sarkhel's (multi. loc.) (D,T)
Seashell (NW1) (T)
Shanghai Blues (WC1) (T)
Shikara (SW3) (T)
Singapore Garden (NW6) (D,T)
Singapura (multi. loc.) (T)
Six-13 (W1) (D,T)
Solly's (NW11) (T)
Spago (SW7) (T)
Spiga (W1) (T)
Spighetta (W1) (T)
Star of India (SW5) (T)
Sticky Fingers (W8) (T)
St. John Bread/Wine (E1) (T)
Strada (multi. loc.) (T)

Tamarind (W1) (D,T)
Tas (SE1) (T)
Thai Square (multi. loc.) (T)
Tom's Deli (W11) (T)
Troubadour (SW5) (T)
Truc Vert (W1) (D,T)
Two Bros. Fish (N3) (T)
Ubon (E14) (T)
Vama (SW10) (D,T)
Veeraswamy (W1) (T)
Villandry (W1) (T)
Vrisaki (N22) (T)
Yoshino (W1) (T)
Yo! Sushi (multi. loc.) (D,T)
Zamoyski (NW3) (T)
Zen Central (W1) (D,T)
ZeNW3 (NW3) (D,T)

Dining Alone

(Plus hotels and places with counter service)
Amaya (SW1)
Aubaine (SW3)
Baker & Spice (multi. loc.)
Bibendum Oyster (SW3)
Books for Cooks (W11)
Busaba Eathai (multi. loc.)
Cafe at Sotheby's (W1)
Café Rouge (multi. loc.)
Carluccio's (multi. loc.)
Chowki Bar (W1)
Chuen Cheng Ku (W1)
Coach & Horses (EC1)
Eat & Two Veg (W1)
Ed's Easy Diner (multi. loc.)
Emporio Armani (SW3)
Fifth Floor Cafe (SW1)
Fino (W1)
Fortnum's Fountain (W1)
Hakkasan (W1)
Inn The Park (SW1)
Jenny Lo's Tea Hse. (SW1)
Joe's Rest./Bar (SW1)
La Fromagerie (W1)
Le Colombier (SW3)
Manicomio (SW3)
Matsuri (multi. loc.)
Mildreds (W1)
Mitsukoshi (SW1)
Mon Plaisir (WC2)
New Culture Rev. (multi. loc.)
Nicole's (W1)
Oriel (SW1)
Ottolenghi (N1)
Pat. Valerie (multi. loc.)
Porters (WC2)
Portrait (WC2)
Providores/Tapa (W1)
Randall & Aubin (multi. loc.)
Richoux (multi. loc.)
St. John Bread/Wine (E1)
Tampopo (SW10)
Tate Modern (SE1)
Tom's Deli (W11)
Truc Vert (W1)
Villandry (W1)
Wagamama (multi. loc.)
Wolseley (W1)
Yauatcha (W1)
Yo! Sushi (multi. loc.)

Entertainment

(Call for days and times of performances)
Atlantic B&G (W1) (DJ)
Baltic (SE1) (jazz)
Bank Aldwych (WC2) (jazz)
Bank Westminster (SW1) (DJ)
Bengal Clipper (SE1) (piano)
Big Easy (SW3) (bands)
Bingham (Richmond) (jazz)
Bluebird Club (SW3) (varies)
Boisdale (multi. loc.) (jazz)
Cantaloupe (EC2) (DJ)
Canyon (Richmond) (jazz/piano)
Cheyne Walk (SW3) (jazz)
Chutney Mary (SW10) (jazz)
Circus (W1) (DJ)
Coq d'Argent (EC2) (jazz)
Duke/Clarence (SW5) (quiz nights)
Efes Kebab (W1) (belly dancing)
1802 (E14) (DJ)
Embassy (W1) (DJ)
Floridita (W1) (Cuban)

43 South Molton (W1) (DJ)
Globe (NW3) (cabaret)
Goring Din. Rm. (SW1) (piano)
Hakkasan (W1) (DJ)
Harlem (multi. loc.) (DJ)
Ishbilia (SW1) (belly dancing)
I-Thai (W2) (harp)
Joe Allen (WC2) (jazz/piano)
Lanesborough (SW1) (jazz)
Langan's Brasserie (W1) (jazz)
Le Café du Jardin (WC2) (piano)
Le Café du Marché (EC1) (jazz)
Le Caprice (SW1) (piano)
Le Pont de la Tour (SE1) (piano)
Le Soufflé (W1) (piano)
Levant (W1) (belly dancing)
Levantine (W2) (belly dancing)
Little Italy (W1) (DJ)
Lola's (N1) (piano)
Maroush (multi. loc.) (varies)
Mash (W1) (DJ)
Meson Don Felipe (SE1) (guitar)
Mirabelle (W1) (piano)
Momo (W1) (varies)
Mon Plaisir (WC2) (accordion)
Naked Turtle (SW14) (jazz)
noble rot. (W1) (DJ)
Oxo Tower Brass. (SE1) (jazz)
Pearl (WC1) (varies)
Pizza on Park (SW1) (varies)
PJ's B&G (WC2) (jazz)
Planet Hollywood (W1) (DJ)
Quaglino's (SW1) (jazz)
Rib Room (SW1) (piano/vocals)
Ritz (W1) (band)
Sartoria (W1) (piano/vocals)
Shanghai Blues (WC1) (varies)
Silks/Spice (multi. loc.) (varies)
Simpson's (WC2) (piano)
Smollensky's (multi.) (DJ/piano)
Soho Spice (W1) (DJ)
Souk (WC2) (belly dancing)
Sugar Reef (W1) (nightclub)
Sumosan (W1) (DJ)
Tas (SE1) (guitar)
Thai Square (multi.) (DJ/varies)
Tugga (SW3) (DJ)
Vineyard/Stock. (Berks) (jazz/piano)
Windows on World (W1) (band)

Fireplaces

Abbeville (SW4)
Abbey Rd. Pub (NW8)
Admiral Codrington (SW3)
Angela Hartnett's (W1)
Anglesea Arms (W6)
Balham Kitchen (SW12)
Bam-Bou (W1)
Barnsbury (N1)
Bierodrome (WC2)
Bleeding Heart (EC1)
Brunello (SW7)
Builders Arms (SW3)
Butlers Wharf (SE1)
Cambio de Tercio (SW5)
Cheyne Walk (SW3)
Christopher's (WC2)
Cicada (EC1)
Clerkenwell (EC1)
Coach & Horses (EC1)
Crazy Bear (W1)
Daphne's (SW3)
Draper's Arms (N1)
Edera (W11)
French Horn (Berks)
Gravetye Manor (W. Sus)
Grenadier (SW1)
Havelock Tavern (W14)
I-Thai (W2)
Julie's (W11)
La Poule au Pot (SW1)
Le Cercle (SW1)
Le Manoir/Quat (Oxon)
Lemonia (NW1)
L'Escargot (W1)
LMNT (E8)
Lundum's (SW7)
Maggiores (WC2)
Malmaison Hotel (EC1)
Maroush (SW3)
Montagu (W1)
Naked Turtle (SW14)
Palmerston (SE22)
Prince Bonaparte (W2)
Richard Corrigan (W1)
Rules (WC2)

Salusbury Pub (NW6)
Sir Charles Napier (Oxon)
Sonny's (SW13)
Vine (NW5)
Waterside Inn (Berks)
Wells (NW3)
Westbourne (W2)

Game in Season

Abbeville (SW4)
Admiralty (WC2)
Alastair Little (W1)
Albannach (WC2)
Allium (SW1)
Almeida (N1)
Anchor & Hope (SE1)
Andrew Edmunds (W1)
Angela Hartnett's (W1)
Archipelago (W1)
Aurora (EC2)
Avenue (SW1)
Axis (WC2)
Baltic (SE1)
Barnsbury (N1)
Belvedere (W8)
Berkeley Square (W1)
Bibendum (SW3)
Bistrotheque (E2)
Blandford St. (W1)
Bleeding Heart (EC1)
Blue Print Café (SE1)
Boxwood Café (SW1)
Brackenbury (W6)
Brasserie Roux (SW1)
Brass. St. Quentin (SW3)
Brian Turner (W1)
Brunello (SW7)
Butlers Wharf (SE1)
Capital (SW3)
Caraffini (SW1)
Caravaggio (EC3)
Cellar Gascon (EC1)
Chez Bruce (SW17)
Chez Gérard (SW1)
Chutney Mary (SW10)
Cinnamon Club (SW1)
Cipriani (W1)
Circus (W1)
Club Gascon (EC1)
Coach & Horses (EC1)
Criterion Grill (W1)
1802 (E14)
Electric Brasserie (W11)
Embassy (W1)
Enoteca Turi (SW15)
Enterprise (SW3)
Farm (SW6)
ffiona's (W8)
Fifteen (N1)
Fino (W1)
Foliage (SW1)
French Horn (Berks)
Glas (SE1)
Glasshouse (Richmond)
Gordon Ramsay/Claridge's (W1)
Gordon Ramsay/68 Royal (SW3)
Goring Din. Rm. (SW1)
Gravetye Manor (W. Sus)
Green Olive (W9)
Green's (SW1)
Grenadier (SW1)
Greyhound (SW11)
Grill Room (W1)
Grumbles (SW1)
Havelock Tavern (W14)
Il Convivio (SW1)
Il Portico (W8)
Julie's (W11)
Kensington Pl. (W8)
Kew Grill (Richmond)
La Famiglia (SW10)
La Fontana (SW1)
La Genova (W1)
Lanesborough (SW1)
Langan's Bistro (W1)
Langan's Brasserie (W1)
La Poule au Pot (SW1)
La Trompette (W4)
La Trouvaille (W1)
Le Cercle (SW1)
Ledbury (W11)
Le Gavroche (W1)
Le Manoir/Quat (Oxon)
Le Pont de la Tour (SE1)
L'Escargot (W1)
Le Soufflé (W1)
Les Trois Garçons (E1)
L'Etranger (SW7)

L'Incontro (SW1)
Locanda Locatelli (W1)
Lola's (N1)
L'Oranger (SW1)
Lundum's (SW7)
Malmaison Hotel (EC1)
Michael Moore (W1)
Mirabelle (W1)
Montpeliano (SW7)
Monza (SW3)
Morgan M (N7)
Moro (EC1)
Motcombs (SW1)
MVH (SW13)
Naked Turtle (SW14)
Nathalie (SW3)
Neal Street (WC2)
noble rot. (W1)
Notting Grill (W11)
Notting Hill Brass. (W11)
Novelli/Auberge du Lac (Herts)
Odette's (NW1)
Odin's (W1)
Olivo (SW1)
1 Lombard St. (EC3)
Orrery (W1)
Oslo Court (NW8)
Osteria Antica (SW11)
Oxo Tower (SE1)
Passione (W1)
Paternoster Chop (EC4)
Pearl (WC1)
Pétrus (SW1)
Pig's Ear (SW3)
Prism (EC3)
Providores/Tapa (W1)
Quadrato (E14)
Quaglino's (SW1)
Quirinale (SW1)
Racine (SW3)
Randall & Aubin (SW10)
Ransome's Dock (SW11)
Rhodes 24 (EC2)
Riccardo's (SW3)
Richard Corrigan (W1)
Ritz (W1)
Riva (SW13)
River Café (W6)
Rodizio Rico (W2)
Roussillon (SW1)
Rules (WC2)
Santini (SW1)
Sartoria (W1)
Savoy Grill (WC2)
Simpson's (WC2)
Sir Charles Napier (Oxon)
Sketch/Lecture Rm. (W1)
Snows on Green (W6)
Sonny's (SW13)
Square (W1)
St. John (EC1)
Tate Gallery (SW1)
Tom Aikens (SW3)
Villandry (W1)
Waterside Inn (Berks)
Wheeler's (SW1)
Wilton's (SW1)
Windows on World (W1)
Wolseley (W1)
W'Sens (SW1)
Zafferano (SW1)
Zetter (EC1)

Historic Places

(Year opened; * building)
1520 Just St. James's (SW1)*
1550 Fat Duck (Berks)*
1571 Royal Exchange (EC3)*
1598 Gravetye Manor (W. Sus)*
1662 Bleeding Heart (EC1)*
1667 Ye Olde Cheshire (EC4)*
1680 French Horn (Berks)*
1692 Giovanni's (WC2)*
1700 Admiralty (WC2)*
1700 Cru (N1)*
1700 Ransome's Dock (SW11)*
1700 Sir Charles (Oxon)*
1740 Richard Corrigan (W1)*
1742 Grenadier (SW1)*
1742 Wilton's (SW1)
1780 Andrew Edmunds (W1)*
1790 Rowley's (SW1)*
1798 Rules (WC2)*
1800 Anglesea Arms (W6)*
1800 Hoxton Apprentice (N1)*
1800 Snows on Green (W6)*
1802 1802 (E14)*

1810 Pig's Ear (SW3)*
1828 Simpson's (WC2)*
1875 Quality Chop Hse. (EC1)*
1889 Foliage (SW1)*
1889 Savoy Grill (WC2)
1889 Sweetings (EC4)
1890 Aurora (EC2)*
1890 R.S.J. (SE1)*
1896 J. Sheekey (WC2)*
1897 Angela Hartnett's (W1)*
1900 Blakes (SW7)*
1900 Fina Estampa (SE1)*
1900 Frontline (W2)*
1905 Almeida (N1)*
1906 Ritz (W1)*
1910 Goring Din. Rm. (SW1)*
1910 Waterloo Fire (SE1)*
1911 Bibendum (SW3)*
1920 Bloom's (NW11)
1920 Orso (WC2)*
1926 Pat. Valerie (multi. loc.)
1926 Veeraswamy (W1)
1927 L'Escargot (W1)
1930 Sonny's (SW13)*
1931 Grill Room (W1)
1935 Bistrotheque (E2)*
1939 Geales Fish (W8)
1942 French House (W1)*
1942 Mon Plaisir (WC2)
1947 Daquise (SW7)
1950 Fortnum's Fountain (W1)
1950 Pomegranates (SW1)*
1952 Wheeler's (SW1)
1953 Gay Hussar (W1)
1953 Guinea Grill (W1)
1954 Troubadour (SW5)

Hotel Dining

Auberge du Lac
  Novelli/Auberge (Herts)
Baglioni
  Brunello (SW7)
Bentley Hotel
  1880 (SW7)
Berkeley Hotel
  Boxwood Café (SW1)
  Pétrus (SW1)
Bingham Hotel
  Bingham (Richmond)
Blakes Hotel
  Blakes (SW7)
Capital Hotel
  Capital (SW3)
Carlton Tower
  Rib Room (SW1)
Claridge's Hotel
  Gordon Ramsay/Claridge's (W1)
Connaught Hotel
  Angela Hartnett's (W1)
Courthouse Hotel Kempinski
  Silk (W1)
Crowne Plaza
  Refettorio (EC4)
Crowne Plaza London St. James
  Quilon (SW1)
Dolphin Square Hotel
  Allium (SW1)
Dorchester
  Grill Room (W1)
Four Seasons Canary Wharf
  Quadrato (E14)
Four Seasons Hotel
  Lanes (W1)
French Horn Hotel
  French Horn (Berks)
Gore Hotel
  Bistrot 190 (SW7)
Goring Hotel
  Goring Din. Rm. (SW1)
Gravetye Manor Hotel
  Gravetye Manor (W. Sus)
Great Eastern Hotel
  Aurora (EC2)
  Fishmarket (EC2)
  Terminus (EC2)
Halkin Hotel
  Nahm (SW1)
Hempel Hotel
  I-Thai (W2)
Hilton Park Lane
  Windows on World (W1)
Hotel InterContinental
  Le Soufflé (W1)

Hyatt Regency
  Locanda Locatelli (W1)
  Montagu (W1)
Lanesborough
  Lanesborough (SW1)
Le Manoir aux Quat'Saisons
  Le Manoir/Quat (Oxon)
Le Meridien Piccadilly
  Terrace (W1)
Malmaison Hotel
  Malmaison Hotel (EC1)
Mandarin Oriental Hyde Park
  Foliage (SW1)
Metropolitan Hotel
  Nobu (W1)
Millennium Hotel Mayfair
  Shogun (W1)
Millennium Knightsbridge Hotel
  Mju (SW1)
Millennium Mayfair Hotel
  Brian Turner (W1)
One Aldwych Hotel
  Axis (WC2)
  Indigo (WC2)
Park Lane Hotel
  Citrus (W1)
Petersham Hotel
  Petersham (Richmond)
Renaissance Chancery Court
  Pearl (WC1)
Ritz Hotel
  Ritz (W1)
Riverbank Park Plaza Hotel
  Chino Latino (SE1)
Royal Lancaster Hotel
  Island Rest. (W2)
Royal National Hotel
  Poons (WC1)
Sanderson Hotel
  Spoon (W1)
Savoy Hotel
  Banquette (WC2)
  Savoy Grill (WC2)
Sheraton Park Tower
  One-O-One (SW1)
Sofitel St. James London
  Brasserie Roux (SW1)
St. Martin's Lane Hotel
  Asia de Cuba (WC2)
Thistle Hotel
  Chez Gérard (SW1)
Vineyard at Stockcross
  Vineyard/Stockcross (Berks)
Waldorf-Hilton
  Homage (WC2)
Waterside Inn
  Waterside Inn (Berks)
Zetter
  Zetter (EC1)

Late Dining

(Weekday closing hour)
Asia de Cuba (WC2) (varies)
Atlantic B&G (W1) (12 AM)
Avenue (SW1) (12 AM)
Balans (multi. loc.) (varies)
Banquette (WC2) (12 AM)
Beiteddine (SW1) (12 AM)
Blakes (SW7) (12 AM)
Blue Elephant (SW6) (12 AM)
Buona Sera (multi. loc.) (12 AM)
Cafe Lazeez (multi. loc.) (varies)
Cantaloupe (EC2) (12 AM)
Circus (W1) (12 AM)
Cocoon (W1) (1 AM)
Efes Kebab (W1) (12 AM)
Fakhreldine (W1) (12 AM)
Floridita (W1) (1 AM)
43 South Molton (W1) (1 AM)
1492 (SW6) (12 AM)
Gallipoli (N1) (12 AM)
Gaucho Grill (NW3) (12 AM)
Giraffe (N1) (12 AM)
Great Eastern (EC2) (12 AM)
Hakkasan (W1) (12 AM)
Halepi (W2) (12 AM)
Hard Rock Cafe (W1) (12:30 AM)
Harlem (multi. loc.) (1 AM)
Imperial China (WC2) (12 AM)
Ishbilia (SW1) (12 AM)
Ivy, The (WC2) (12 AM)
Iznik (N5) (12 AM)

Jim Thompson's (SW6) (varies)
Joe Allen (WC2) (12:45 AM)
J. Sheekey (WC2) (12 AM)
Julie's (W11) (varies)
Kandoo (W2) (12 AM)
Kettners (W1) (1 AM)
La Porchetta (multi.) (12 AM)
La Rueda (SW4) (varies)
Le Café/Jardin (WC2) (12 AM)
Le Caprice (SW1) (12 AM)
Le Deuxième (WC2) (12 AM)
Lee Ho Fook (W1) (12 AM)
Le Mercury (N1) (1 AM)
Le Palais/Jardin (WC2) (1 AM)
Levant (W1) (1 AM)
Levantine (W2) (12 AM)
Little Bay (multi. loc.) (12 AM)
Little Italy (W1) (4 AM)
Lonsdale (W11) (12 AM)
Lou Pescadou (SW5) (12 AM)
Lucky 7 (W2) (12 AM)
Maroush (multi. loc.) (varies)
Meza (W1) (varies)
Mr. Chow (SW1) (12 AM)
Mr. Kong (WC2) (2:45 AM)
Naked Turtle (SW14) (12 AM)
New World (W1) (12 AM)
Noura (multi. loc.) (varies)
Orig. Lah. Kebab (multi.) (12 AM)
Orso (WC2) (12 AM)
Ozer (W1) (12 AM)
Ping Pong (W1) (12 AM)
Pizza Express (multi.) (varies)
Pizza Pomodoro (SW3) (varies)
PJ's B&G (WC2) (varies)
Planet Hollywood (W1) (1 AM)
Quaglino's (SW1) (12 AM)
Quod (SW1) (12 AM)
Randall & Aubin (SW10) (12 AM)
Sofra (W1) (12 AM)
Soho Spice (W1) (varies)
Souk (WC2) (12 AM)
Spago (SW7) (12 AM)
Sugar Hut (SW6) (12:30 AM)
Sugar Reef (W1) (1 AM)
Taman gang (W1) (1 AM)
Tas (SE1) (varies)
Thai Square (SW15) (12 AM)
Tokyo Diner (WC2) (12 AM)
Troubadour (SW5) (12 AM)
Vingt-Quatre (SW10) (24 hrs.)
Wolseley (W1) (12 AM)
W'Sens (SW1) (12 AM)

No-Smoking Sections

Almeida (N1)
Amaya (SW1)
Anglesea Arms (W6)
Arkansas Cafe (E1)
Ask Pizza (multi. loc.)
Balans (multi. loc.)
Bankside (SE1)
Belgo (WC2)
Berkeley Square (W1)
Bertorelli (multi. loc.)
Big Easy (SW3)
Black & Blue (multi. loc.)
Blandford St. (W1)
Bombay Brasserie (SW7)
Brian Turner (W1)
Brinkley's (SW10)
Browns (multi. loc.)
Cafe Fish (W1)
Cafe Lazeez (multi. loc.)
Café Rouge (multi. loc.)
Café Spice Namasté (E1)
Caldesi (W1)
Camden Brasserie (NW1)
Cantaloupe (EC2)
Cantina Vinopolis (SE1)
Canyon (Richmond)
Caraffini (SW1)
Carpaccio (SW3)
Casale Franco (N1)
Chamberlain's (EC3)
Champor (SE1)
Chez Gérard (multi. loc.)
Chowki Bar (W1)
Chuen Cheng Ku (W1)
Chutney Mary (SW10)
Citrus (W1)
Clerkenwell (EC1)
Como Lario (SW1)
Daphne's (SW3)

Daquise (SW7)
Defune (W1)
Dish Dash (SW12)
Duke of Cambridge (N1)
Eat & Two Veg (W1)
ECapital (W1)
Ed's Easy Diner (NW3)
Enoteca Turi (SW15)
Eyre Brothers (EC2)
Fakhreldine (W1)
Fifth Floor Cafe (SW1)
fish! (SE1)
Fish Hoek (W4)
Fish Shop on St. John (EC1)
Fortnum's Fountain (W1)
Frederick's (N1)
Getti (multi. loc.)
Giovanni's (WC2)
Ikkyu (W1)
Indigo (WC2)
Ishbilia (SW1)
Joe Allen (WC2)
Khan's (W2)
Khan's/Kensington (SW7)
Koi (W8)
Lanes (W1)
La Porchetta (N1)
Lee Ho Fook (W1)
Le Soufflé (W1)
L'Etranger (SW7)
Light House (SW19)
Little Italy (W1)
Livebait (multi. loc.)
Locanda Ottoemezzo (W8)
Malabar Junction (WC1)
Mango Tree (SW1)
Mao Tai (multi. loc.)
Maroush (multi. loc.)
Mela (WC2)
Metrogusto (N1)
Mitsukoshi (SW1)
Motcombs (SW1)
Naked Turtle (SW14)
Nathalie (SW3)
Nautilus Fish (NW6)
New Culture Rev. (multi. loc.)
Nicole's (W1)
Nobu (W1)
Notting Grill (W11)
Noura (SW1)
Novelli/Auberge du Lac (Herts)
Odin's (W1)
One-O-One (SW1)
Oriel (SW1)
Original Tagine (W1)
Orrery (W1)
Orso (WC2)
Osteria dell'Arancio (SW10)
Painted Heron (multi. loc.)
Palmerston (SE22)
Parsee (N19)
Patara (multi. loc.)
Pat. Valerie (multi. loc.)
Patterson's (W1)
Pescatori (W1)
Phoenix Palace (NW1)
Pizza Express (multi. loc.)
Pizza Metro (SW11)
Pizza on Park (SW1)
Pizza Pomodoro (EC2)
PJ's B&G (WC2)
Planet Hollywood (W1)
Pomino (SW17)
Pomodorino (SW1)
Poons (WC2)
Porters (WC2)
Quadrato (E14)
Quod (SW1)
Racine (SW3)
Rasa (W1)
Ravi Shankar (NW1)
Reubens (W1)
Richoux (multi. loc.)
Rocket (multi. loc.)
Rosmarino (NW8)
Santa Lucia (SW10)
Sarkhel's (multi. loc.)
Seashell (NW1)
Shanghai Blues (WC1)
Shepherd's (SW1)
Shikara (SW3)
Sir Charles Napier (Oxon)
Smollensky's (multi. loc.)
Spighetta (W1)

Sticky Fingers (W8)
Strada (multi. loc.)
Sumosan (W1)
Suze (W1)
Tas (SE1)
Terminus (EC2)
Terrace (W1)
Thierry's (SW3)
Union Cafe (W1)
Vale (W9)
Verbanella (SW3)
Vivat Bacchus (EC4)
Waterside Inn (Berks)
Windows on World (W1)
W'Sens (SW1)
Zizzi (multi. loc.)

Noteworthy Newcomers

Abbey (NW1)
Albannach (WC2)
Amaya (SW1)
Aubaine (SW3)
Bellamy's (W1)
Bingham (Richmond)
Bistrotheque (E2)
Bluebird Club (SW3)
Camerino (W1)
Chalcot (NW1)
Chinese Exp. (W1)
Chino Latino (SE1)
Cocoon (W1)
Crazy Homies (W2)
deep (SW6)
Farm (SW6)
Fiore (SW1)
Floridita (W1)
Food Room (SW8)
43 South Molton (W1)
Frankie's Italian (SW3)
Glas (SE1)
Graze (W9)
Greyhound (SW11)
Grocer on Warwick (W1)
Gun (E14)
Homage (WC2)
Iniga (SW3)
Island Rest. (W2)
Ledbury (W11)
Le Vacherin (W4)
Lilly's (E1)
Maze (W1)
Meza (W1)
Michiaki (W1)
Montagu (W1)
OCCO (W14)
Osteria dell'Arancio (SW10)
Ottolenghi (N1)
Paternoster Chop (EC4)
Pengelley's (SW1)
Pig's Ear (SW3)
Ping Pong (W1)
Pomino (SW17)
Pomodorino (SW1)
Roka (W1)
Salt Yard (W1)
Sardo Canale (NW1)
Shanghai Blues (WC1)
Shikara (SW3)
Silk (W1)
Tugga (SW3)
Umu (W1)
Vivat Bacchus (EC4)
Wizzy (SW6)
W'Sens (SW1)

Offbeat

Albannach (WC2)
Alounak (multi. loc.)
Annie's (multi. loc.)
Aperitivo (W1)
Archipelago (W1)
Arkansas Cafe (E1)
Asia de Cuba (WC2)
Baker & Spice (multi. loc.)
Belgo (multi. loc.)
Benihana (multi. loc.)
Bierodrome (multi. loc.)
Blah! Blah! Blah! (W12)
Bloom's (NW11)
Blue Elephant (SW6)
Boisdale (multi. loc.)
Books for Cooks (W11)
Cambio de Tercio (SW5)
Cellar Gascon (EC1)

Chor Bizarre (W1)
Chowki Bar (W1)
Club Gascon (EC1)
Cocoon (W1)
Costas Grill (W8)
Crazy Bear (W1)
Crazy Homies (W2)
Cru (N1)
Daquise (SW7)
Dish Dash (SW12)
Fat Duck (Berks)
ffiona's (W8)
Fifteen (N1)
FishWorks (W4)
Food for Thought (WC2)
Hoxton Apprentice (N1)
itsu (multi. loc.)
Jenny Lo's Tea Hse. (SW1)
Jim Thompson's (multi. loc.)
Kulu Kulu Sushi (multi. loc.)
La Fromagerie (W1)
La Porte des Indes (W1)
Le Cercle (SW1)
Les Trois Garçons (E1)
Levant (W1)
Levantine (W2)
LMNT (E8)
Lola's (N1)
Lucky 7 (W2)
Maggie Jones's (W8)
Mju (SW1)
Momo (W1)
Moro (EC1)
Moshi Moshi (EC2)
MVH (SW13)
Nahm (SW1)
Nautilus Fish (NW6)
Ottolenghi (multi. loc.)
Ozer (W1)
Pizza Metro (SW11)
Providores/Tapa (W1)
Quality Chop Hse. (EC1)
Rainforest Cafe (W1)
Randall & Aubin (W1)
Ransome's Dock (SW11)
Rasoi Vineet Bhatia (SW3)
Real Greek (EC1)
Richard Corrigan (W1)
Rivington Grill (EC2)
Sale e Pepe (SW1)
Sketch/Gallery (W1)
Solly's (NW11)
Souk (WC2)
Spoon (W1)
St. John (EC1)
St. John Bread/Wine (E1)
Tate Gallery (SW1)
Tom's Deli (W11)
Troubadour (SW5)
Truc Vert (W1)
Tsunami (SW4)
Wagamama (multi. loc.)
Wapping Food (E1)
Yo! Sushi (multi. loc.)

Outdoor Dining

(G=garden; P=patio; PV=pavement; T=terrace; W=waterside)

Abbeville (SW4) (PV)
Abbey Rd. Pub (NW8) (P)
Abingdon (W8) (PV)
Admiral Codrington (SW3) (P)
Al Hamra (W1) (P)
Anglesea Arms (W6) (P)
Archipelago (W1) (P)
Ark (W8) (T)
Arkansas Cafe (E1) (PV)
Artigiano (NW3) (PV)
Aubaine (SW3) (PV)
Babylon (W8) (T)
Balham Kitchen (SW12) (PV)
Bam-Bou (W1) (T)
Bank Westminster (SW1) (T)
Belvedere (W8) (T)
Berkeley Square (W1) (P)
Blandford St. (W1) (PV)
Blue Print Café (SE1) (T,W)
Brackenbury (W6) (P)
Brian Turner (W1) (P)
Brunello (SW7) (G)
Builders Arms (SW3) (PV)
Butlers Wharf (SE1) (P,W)
Cantina del Ponte (SE1) (P,W)

Canyon (Richmond) (P,T)
Caraffini (SW1) (PV)
Casale Franco (N1) (P)
Chamberlain's (EC3) (PV)
Chez Kristof (W6) (T)
Churchill Arms (W8) (P)
Coq d'Argent (EC2) (G,T)
Daphne's (SW3) (G)
Eagle (EC1) (PV)
e&o (W11) (PV)
Edera (W11) (P)
1802 (E14) (T,W)
Elistano (SW3) (PV)
Embassy (W1) (P)
Engineer (NW1) (G)
Fifth Floor Cafe (SW1) (T)
fish! (SE1) (T)
FishWorks (W4) (G)
Hard Rock Cafe (W1) (T)
Havelock Tavern (W14) (G,PV)
Hoxton Apprentice (N1) (T)
Hush (W1) (P)
Inn The Park (SW1) (T)
Ishbilia (SW1) (PV)
Joe's (SW3) (PV)
Julie's (W11) (P,PV)
Kandoo (W2) (G)
La Famiglia (SW10) (G)
La Poule au Pot (SW1) (P)
La Trompette (W4) (T)
L'Aventure (NW8) (T)
Le Colombier (SW3) (T)
Le Petit Max (SW11) (T)
Le Pont de la Tour (SE1) (P,W)
Locanda Ottoemezzo (W8) (PV)
L'Oranger (SW1) (P)
Lundum's (SW7) (T)
Made in Italy (SW3) (T)
Manicomio (SW3) (P)
Mediterraneo (W11) (PV)
Mildreds (W1) (PV)
Mirabelle (W1) (P)
Momo (W1) (T)
Monza (SW3) (PV)
Moro (EC1) (PV)
Motcombs (SW1) (PV)
Notting Grill (W11) (T)
OCCO (W14) (PV)
Odette's (NW1) (G,PV)
Oriel (SW1) (PV)
Orrery (W1) (T)
Osteria Antica (SW11) (PV)
Osteria Basilico (W11) (P)
Oxo Tower (SE1) (T,W)
Oxo Tower Brass. (SE1) (T,W)
Ozer (W1) (PV)
Painted Heron (multi. loc.) (G,T)
Passione (W1) (P)
Pellicano (SW3) (PV)
Petersham (Richmond) (T)
Pizza on Park (SW1) (PV)
PJ's B&G (multi. loc.) (PV)
Plateau (E14) (T)
Porters (WC2) (PV)
Quadrato (E14) (T)
Ransome's Dock (SW11) (T)
Real Greek (multi. loc.) (PV)
Riccardo's (SW3) (P)
Ritz (W1) (T)
River Café (W6) (P)
Rocket (multi. loc.) (PV,T,W)
Rosmarino (NW8) (T)
Santini (SW1) (T)
Sir Charles Napier (Oxon) (G,T)
Smiths/Top Floor (EC1) (T)
Spoon (W1) (G,P)
Texas Embassy (SW1) (PV)
Tom's Deli (W11) (G)
Toto's (SW3) (G)
202 (W11) (G,PV)
Uli (W11) (P)
Vama (SW10) (P)
Villandry (W1) (PV)
Vine (NW5) (G)
Vineyard/Stock (Berks) (T,W)
Wapping Food (E1) (G,P)
Westbourne (W2) (T)

People-Watching

Admiral Codrington (SW3)
Amaya (SW1)
Angela Hartnett's (W1)
Asia de Cuba (WC2)
Aubaine (SW3)

Avenue (SW1)
Bam-Bou (W1)
Bellamy's (W1)
Belvedere (W8)
Benares (W1)
Bibendum (SW3)
Bibendum Oyster (SW3)
Blakes (SW7)
Boxwood Café (SW1)
Brunello (SW7)
Cafe at Sotheby's (W1)
Caraffini (SW1)
Carpaccio (SW3)
Cellar Gascon (EC1)
Christopher's (WC2)
Cinnamon Club (SW1)
Cipriani (W1)
Circus (W1)
Club Gascon (EC1)
Daphne's (SW3)
Drones (SW1)
e&o (W11)
Eight Over Eight (SW3)
Electric Brasserie (W11)
Emporio Armani (SW3)
Fifteen (N1)
Fifth Floor (SW1)
Fifth Floor Cafe (SW1)
Fino (W1)
Frankie's Italian (SW3)
Glasshouse (Richmond)
Gordon Ramsay/Claridge's (W1)
Gordon Ramsay/68 Royal (SW3)
Hakkasan (W1)
Hush (W1)
Ivy, The (WC2)
Joe's (SW3)
J. Sheekey (WC2)
Kensington Pl. (W8)
La Famiglia (SW10)
Langan's Bistro (W1)
Langan's Brasserie (W1)
La Trompette (W4)
Le Caprice (SW1)
Le Cercle (SW1)
Ledbury (W11)
Le Gavroche (W1)
L'Incontro (SW1)
Locanda Locatelli (W1)
Manicomio (SW3)
Maze (W1)
Mirabelle (W1)
Momo (W1)
Nicole's (W1)
Nobu (W1)
Orso (WC2)
Pasha (SW7)
Pengelley's (SW1)
Pétrus (SW1)
PJ's B&G (SW3)
Providores/Tapa (W1)
Quaglino's (SW1)
Quo Vadis (W1)
Racine (SW3)
Riccardo's (SW3)
River Café (W6)
Roka (W1)
San Lorenzo (SW3)
Santini (SW1)
Savoy Grill (WC2)
Sketch/Gallery (W1)
Sketch/Lecture Rm. (W1)
Smiths/Dining Rm. (EC1)
Sophie's Steak (SW10)
Spoon (W1)
Sumosan (W1)
Timo (W8)
Tom Aikens (SW3)
Tom's Deli (W11)
202 (W11)
Ubon (E14)
Vingt-Quatre (SW10)
Waterside Inn (Berks)
Wilton's (SW1)
Wolseley (W1)
Yauatcha (W1)
Zafferano (SW1)
Zetter (EC1)
Zilli Fish (W1)
Zinc B&G (W1)
Zuma (SW7)

Power Scenes

Angela Hartnett's (W1)
Aurora (EC2)
Avenue (SW1)
Bank Aldwych (WC2)
Belvedere (W8)

Blue Print Café (SE1)
Boxwood Café (SW1)
Caravaggio (EC3)
Cecconi's (W1)
Cellar Gascon (EC1)
Cinnamon Club (SW1)
Cipriani (W1)
Circus (W1)
Club Gascon (EC1)
Daphne's (SW3)
Drones (SW1)
Gordon Ramsay/Claridge's (W1)
Gordon Ramsay/68 Royal (SW3)
Goring Din. Rm. (SW1)
Greenhouse (W1)
Green's (SW1)
Grill Room (W1)
Ivy, The (WC2)
J. Sheekey (WC2)
Lanes (W1)
Langan's Brasserie (W1)
Launceston Place (W8)
Le Caprice (SW1)
Ledbury (W11)
Le Gavroche (W1)
Le Manoir/Quat (Oxon)
Le Pont de la Tour (SE1)
Le Soufflé (W1)
L'Incontro (SW1)
Maze (W1)
Mirabelle (W1)
Nahm (SW1)
Neal Street (WC2)
Nobu (W1)
Odin's (W1)
1 Lombard St. (EC3)
Pétrus (SW1)
Prism (EC3)
Quirinale (SW1)
Rhodes 24 (EC2)
Ritz (W1)
San Lorenzo (SW3)
Savoy Grill (WC2)
Shepherd's (SW1)
Sketch/Lecture Rm. (W1)
Spoon (W1)
Square (W1)
Tom Aikens (SW3)
Umu (W1)
Waterside Inn (Berks)
Wheeler's (SW1)
Wilton's (SW1)
Wolseley (W1)
Zafferano (SW1)
Zuma (SW7)

Pre-Theatre Menus

(Call for prices and times)
Al Duca (SW1)
Almeida (N1)
Angela Hartnett's (W1)
Asia de Cuba (WC2)
Atlantic B&G (W1)
Axis (WC2)
Baltic (SE1)
Bank Westminster (SW1)
Benares (W1)
Brasserie Roux (SW1)
Brass. St. Quentin (SW3)
Christopher's (WC2)
Cinnamon Club (SW1)
Embassy (W1)
Gordon Ramsay/Claridge's (W1)
Goring Din. Rm. (SW1)
Indigo (WC2)
Joe Allen (WC2)
La Bouchée (SW7)
Lanesborough (SW1)
La Trouvaille (multi. loc.)
Le Deuxième (WC2)
L'Escargot (W1)
L'Estaminet (WC2)
L'Etranger (SW7)
Lola's (N1)
Matsuri (multi. loc.)
Mint Leaf (SW1)
Mon Plaisir (WC2)
Orso (WC2)
Oxo Tower Brass. (SE1)
Pearl (WC1)
Porters (WC2)
Quaglino's (SW1)
Quo Vadis (W1)
Racine (SW3)

Red Fort (W1)
Richard Corrigan (W1)
Ritz (W1)
R.S.J. (SE1)
Savoy Grill (WC2)
Spoon (W1)
Veeraswamy (W1)
Villandry (W1)
Zaika (W8)

Private Rooms
(Call for capacity)
Abbey Rd. Pub (NW8)
Admiralty (WC2)
Alastair Little (W1)
Albannach (WC2)
Allium (SW1)
Alloro (W1)
Almeida (N1)
Amaya (SW1)
Angela Hartnett's (W1)
Arkansas Cafe (E1)
Asia de Cuba (WC2)
Babylon (W8)
Baltic (SE1)
Bam-Bou (W1)
Belgo (multi. loc.)
Belvedere (W8)
Benares (W1)
Benihana (multi. loc.)
Berkeley Square (W1)
Blakes (SW7)
Blue Elephant (SW6)
Bodeans (multi. loc.)
Bombay Bicycle (multi. loc.)
Boxwood Café (SW1)
Brackenbury (W6)
Brasserie Roux (SW1)
Brian Turner (W1)
Brunello (SW7)
Café Spice Namasté (E1)
Cambio de Tercio (SW5)
Cantina Vinopolis (SE1)
Capital (SW3)
Chez Bruce (SW17)
Chez Kristof (W6)
Christopher's (WC2)
Chuen Cheng Ku (W1)
Chutney Mary (SW10)
Chutney's (NW1)
Cinnamon Club (SW1)
Cipriani (W1)
Circus (W1)
Clerkenwell (EC1)
Cocoon (W1)
Cru (N1)
Daphne's (SW3)
Drones (SW1)
e&o (W11)
Edera (W11)
1880 (SW7)
1802 (E14)
Eight Over Eight (SW3)
Embassy (W1)
Fairuz (multi. loc.)
Floridita (W1)
French Horn (Berks)
Gordon Ramsay/Claridge's (W1)
Goring Din. Rm. (SW1)
Gravetye Manor (W. Sus)
Greenhouse (W1)
Green's (SW1)
Guinea Grill (W1)
Hakkasan (W1)
Hard Rock Cafe (W1)
Hush (W1)
Ishbilia (SW1)
I-Thai (W2)
itsu (multi. loc.)
Ivy, The (WC2)
Julie's (W11)
Just St. James's (SW1)
Kai Mayfair (W1)
Kensington Pl. (W8)
La Porte des Indes (W1)
La Poule au Pot (SW1)
La Trouvaille (multi. loc.)
Launceston Place (W8)
Le Cercle (SW1)
Le Colombier (SW3)
Le Manoir/Quat (Oxon)
Le Pont de la Tour (SE1)
L'Escargot (W1)
L'Estaminet (WC2)

Les Trois Garçons (E1)
Le Suquet (SW3)
L'Etranger (SW7)
L'Incontro (SW1)
Lola's (N1)
L'Oranger (SW1)
Lundum's (SW7)
Made in Italy (SW3)
Malmaison Hotel (EC1)
Manicomio (SW3)
Mao Tai (multi. loc.)
Masala Zone (multi. loc.)
Matsuri (multi. loc.)
Memories/China (multi. loc.)
Metrogusto (N1)
Mimmo d'Ischia (SW1)
Mint Leaf (SW1)
Mirabelle (W1)
Mitsukoshi (SW1)
Momo (W1)
Mon Plaisir (WC2)
Montpeliano (SW7)
Morgan M (N7)
Motcombs (SW1)
Mr. Chow (SW1)
MVH (SW13)
Nahm (SW1)
Nathalie (SW3)
Neal Street (WC2)
noble rot. (W1)
Nobu (W1)
Notting Grill (W11)
Notting Hill Brass. (W11)
Noura (multi. loc.)
Novelli/Auberge du Lac (Herts)
Nyonya (W11)
1 Lombard St. (EC3)
1 Lombard Brass. (EC3)
One-O-One (SW1)
Palmerston (SE22)
Pasha (SW7)
Passione (W1)
Patara (multi. loc.)
Patterson's (W1)
Pearl (WC1)
Pellicano (SW3)
Pétrus (SW1)
Plateau (E14)
Poissonnerie/l'Ave. (SW3)
Prism (EC3)
Quaglino's (SW1)
Quo Vadis (W1)
Rainforest Cafe (W1)
Rasa (multi. loc.)
Rasoi Vineet Bhatia (SW3)
Real Greek (multi. loc.)
Rib Room (SW1)
Richard Corrigan (W1)
Ritz (W1)
Rivington Grill (EC2)
Rocket (multi. loc.)
Roussillon (SW1)
Royal China (multi. loc.)
Rules (WC2)
San Lorenzo (SW19)
Santa Fe (N1)
Santini (SW1)
Sarkhel's (multi. loc.)
Sartoria (W1)
Savoy Grill (WC2)
Shepherd's (SW1)
Signor Zilli (W1)
Sir Charles Napier (Oxon)
Six-13 (W1)
Smiths/Dining Rm. (EC1)
Smiths/Top Floor (EC1)
Solly's (NW11)
Square (W1)
Star of India (SW5)
St. John (EC1)
Sumosan (W1)
Tatsuso (EC2)
Tentazioni (SE1)
Texas Embassy (SW1)
Thai Square (multi. loc.)
Timo (W8)
Tugga (SW3)
Vale (W9)
Vasco & Piero's (W1)
Veeraswamy (W1)
Villandry (W1)
Vineyard/Stockcross (Berks)
Vivat Bacchus (EC4)
Waterloo Fire (SE1)

Waterside Inn (Berks)
Wells (NW3)
Wheeler's (SW1)
White Swan (EC4)
Wilton's (SW1)
Wòdka (W8)
Ye Olde Cheshire (EC4)
Zetter (EC1)

Pubs/Microbreweries

Abbeville (SW4)
Abbey Rd. Pub (NW8)
Admiral Codrington (SW3)
Anchor & Hope (SE1)
Anglesea Arms (W6)
Barnsbury (N1)
Builders Arms (SW3)
Churchill Arms (W8)
Coach & Horses (EC1)
Cow Din. Rm. (W2)
Draper's Arms (N1)
Duke of Cambridge (N1)
Duke of Clarence (SW5)
Eagle (EC1)
Ebury Din. Rm. (SW1)
Engineer (NW1)
Farm (SW6)
Grenadier (SW1)
Gun (E14)
Havelock Tavern (W14)
Ladbroke Arms (W11)
Lansdowne (NW1)
Mash (W1)
Oak (W2)
Palmerston (SE22)
Pig's Ear (SW3)
Prince Bonaparte (W2)
Salusbury Pub (NW6)
Vine (NW5)
Wells (NW3)
Westbourne (W2)
White Swan (EC4)
Ye Olde Cheshire (EC4)

Pudding Specialists

Alastair Little (W1)
Almeida (N1)
Amaya (SW1)
Angela Hartnett's (W1)
Asia de Cuba (WC2)
Aubaine (SW3)
Aubergine (SW10)
Aurora (EC2)
Baker & Spice (multi. loc.)
Belvedere (W8)
Bibendum Oyster (SW3)
Blakes (SW7)
Boxwood Café (SW1)
Capital (SW3)
Chez Bruce (SW17)
Cipriani (W1)
Clarke's (W8)
Club Gascon (EC1)
Embassy (W1)
Fat Duck (Berks)
Fifth Floor (SW1)
Foliage (SW1)
Fortnum's Fountain (W1)
Glasshouse (Richmond)
Gordon Ramsay/Claridge's (W1)
Gordon Ramsay/68 Royal (SW3)
Greenhouse (W1)
Homage (WC2)
Lanes (W1)
Lanesborough (SW1)
La Trompette (W4)
Le Cercle (SW1)
Ledbury (W11)
Le Gavroche (W1)
Le Manoir/Quat (Oxon)
Le Soufflé (W1)
Locanda Locatelli (W1)
L'Oranger (SW1)
Maze (W1)
Mirabelle (W1)
Nobu (W1)
Novelli/Auberge du Lac (Herts)
Orrery (W1)
Ottolenghi (multi. loc.)
Pat. Valerie (multi. loc.)
Pétrus (SW1)
Plateau (E14)
Providores/Tapa (W1)
Rasoi Vineet Bhatia (SW3)
Richard Corrigan (W1)

Richoux (multi. loc.)
Ritz (W1)
River Café (W6)
Savoy Grill (WC2)
Sketch/Gallery (W1)
Sketch/Lecture Rm. (W1)
Spoon (W1)
Square (W1)
Tom Aikens (SW3)
Ubon (E14)
Waterside Inn (Berks)
Wolseley (W1)
W'Sens (SW1)
Yauatcha (W1)
Zafferano (SW1)
Zuma (SW7)

Quiet Conversation

Al Sultan (W1)
Aubergine (SW10)
Aurora (EC2)
Axis (WC2)
Banquette (WC2)
Benares (W1)
Bengal Clipper (SE1)
Bentley's (W1)
Berkeley Square (W1)
Bingham (Richmond)
Blakes (SW7)
Brian Turner (W1)
Capital (SW3)
Chalcot (NW1)
1880 (SW7)
Embassy (W1)
Foliage (SW1)
Goring Din. Rm. (SW1)
Green's (SW1)
Il Convivio (SW1)
Indigo (WC2)
La Genova (W1)
Lanes (W1)
Lanesborough (SW1)
Launceston Place (W8)
Le Gavroche (W1)
Le Manoir/Quat (Oxon)
L'Oranger (SW1)
Lundum's (SW7)
Mitsukoshi (SW1)
Mju (SW1)
Nahm (SW1)
Nathalie (SW3)
Odin's (W1)
One-O-One (SW1)
Orrery (W1)
Quadrato (E14)
Quirinale (SW1)
Rasoi Vineet Bhatia (SW3)
Ritz (W1)
Roussillon (SW1)
Salloos (SW1)
Shikara (SW3)
Sketch/Lecture Rm. (W1)
Stratford's (W8)
Waterside Inn (Berks)
Wilton's (SW1)
Windows on World (W1)

Romantic Places

Amaya (SW1)
Andrew Edmunds (W1)
Angela Hartnett's (W1)
Archipelago (W1)
Aurora (EC2)
Babylon (W8)
Belvedere (W8)
Bingham (Richmond)
Blakes (SW7)
Blue Elephant (SW6)
Brunello (SW7)
Capital (SW3)
Cellar Gascon (EC1)
Chez Bruce (SW17)
Chutney Mary (SW10)
Cipriani (W1)
Clarke's (W8)
Club Gascon (EC1)
Crazy Bear (W1)
Criterion Grill (W1)
Daphne's (SW3)
Drones (SW1)
Frederick's (N1)
French Horn (Berks)
Glasshouse (Richmond)
Gordon Ramsay/Claridge's (W1)

Gordon Ramsay/68 Royal (SW3)
Gravetye Manor (W. Sus)
Greenhouse (W1)
Hakkasan (W1)
Julie's (W11)
Lanesborough (SW1)
La Poule au Pot (SW1)
La Trompette (W4)
Launceston Place (W8)
L'Aventure (NW8)
Le Café du Marché (EC1)
Le Caprice (SW1)
Le Cercle (SW1)
Ledbury (W11)
Le Gavroche (W1)
Le Manoir/Quat (Oxon)
Le Pont de la Tour (SE1)
Les Trois Garçons (E1)
Locanda Locatelli (W1)
L'Oranger (SW1)
Lundum's (SW7)
Maggie Jones's (W8)
Mirabelle (W1)
Momo (W1)
Nathalie (SW3)
Nobu (W1)
Odette's (NW1)
Odin's (W1)
Orrery (W1)
Pétrus (SW1)
Pomegranates (SW1)
Prism (EC3)
Rasoi Vineet Bhatia (SW3)
Richard Corrigan (W1)
Ritz (W1)
River Café (W6)
Roussillon (SW1)
San Lorenzo (SW3)
Sketch/Lecture Rm. (W1)
Snows on Green (W6)
Square (W1)
Tom Aikens (SW3)
Toto's (SW3)
Waterside Inn (Berks)
Windows on World (W1)
Zafferano (SW1)
Zuma (SW7)

Senior Appeal

Al Duca (SW1)
Amaya (SW1)
Angela Hartnett's (W1)
Aubaine (SW3)
Aubergine (SW10)
Bellamy's (W1)
Belvedere (W8)
Bentley's (W1)
Berkeley Square (W1)
Bibendum (SW3)
Bloom's (NW11)
Boxwood Café (SW1)
Brasserie Roux (SW1)
Brass. St. Quentin (SW3)
Brian Turner (W1)
Cafe at Sotheby's (W1)
Capital (SW3)
Cecconi's (W1)
Cipriani (W1)
Citrus (W1)
Drones (SW1)
Elena's l'Etoile (W1)
Foliage (SW1)
Fortnum's Fountain (W1)
Glasshouse (Richmond)
Gordon Ramsay/Claridge's (W1)
Gordon Ramsay/68 Royal (SW3)
Goring Din. Rm. (SW1)
Gravetye Manor (W. Sus)
Greenhouse (W1)
Green's (SW1)
Grill Room (W1)
Ivy, The (WC2)
J. Sheekey (WC2)
Kai Mayfair (W1)
La Genova (W1)
Lanes (W1)
Lanesborough (SW1)
Langan's Bistro (W1)
La Poule au Pot (SW1)
Launceston Place (W8)
Le Caprice (SW1)
Ledbury (W11)
Le Gavroche (W1)
Le Manoir/Quat (Oxon)
Le Soufflé (W1)

Le Suquet (SW3)
L'Etranger (SW7)
L'Incontro (SW1)
Locanda Locatelli (W1)
L'Oranger (SW1)
Lundum's (SW7)
Manzi's (WC2)
Mimmo d'Ischia (SW1)
Mirabelle (W1)
Montpeliano (SW7)
Motcombs (SW1)
Nathalie (SW3)
Neal Street (WC2)
Noura (multi. loc.)
Odin's (W1)
One-O-One (SW1)
Orrery (W1)
Pat. Valerie (multi. loc.)
Pétrus (SW1)
Poissonnerie/l'Ave. (SW3)
Quadrato (E14)
Quirinale (SW1)
Racine (SW3)
Red Fort (W1)
Reubens (W1)
Rib Room (SW1)
Richoux (multi. loc.)
Ritz (W1)
Riva (SW13)
Rosmarino (NW8)
Rowley's (SW1)
Rules (WC2)
Santini (SW1)
Sartoria (W1)
Savoy Grill (WC2)
Scalini (SW3)
Shepherd's (SW1)
Shikara (SW3)
Shogun (W1)
Simpson's (WC2)
Sketch/Lecture Rm. (W1)
Square (W1)
Stratford's (W8)
Tate Gallery (SW1)
Tom Aikens (SW3)
Toto's (SW3)
Waterside Inn (Berks)
Wilton's (SW1)
Wolseley (W1)
Zafferano (SW1)
Zen Central (W1)

Set-Price Menus

(Call for prices and times)
Abingdon (W8)
Alastair Little (W1)
Albannach (WC2)
Al Duca (SW1)
Allium (SW1)
Alloro (W1)
Almeida (N1)
Amaya (SW1)
Angela Hartnett's (W1)
Anglesea Arms (W6)
Archipelago (W1)
Asia de Cuba (WC2)
Aubergine (SW10)
Aurora (EC2)
Avenue (SW1)
Axis (WC2)
Baltic (SE1)
Bellamy's (W1)
Belvedere (W8)
Benares (W1)
Bengal Clipper (SE1)
Benihana (multi. loc.)
Berkeley Square (W1)
Bibendum (SW3)
Blue Elephant (SW6)
Boxwood Café (SW1)
Brasserie Roux (SW1)
Brass. St. Quentin (SW3)
Brian Turner (W1)
Brunello (SW7)
Butlers Wharf (SE1)
Café Japan (NW11)
Café Spice Namasté (E1)
Capital (SW3)
Caravaggio (EC3)
Cellar Gascon (EC1)
Champor (SE1)
Chez Bruce (SW17)
Chez Kristof (W6)
Chor Bizarre (W1)

Christopher's (WC2)
Chutney Mary (SW10)
Cigala (WC1)
Cinnamon Club (SW1)
Cipriani (W1)
Citrus (W1)
City Miyama (EC4)
Clarke's (W8)
Clerkenwell (EC1)
Club Gascon (EC1)
Cocoon (W1)
Coq d'Argent (EC2)
Crazy Bear (W1)
Criterion Grill (W1)
Deya (W1)
Drones (SW1)
ECapital (W1)
1880 (SW7)
Eight Over Eight (SW3)
El Pirata (W1)
Embassy (W1)
Enoteca Turi (SW15)
Essenza (W11)
Fakhreldine (W1)
Fat Duck (Berks)
Fino (W1)
Fish Shop on St. John (EC1)
Foliage (SW1)
French Horn (Berks)
Glasshouse (Richmond)
Gordon Ramsay/Claridge's (W1)
Gordon Ramsay/68 Royal (SW3)
Goring Din. Rm. (SW1)
Gravetye Manor (W. Sus)
Greenhouse (W1)
Grill Room (W1)
Ikeda (W1)
Il Convivio (SW1)
Indigo (WC2)
Ivy, The (WC2)
Joy King Lau (WC2)
J. Sheekey (WC2)
Kai Mayfair (W1)
Kensington Pl. (W8)
Kiku (W1)
Lanes (W1)
Lanesborough (SW1)
Langan's Bistro (W1)
Lansdowne (NW1)
La Porte des Indes (W1)
La Poule au Pot (SW1)
Latium (W1)
La Trompette (W4)
Launceston Place (W8)
L'Aventure (NW8)
Le Boudin Blanc (W1)
Le Café du Marché (EC1)
Le Cercle (SW1)
Le Colombier (SW3)
Le Gavroche (W1)
Le Manoir/Quat (Oxon)
Le Petit Max (SW11)
Le Pont de la Tour (SE1)
L'Escargot (W1)
Le Soufflé (W1)
Les Trois Garçons (E1)
Le Suquet (SW3)
L'Etranger (SW7)
Levant (W1)
L'Incontro (SW1)
Livebait (multi. loc.)
Locanda Ottoemezzo (W8)
Lola's (N1)
L'Oranger (SW1)
Lucio (SW3)
Lundum's (SW7)
Maggie Jones's (W8)
Malmaison Hotel (EC1)
Mango Tree (SW1)
Mao Tai (multi. loc.)
Matsuri (multi. loc.)
Mela (WC2)
Memories/China (multi. loc.)
Mint Leaf (SW1)
Mirabelle (W1)
Mitsukoshi (SW1)
Mju (SW1)
Momo (W1)
Motcombs (SW1)
Mr. Chow (SW1)
MVH (SW13)
Nathalie (SW3)
Neal Street (WC2)
Nobu (W1)

Noura (multi. loc.)
Novelli/Auberge du Lac (Herts)
Olivo (SW1)
1 Lombard St. (EC3)
One-O-One (SW1)
Orrery (W1)
Oslo Court (NW8)
Oxo Tower (SE1)
Ozer (W1)
Painted Heron (multi. loc.)
Patara (multi. loc.)
Patterson's (W1)
Pearl (WC1)
Pellicano (SW3)
Pétrus (SW1)
Plateau (E14)
Poissonnerie/l'Ave. (SW3)
Pomino (SW17)
Porters (WC2)
Princess Garden (W1)
Quadrato (E14)
Quaglino's (SW1)
Quilon (SW1)
Racine (SW3)
Rasa (multi. loc.)
Rasoi Vineet Bhatia (SW3)
Rib Room (SW1)
Richard Corrigan (W1)
Ritz (W1)
Roka (W1)
Rosmarino (NW8)
Roussillon (SW1)
Royal China (multi. loc.)
Salloos (SW1)
Sardo Canale (NW1)
Sarkhel's (multi. loc.)
Sartoria (W1)
Savoy Grill (WC2)
Shogun (W1)
Six-13 (W1)
Sketch/Lecture Rm. (W1)
Snows on Green (W6)
Sonny's (SW13)
Sophie's Steak (SW10)
Square (W1)
Taman gang (W1)
Tamarind (W1)
Tatsuso (EC2)
Tentazioni (SE1)
Tom Aikens (SW3)
Toto's (SW3)
Vasco & Piero's (W1)
Veeraswamy (W1)
Vineyard/Stockcross (Berks)
Vivat Bacchus (EC4)
Waterside Inn (Berks)
Windows on World (W1)
Wòdka (W8)
W'Sens (SW1)
Yoshino (W1)
Zafferano (SW1)
Zaika (W8)
Zen Central (W1)
Ziani (SW3)
Zuma (SW7)

Singles Scenes

Admiral Codrington (SW3)
Albannach (WC2)
Amaya (SW1)
Asia de Cuba (WC2)
Atlantic B&G (W1)
Avenue (SW1)
Balans (multi. loc.)
Bank Aldwych (WC2)
Bank Westminster (SW1)
Belgo (multi. loc.)
Bierodrome (multi. loc.)
Big Easy (SW3)
Bistrot 190 (SW7)
Bluebird Club (SW3)
Brinkley's (SW10)
Browns (multi. loc.)
Buona Sera (SW3)
Cafe Pacifico (WC2)
Cantaloupe (EC2)
Cecconi's (W1)
Cellar Gascon (EC1)
Christopher's (WC2)
Circus (W1)
Cocoon (W1)
Collection (SW3)
Dish Dash (SW12)
Draper's Arms (N1)

e&o (W11)
Ebury Wine Bar (SW1)
Eight Over Eight (SW3)
Engineer (NW1)
Enterprise (SW3)
Fifteen (N1)
Fifth Floor Cafe (SW1)
Fino (W1)
First Floor (W11)
Floridita (W1)
43 South Molton (W1)
Hakkasan (W1)
Hush (W1)
Just St. James's (SW1)
Kettners (W1)
La Rueda (multi. loc.)
Le Cercle (SW1)
Maroush (multi. loc.)
Maze (W1)
Medcalf (EC1)
Momo (W1)
Moro (EC1)
Motcombs (SW1)
Nam Long-Le Shaker (SW5)
noble rot. (W1)
Nobu (W1)
Oriel (SW1)
Oxo Tower (SE1)
Oxo Tower Brass. (SE1)
Pengelley's (SW1)
Pizza on Park (SW1)
PJ's B&G (SW3)
Quaglino's (SW1)
Roka (W1)
Sketch/Gallery (W1)
Smiths/Dining Rm. (EC1)
Sophie's Steak (SW10)
Spiga (W1)
Spighetta (W1)
Spoon (W1)
Sticky Fingers (W8)
Sugar Reef (W1)
Sumosan (W1)
Terminus (EC2)
Texas Embassy (SW1)
Tugga (SW3)
Waterloo Fire (SE1)
Zinc B&G (multi. loc.)
Zuma (SW7)

Sleepers

(Good to excellent food, but little known)

Abeno (WC1)
Al Waha (W2)
Archipelago (W1)
Beiteddine (SW1)
Blah! Blah! Blah! (W12)
Brunello (SW7)
Bush B&G (W12)
Casale Franco (N1)
Cellar Gascon (EC1)
Chamberlain's (EC3)
Chancery (EC4)
Chutney's (NW1)
Cigala (WC1)
City Miyama (EC4)
Coach & Horses (EC1)
Crazy Bear (W1)
Del Buongustaio (SW15)
Deya (W1)
ECapital (W1)
Edera (W11)
1880 (SW7)
Essenza (W11)
Fina Estampa (SE1)
Ginger (W2)
Great Eastern (EC2)
Green Olive (W9)
Gun (E14)
Havelock Tavern (W14)
I-Thai (W2)
Iznik (N5)
Kastoori (SW17)
Kew Grill (Richmond)
Kiku (W1)
Koi (W8)
La Fontana (SW1)
Latium (W1)
Lilly's (E1)
Lola's (N1)
Lou Pescadou (SW5)
Ma Goa (SW15)
Metrogusto (N1)
Mildreds (W1)
Mitsukoshi (SW1)

Miyama (W1)
Nathalie (SW3)
Noto (multi. loc.)
Novelli/Auberge du Lac (Herts)
Original Tagine (W1)
Osteria dell'Arancio (SW10)
Pasha (N1)
Petersham (Richmond)
Redmonds (SW14)
Refettorio (EC4)
Sarkhel's (multi. loc.)
Sir Charles Napier (Oxon)
Snows on Green (W6)
Song Que Café (E2)
Sonny's (SW13)
Sri Thai Soho (W1)
Stratford's (W8)
Sugar Hut (SW6)
Tatsuso (EC2)
Uli (W11)
Vasco & Piero's (W1)
Vine (NW5)
Vineyard/Stockcross (Berks)
Vrisaki (N22)
Zamoyski (NW3)

Smoking Prohibited

(May be permissible at bar)
Admiralty (WC2)
Albannach (WC2)
Angela Hartnett's (W1)
Baker & Spice (SW3)
Banquette (WC2)
Benares (W1)
Bengal Clipper (SE1)
Benihana (multi. loc.)
Bibendum (SW3)
Bingham (Richmond)
Bloom's (NW11)
Books for Cooks (W11)
Boxwood Café (SW1)
Brackenbury (W6)
Busaba Eathai (multi. loc.)
Cafe at Sotheby's (W1)
Café Japan (NW11)
Capital (SW3)
Chez Bruce (SW17)
Clarke's (W8)
Cocoon (W1)
1880 (SW7)
Fat Duck (Berks)
Fifteen (N1)
FishWorks (multi. loc.)
Food for Thought (WC2)
French Horn (Berks)
Gate (W6)
Giraffe (multi. loc.)
Glas (SE1)
Glasshouse (Richmond)
Globe (NW3)
Gordon Ramsay/Claridge's (W1)
Gordon Ramsay/68 Royal (SW3)
Gourmet Burger (multi. loc.)
Gravetye Manor (W. Sus)
Greenhouse (W1)
Grocer on Warwick (W1)
Hard Rock Cafe (W1)
Inn The Park (SW1)
itsu (multi. loc.)
Jenny Lo's Tea Hse. (SW1)
Kulu Kulu Sushi (multi. loc.)
La Fromagerie (W1)
La Trompette (W4)
Le Cercle (SW1)
Ledbury (W11)
Le Gavroche (W1)
Le Manoir/Quat (Oxon)
Le Vacherin (W4)
Maggiores (WC2)
Mandalay (W2)
Masala Zone (multi. loc.)
Maze (W1)
Michael Moore (W1)
Michiaki (W1)
Mju (SW1)
Morgan M (N7)
Moshi Moshi (multi. loc.)
Noto (SW1)
Nyonya (W11)
OCCO (W14)
Odette's (NW1)
Ottolenghi (multi. loc.)
Pat. Valerie (multi. loc.)
Pearl (WC1)
Pengelley's (SW1)
Pepper Tree (SW4)
Pétrus (SW1)
Pied à Terre (W1)

Ping Pong (W1)
Portrait (WC2)
Providores/Tapa (W1)
Quilon (SW1)
Rainforest Cafe (W1)
Ransome's Dock (SW11)
Raoul's (W9)
Rasoi Vineet Bhatia (SW3)
River Café (W6)
Rodizio Rico (N1)
Roka (W1)
Roussillon (SW1)
Rules (WC2)
Sardo Canale (NW1)
Satsuma (W1)
Savoy Grill (WC2)
Silk (W1)
Simply Nico (SW1)
Solly's (NW11)
Square (W1)
Tampopo (SW10)
Tate Modern (SE1)
Timo (W8)
Tom Aikens (SW3)
Tom's Deli (W11)
Tootsies (multi. loc.)
Truc Vert (W1)
Two Bros. Fish (N3)
202 (W11)
Ubon (E14)
Umu (W1)
Villandry (W1)
Vineyard/Stockcross (Berks)
Wagamama (multi. loc.)
Wells (NW3)
Wizzy (SW6)
Yauatcha (W1)
Yo! Sushi (multi. loc.)
Zamoyski (NW3)
Zuma (SW7)

Special Occasions

Almeida (N1)
Amaya (SW1)
Angela Hartnett's (W1)
Asia de Cuba (WC2)
Aubergine (SW10)
Avenue (SW1)
Belvedere (W8)
Berkeley Square (W1)
Bibendum (SW3)
Blakes (SW7)
Bluebird Club (SW3)
Blue Elephant (SW6)
Boxwood Café (SW1)
Brunello (SW7)
Capital (SW3)
Cecconi's (W1)
Chez Bruce (SW17)
Chutney Mary (SW10)
Cinnamon Club (SW1)
Cipriani (W1)
Clarke's (W8)
Club Gascon (EC1)
Crazy Bear (W1)
Criterion Grill (W1)
Daphne's (SW3)
Drones (SW1)
Fat Duck (Berks)
Fifteen (N1)
Fino (W1)
Floridita (W1)
Foliage (SW1)
French Horn (Berks)
Glasshouse (Richmond)
Gordon Ramsay/Claridge's (W1)
Gordon Ramsay/68 Royal (SW3)
Goring Din. Rm. (SW1)
Gravetye Manor (W. Sus)
Greenhouse (W1)
Grill Room (W1)
Hakkasan (W1)
Ivy, The (WC2)
J. Sheekey (WC2)
Lanesborough (SW1)
La Trompette (W4)
Launceston Place (W8)
Le Caprice (SW1)
Le Cercle (SW1)
Ledbury (W11)
Le Gavroche (W1)
Le Manoir/Quat (Oxon)
Le Pont de la Tour (SE1)
Le Soufflé (W1)
Locanda Locatelli (W1)
L'Oranger (SW1)
Lundum's (SW7)
Maze (W1)

Mirabelle (W1)
Mju (SW1)
Momo (W1)
Morgan M (N7)
Nahm (SW1)
Neal Street (WC2)
Nobu (W1)
Novelli/Auberge du Lac (Herts)
Orrery (W1)
Ottolenghi (multi. loc.)
Pétrus (SW1)
Plateau (E14)
Providores/Tapa (W1)
Quaglino's (SW1)
Rasoi Vineet Bhatia (SW3)
Richard Corrigan (W1)
Ritz (W1)
River Café (W6)
San Lorenzo (SW3)
Santini (SW1)
Sartoria (W1)
Savoy Grill (WC2)
Sketch/Lecture Rm. (W1)
Smiths/Dining Rm. (EC1)
Smiths/Top Floor (EC1)
Spoon (W1)
Square (W1)
Tom Aikens (SW3)
Ubon (E14)
Umu (W1)
Vineyard/Stockcross (Berks)
Waterside Inn (Berks)
Wilton's (SW1)
Windows on World (W1)
Wolseley (W1)
Zafferano (SW1)
Zaika (W8)
Zuma (SW7)

Tea Service

(See also Hotel Dining)
Cafe at Sotheby's (W1)
Café Rouge (multi. loc.)
Chor Bizarre (W1)
Cipriani (W1)
Criterion Grill (W1)
Del Buongustaio (SW15)
1802 (E14)
Emporio Armani (SW3)
Fifth Floor Cafe (SW1)
Food for Thought (WC2)
Inn The Park (SW1)
Joe's Rest./Bar (SW1)
Julie's (W11)
La Brasserie (SW3)
La Fromagerie (W1)
Momo (W1)
Nicole's (W1)
Pat. Valerie (multi. loc.)
Pizza on Park (SW1)
Porters (WC2)
Portrait (WC2)
Quaglino's (SW1)
Richoux (multi. loc.)
Royal Exchange (EC3)
Tate Gallery (SW1)
Tate Modern (SE1)
Tom's Deli (W11)
Truc Vert (W1)
202 (W11)
Wolseley (W1)
Yauatcha (W1)

Trendy

Admiral Codrington (SW3)
Alloro (W1)
Amaya (SW1)
Anchor & Hope (SE1)
Angela Hartnett's (W1)
Aperitivo (W1)
Asia de Cuba (WC2)
Assaggi (W2)
Aubaine (SW3)
Avenue (SW1)
Axis (WC2)
Baker & Spice (multi. loc.)
Baltic (SE1)
Bam-Bou (W1)
Belgo (multi. loc.)
Belvedere (W8)
Benares (W1)
Bibendum (SW3)
Bibendum Oyster (SW3)
Bierodrome (multi. loc.)
Blakes (SW7)
Boxwood Café (SW1)
Busaba Eathai (multi. loc.)
Bush B&G (W12)

Cafe at Sotheby's (W1)
Cafe Lazeez (multi. loc.)
Canyon (Richmond)
Caraffini (SW1)
Carluccio's (multi. loc.)
Cecconi's (W1)
Cellar Gascon (EC1)
Cheyne Walk (SW3)
Chez Bruce (SW17)
Christopher's (WC2)
Cicada (EC1)
Cinnamon Club (SW1)
Cipriani (W1)
Circus (W1)
Clarke's (W8)
Club Gascon (EC1)
Cocoon (W1)
Crazy Bear (W1)
Crazy Homies (W2)
Daphne's (SW3)
Drones (SW1)
e&o (W11)
ECapital (W1)
Edera (W11)
Eight Over Eight (SW3)
Electric Brasserie (W11)
Elistano (SW3)
Emporio Armani (SW3)
Enterprise (SW3)
Fifteen (N1)
Fifth Floor (SW1)
Fifth Floor Cafe (SW1)
Fino (W1)
fish! (SE1)
Fish Shop on St. John (EC1)
43 South Molton (W1)
Frankie's Italian (SW3)
Glasshouse (Richmond)
Gordon Ramsay/Claridge's (W1)
Gordon Ramsay/68 Royal (SW3)
Greenhouse (W1)
Hakkasan (W1)
Harlem (W2)
Hush (W1)
Incognico (WC2)
itsu (multi. loc.)
Ivy, The (WC2)
Joe's (SW3)
Joe's Rest./Bar (SW1)
J. Sheekey (WC2)
Kensington Pl. (W8)
La Fromagerie (W1)
Langan's Brasserie (W1)
La Trompette (W4)
Le Caprice (SW1)
Le Cercle (SW1)
Le Colombier (SW3)
Ledbury (W11)
Les Trois Garçons (E1)
L'Etranger (SW7)
Livebait (multi. loc.)
Locanda Locatelli (W1)
Lola's (N1)
Lucky 7 (W2)
Manicomio (SW3)
Masala Zone (multi. loc.)
Maze (W1)
Mirabelle (W1)
Momo (W1)
Moro (EC1)
Nahm (SW1)
Nam Long-Le Shaker (SW5)
Nicole's (W1)
Nobu (W1)
Oliveto (SW1)
Olivo (SW1)
Orrery (W1)
Orso (WC2)
Ottolenghi (multi. loc.)
Oxo Tower (SE1)
Pasha (SW7)
Pengelley's (SW1)
Pétrus (SW1)
Pizza Metro (SW11)
PJ's B&G (SW3)
Providores/Tapa (W1)
Quo Vadis (W1)
Racine (SW3)
Randall & Aubin (multi. loc.)
Rasoi Vineet Bhatia (SW3)
Real Greek (multi. loc.)
Refettorio (EC4)
Richard Corrigan (W1)
River Café (W6)
Roka (W1)
Rosmarino (NW8)
Salt Yard (W1)
San Lorenzo (SW3)

Savoy Grill (WC2)
Sketch/Gallery (W1)
Smiths/Dining Rm. (EC1)
Sophie's Steak (SW10)
Spiga (W1)
Spighetta (W1)
Spoon (W1)
Square (W1)
St. John (EC1)
St. John Bread/Wine (E1)
Taman gang (W1)
Tom Aikens (SW3)
Tom's Deli (W11)
Tsunami (SW4)
Tugga (SW3)
202 (W11)
Ubon (E14)
Vama (SW10)
Vingt-Quatre (SW10)
Wagamama (multi. loc.)
Wapping Food (E1)
Wells (NW3)
Wolseley (W1)
Yauatcha (W1)
Yo! Sushi (multi. loc.)
Zafferano (SW1)
Zetter (EC1)
Ziani (SW3)
Zilli Fish (W1)
Zuma (SW7)

Views

Babylon (W8)
Belvedere (W8)
Blue Print Café (SE1)
Butlers Wharf (SE1)
Café Spice Namasté (E1)
Cantina del Ponte (SE1)
Canyon (Richmond)
Cheyne Walk (SW3)
Coq d'Argent (EC2)
1802 (E14)
Fakhreldine (W1)
Fifth Floor (SW1)
Foliage (SW1)
French Horn (Berks)
Gaucho Grill (E14)
Gravetye Manor (W. Sus)
Greenhouse (W1)
Lanes (W1)
Le Manoir/Quat (Oxon)
Le Pont de la Tour (SE1)
Maze (W1)
Nobu (W1)
Novelli/Auberge du Lac (Herts)
Orrery (W1)
Oxo Tower (SE1)
Oxo Tower Brass. (SE1)
Petersham (Richmond)
Pizza on Park (SW1)
Plateau (E14)
Pomino (SW17)
Portrait (WC2)
Quadrato (E14)
Ransome's Dock (SW11)
Rhodes 24 (EC2)
River Café (W6)
Rocket (SW15)
Roka (W1)
Royal China (E14)
Sir Charles Napier (Oxon)
Smiths/Top Floor (EC1)
Tate Modern (SE1)
Thai Square (SW15)
Ubon (E14)
Waterside Inn (Berks)
Windows on World (W1)

Visitors on Expense Account

Almeida (N1)
Amaya (SW1)
Angela Hartnett's (W1)
Asia de Cuba (WC2)
Aubergine (SW10)
Aurora (EC2)
Bank Aldwych (WC2)
Bank Westminster (SW1)
Belvedere (W8)
Benares (W1)
Bentley's (W1)
Berkeley Square (W1)
Bibendum (SW3)
Blakes (SW7)
Boxwood Café (SW1)
Brian Turner (W1)
Capital (SW3)
Caravaggio (EC3)

Cecconi's (W1)
Chez Bruce (SW17)
Christopher's (WC2)
Chutney Mary (SW10)
Cinnamon Club (SW1)
Cipriani (W1)
Clarke's (W8)
Club Gascon (EC1)
Coq d'Argent (EC2)
Criterion Grill (W1)
Daphne's (SW3)
Deya (W1)
Drones (SW1)
Edera (W11)
1880 (SW7)
Elena's l'Etoile (W1)
Embassy (W1)
Fat Duck (Berks)
Fifteen (N1)
Fifth Floor (SW1)
Fino (W1)
Foliage (SW1)
Glasshouse (Richmond)
Gordon Ramsay/Claridge's (W1)
Gordon Ramsay/68 Royal (SW3)
Gravetye Manor (W. Sus)
Greenhouse (W1)
Green's (SW1)
Grill Room (W1)
Hakkasan (W1)
Incognico (WC2)
Ivy, The (WC2)
J. Sheekey (WC2)
Kai Mayfair (W1)
Lanes (W1)
Lanesborough (SW1)
Langan's Brasserie (W1)
Launceston Place (W8)
Le Caprice (SW1)
Ledbury (W11)
Le Gavroche (W1)
Le Manoir/Quat (Oxon)
Le Pont de la Tour (SE1)
L'Incontro (SW1)
Locanda Locatelli (W1)
L'Oranger (SW1)
Matsuri (multi. loc.)
Maze (W1)
Mirabelle (W1)
Mitsukoshi (SW1)
Mju (SW1)
Nahm (SW1)
Neal Street (WC2)
Nobu (W1)
Novelli/Auberge du Lac (Herts)
Odin's (W1)
One-O-One (SW1)
Orrery (W1)
Oxo Tower (SE1)
Pétrus (SW1)
Plateau (E14)
Poissonnerie/l'Ave. (SW3)
Providores/Tapa (W1)
Quaglino's (SW1)
Quirinale (SW1)
Rasoi Vineet Bhatia (SW3)
Red Fort (W1)
Rhodes 24 (EC2)
Ritz (W1)
Riva (SW13)
River Café (W6)
Roka (W1)
San Lorenzo (SW3)
Santini (SW1)
Sartoria (W1)
Savoy Grill (WC2)
Shanghai Blues (WC1)
Shogun (W1)
Silk (W1)
Sketch/Lecture Rm. (W1)
Smiths/Top Floor (EC1)
Spoon (W1)
Square (W1)
Sumosan (W1)
Tamarind (W1)
Tatsuso (EC2)
Tom Aikens (SW3)
Ubon (E14)
Umu (W1)
Vineyard/Stockcross (Berks)
Waterside Inn (Berks)
Wilton's (SW1)
Windows on World (W1)
W'Sens (SW1)
Zafferano (SW1)
Zaika (W8)
Zen Central (W1)
Zuma (SW7)

Winning Wine Lists

Andrew Edmunds (W1)
Angela Hartnett's (W1)
Aubergine (SW10)
Aurora (EC2)
Belvedere (W8)
Bibendum (SW3)
Bleeding Heart (EC1)
Boisdale (multi. loc.)
Cafe at Sotheby's (W1)
Cantina Vinopolis (SE1)
Capital (SW3)
Caravaggio (EC3)
Cecconi's (W1)
Cellar Gascon (EC1)
Chez Bruce (SW17)
Christopher's (WC2)
Chutney Mary (SW10)
Cinnamon Club (SW1)
Cipriani (W1)
Clarke's (W8)
Club Gascon (EC1)
Coq d'Argent (EC2)
Criterion Grill (W1)
Cru (N1)
Drones (SW1)
Ebury Wine Bar (SW1)
ECapital (W1)
Edera (W11)
1880 (SW7)
Embassy (W1)
Enoteca Turi (SW15)
Fat Duck (Berks)
Fifteen (N1)
Fifth Floor (SW1)
Fino (W1)
Foliage (SW1)
Glasshouse (Richmond)
Gordon Ramsay/Claridge's (W1)
Gordon Ramsay/68 Royal (SW3)
Gravetye Manor (W. Sus)
Greenhouse (W1)
Grill Room (W1)
Hakkasan (W1)
Il Convivio (SW1)
Lanes (W1)
Lanesborough (SW1)
Langan's Bistro (W1)
Latium (W1)
La Trompette (W4)
Le Cercle (SW1)
Ledbury (W11)
Le Gavroche (W1)
Le Manoir/Quat (Oxon)
Le Pont de la Tour (SE1)
L'Escargot (W1)
Le Soufflé (W1)
L'Etranger (SW7)
L'Incontro (SW1)
Locanda Locatelli (W1)
Lola's (N1)
L'Oranger (SW1)
Maze (W1)
Mirabelle (W1)
Mju (SW1)
Morgan M (N7)
Nahm (SW1)
noble rot. (W1)
Novelli/Auberge du Lac (Herts)
Odette's (NW1)
1 Lombard St. (EC3)
One-O-One (SW1)
Orrery (W1)
Pétrus (SW1)
Plateau (E14)
Prism (EC3)
Ransome's Dock (SW11)
Refettorio (EC4)
Rib Room (SW1)
Richard Corrigan (W1)
Ritz (W1)
R.S.J. (SE1)
Sartoria (W1)
Savoy Grill (WC2)
Sketch/Lecture Rm. (W1)
Square (W1)
Tate Gallery (SW1)
TECA (W1)
Tom Aikens (SW3)
Umu (W1)
Vineyard/Stockcross (Berks)
Vivat Bacchus (EC4)
Waterside Inn (Berks)
Wilton's (SW1)
Windows on World (W1)
Zafferano (SW1)

Wine Vintage Chart

This chart is designed to help you select wine to go with your meal. It is based on the same 0 to 30 scale used throughout this *Survey*. The ratings (prepared by our friend **Howard Stravitz,** a law professor at the University of South Carolina) reflect both the quality of the vintage and the wine's readiness for present consumption. Thus, if a wine is not fully mature or is over the hill, its rating has been reduced. We do not include 1987, 1991–1993 vintages because they are not especially recommended for most areas. A dash indicates that a wine is either past its peak or too young to rate.

	'85	'86	'88	'89	'90	'94	'95	'96	'97	'98	'99	'00	'01	'02	'03
WHITES															
French:															
Alsace	24	–	22	28	28	27	26	25	25	26	25	26	27	25	–
Burgundy	26	25	–	24	22	–	28	29	24	23	26	25	23	27	24
Loire Valley	–	–	–	–	24	–	20	23	22	–	24	25	23	27	26
Champagne	28	25	24	26	29	–	26	27	24	24	25	25	26	–	–
Sauternes	21	28	29	25	27	–	21	23	26	24	24	24	28	25	26
Germany	25	–	25	26	27	25	24	27	24	23	25	24	29	27	–
California (Napa, Sonoma, Mendocino):															
Chardonnay	–	–	–	–	–	–	–	24	26	25	25	24	27	29	–
Sauvignon Blanc/Semillon	–	–	–	–	–	–	–	–	–	25	25	23	27	28	26
REDS															
French:															
Bordeaux	24	25	24	26	29	22	26	25	23	25	24	28	26	23	24
Burgundy	23	–	21	24	26	–	26	28	25	22	28	22	24	27	–
Rhône	25	19	27	29	29	24	25	23	24	28	27	27	26	–	25
Beaujolais	–	–	–	–	–	–	–	–	–	–	23	24	–	25	28
California (Napa, Sonoma, Mendocino):															
Cab./Merlot	27	26	–	21	28	29	27	25	28	23	26	23	27	25	–
Pinot Noir	–	–	–	–	–	–	–	–	24	24	25	24	26	29	–
Zinfandel	–	–	–	–	–	–	–	–	–	–	–	–	26	26	–
Italian:															
Tuscany	–	–	–	–	25	22	25	20	29	24	28	26	25	–	–
Piedmont	–	–	–	27	28	–	23	27	27	25	25	28	23	–	–